ART AND OUTRAGE

ART AND OUTRAGE:
Provocation, Controversy and the Visual Arts

JOHN A. WALKER

Pluto Press

LONDON • STERLING, VIRGINIA

First published 1999 by
PLUTO PRESS
345 Archway Road, London N6 5AA
and 22883 Quicksilver Drive, Sterling,
VA 20166–2012, USA

British Library Cataloguing in Publication Data
A catalogue record for this book is available from the
British Library

ISBN 0 7453 1359 0 hardback

Library of Congress Cataloging in Publication Data
Walker, John Albert, 1938–
    Art and outrage : provocation, controversy and the visual arts /
John A. Walker
    p.   cm.
    Includes bibliographical references and index.
    ISBN 0–7453–1359–0 (hbk)
    1. Arts, Modern—20th century—Great Britain—Public opinion.
2. Public opinion—Great Britain. I. Title.
NX543.W345   1999
709'.04'007441—dc21   98–29582
                                                              CIP

Designed, typeset and produced for Pluto Press by
Chase Production Services, Chadlington, OX7 3LN
Printed in the EC by T.J. International Ltd, Padstow

Contents

Acknowledgements

I am grateful to Anne Beech and Robert Webb of Pluto Press for their encouragement and editorial skills, and to Middlesex University for research funds which have provided some relief from teaching duties and contributed towards the cost of illustrations.

A book of this kind is necessarily dependent upon the published writings of many newspaper and magazine journalists, art critics and historians. I would like to thank all those whose work I have consulted and used. Thanks are also due to the Artangel Trust, the Angela Flowers Gallery, Mark Ashton (of the Camden Local Studies and Archive Centre), Naomi Bache for the loan of her dissertation *Can Art Still Shock?* (Middlesex University, 1996), Bryan Biggs (of the Bluecoat Gallery, Liverpool), Jon Bird (of Middlesex University), Marianne Boesky (of Boesky & Calley Fine Arts, New York), Jenni Boswell-Jones, JoAnne Brooks (director of The Archives of J.S.G. Boggs), Barry Curtis (of Middlesex University), Katy Deepwell, Marianne Dickson (assistant keeper of the Ferens Art Gallery, Hull), Rose Frayn, Margaret Garlake, David Gear, Pamela Griffin (of the Hayward Gallery library), Peter Hagerty, Beth Houghton (head of the Tate Library and Archive), Jay Joplin (of the White Cube Gallery), London Animal Action, Kate Love, Norbert Lynton, Elisabeth McCrae (of the Lisson Gallery), Walter Macauley (chief librarian of the *Belfast Telegraph*, *Daily Mail* and *The Evening News*/Associated Newspapers Ltd), Derek Manley, Jayne Marsden (deputy chief librarian of the *Yorkshire Post*), Anne Massey, Ian Ritchie (of the National Portrait Gallery Archive), Steve Robb, Richard Sewell, Kate Smith, R. Schopen (of the PR department of Gateshead Metropolitan Borough Council), Express Newspapers PLC, the *Hull Daily Mail*, the *Liverpool Post & Echo*, the *East Anglian Daily Times*, Peter Sylveire, the staff of the Laing Art Gallery, Newcastle-upon-Tyne, Harriet Vyner, Tim Wilcox (of Manchester City Art Gallery), Simon Wilson and Lyndsey Morgan (of the Tate Gallery), Jennifer Wood (of the Imperial War Museum Art Department), and the Tampa Museum of Art, Florida.

I am grateful to the following artists and photographers for information and permission to reproduce their work: Conrad Atkinson,

Alice Beberman/Chute, Anne Berg, J.S.G. Boggs, Sue Coe, Bill Drummond (of the K Foundation), Ian Hamilton Finlay, William Gear, William Green, Antony Gormley, Rick Gibson, Newton Harrison, Marcus Harvey, Anthony-Noel Kelly, Mary Kelly, John Latham, Leeds United, David Mach, Kippa Matthews, Gustav Metzger, Elizabeth Moore, Jacqueline Morreau, David Muscroft, Hermann Nitsch, Tony Rickaby, Rebecca Scott, Beverly Skinner, Monica Sjöö, Sam Taylor-Wood and Jamie Wagg.

Thanks also to Tim Marlow, editor of *tate: the art magazine*, for permission to reproduce my article about Marcus Harvey's *Myra* painting. (The article has been slightly revised.)

While every effort has been made to trace the copyright owners of the illustrations, the author/publisher will be glad to hear from any we have not been able to contact.

In order to avoid the scholarly apparatus of references and footnotes in the examples, I have dispensed with footnote numbers and simply listed, in date of publication order, the sources of information at the end of the book.

Introduction

Shock in Modern Art

Before 1800 European artists may have set out to astonish, impress and please their patrons and others who viewed their work but the idea of shocking and outraging them would not have crossed their minds. In contrast, during the nineteenth century, French artists such as Cézanne, Courbet, Daumier, Manet and Rodin managed to shock and offend conservative critics and the public with paintings, caricatures and sculptures that were radical in either form or content. The combination of an avant-garde ideology – 'we artists lead the way and march ahead of public taste' – and a capitalist market in art – in which artists competed against one another for sales, commissions, state approval and the attention of dealers, collectors and critics – encouraged individualism and extremism.

There were times, however, when artists collaborated and formed self-help groups – such as the Impressionists and the Nabis – but these were also rival factions which sought to differentiate themselves by means of style and aesthetic philosophy. Market and other imperatives, therefore, put a premium on such values as difference, invention, experiment, originality, newness or novelty. By the early twentieth century harmonious, organic compositions were replaced by fragmented, inconsistent and dissonant compositions. In many instances, the traditional artistic value of beauty was replaced by cults of the primitive and the ugly – witness Picasso's *Demoiselles d'Avignon* (1907). With Kandinsky, Malevich and Mondrian came abstract art, a type of visual sign many lay people found incomprehensible or meaningless.

Shock tactics were increasingly adopted by the radical artists who belonged to the avant-garde movements of the period 1900 to 1939, such as, for instance, by the Futurists, Dadaists, Vorticists and Surrealists. One of the most famous shock effects within Surrealism was the slicing of a woman's eye (actually a dead cow's eye) in *Un Chien Andalou*, the film produced by Luis Buñuel and Salvador Dalí in 1929. It is a tribute to the fevered imaginations of these two artists that this scene still causes those who have not seen it before to gasp in horror.

The artists' desire to startle and outrage audiences – especially those belonging to the ruling bourgeois class – was often politically motivated by a desire to contribute to social change by either reform or revolution, despite the fact that they espoused quite distinct political creeds: there were anarchists, socialists, communists, conservatives and fascists among them.

Peter Bürger has summed up the artists' transformatory ambition, which paradoxically was associated with a refusal to communicate in commonly understood languages, as follows:

> In the historical avant-garde movements, shocking the recipient becomes the dominant principle of artistic intent ... refusal to provide meaning is experienced as shock ... And this is the intention of the avant-garde artist, who hopes that such withdrawal of meaning will direct the reader's attention to the fact that the conduct of one's life is questionable and that it is necessary to change it. Shock is aimed for as a stimulus ... to break through aesthetic immanence and to usher in (initiate) a change in the recipient's life praxis.[1]

That this principle eventually became a convention was confirmed by a statement made in 1989:

> That a work of art might outrage some members of society is a *normal part* of its conditions of existence.[2]

Since art was inexorably associated with the bourgeoisie, radical artists such as the Dadaists and Russian Constructivists found themselves compelled to attack art itself, hence the curious phenomenon of anti-art art and demands from artists for the abolition of art. Yet, as the French sociologist Pierre Bourdieu has noted:

> By a miraculous dialectical renewal, the countless acts of derision and desacrilisation which Modern art has perpetrated against art have always turned, insofar as these are still artistic acts, to the glory of art and artists.[3]

Art, therefore, is still with us. The story of Modern art and its shock tactics is a familiar one but what of the art made and exhibited in Britain in the last 50 years? Is an avant-garde still possible given the fact that avant-garde art is now itself a tradition? Ezra Pound and Harold Rosenberg both referred to 'the tradition of the new'. How can an artist rebel against a culture of rebellion? (Reverting to academic art is a solution some Post-Modern artists have adopted.) Is shock still a potent factor? If so, are the motives still political? And what of the audience? Are we still capable of being surprised and outraged by contemporary art or have we become blasé?

To explore these and other questions this book documents, in chronological order, a series of controversies about the visual arts – excluding architecture – that have occurred in Britain during that period. The pre-1939 British and post-1945 American examples – such as the cases involving Robert Mapplethorpe, Andres Serrano, Richard Serra and others – have been excluded because they are already well documented.[4] However, some examples of works by American and Canadian artists are discussed, namely, those exhibited in, or acquired by, British galleries which have provoked public protests.

The book's aim is to summarise and contextualise each instance, and to examine the social contradictions and conflicts of value involved. It will consider the character of the art itself and report the views of the various parties concerned: artists, critics, curators, patrons, vandals, the police, judges and lawyers, the mass media and the general public. Although complete objectivity on the part of an author is an impossible ideal, an effort has been made to ensure that the views of the various factions are fairly represented and critical assessments of the art have then been attempted.

Shock and the General Public

The term 'general public' refers, of course, to the majority of people who have little knowledge of art and who are not part of the minority group known as 'the art world'. Although 'the general public' is an imprecise category, it is a difficult one to ignore. Letters to the press, quotes derived from journalists' interviews, polls conducted by telephone and acts of vandalism provide some indication of the opinions and feelings of 'the person in the street'.

In regard to shock, therefore, we can distinguish between *prepared* and *unprepared* audiences. The former are familiar with the idea that shock is a recurrent characteristic of Modern art, consequently they half-expect it when visiting exhibitions. But as Peter Bürger has observed, 'Nothing loses its effectiveness more quickly than shock; by its very nature it is a unique experience. As a result of repetition, it changes fundamentally: there is such a thing as expected shock.'[5] As the prepared audience exposed to shock after shock becomes blasé, artists are driven to greater and greater extremes in order to generate the required shock effect. (Another reason for their desperation is probably the competition from electronic media and mass entertainment.) In contrast, the unprepared audience experiences a much greater degree of trauma because for them the shocks are unexpected.

When the general public see or read about new, experimental works of art the questions, 'Is it art? What is art? If it is art, is it any good?' are repeatedly asked. Clearly, before art can be evaluated it has to be distinguished from non-art and often this is not an easy task. In 1996 Marie Woolf reported:

> There is nothing new in the belief that Modern art is rubbish. But nowhere has it been illustrated more clearly than in the London art world, where companies have had to start labelling sculptures to stop cleaners throwing them out with the trash.
>
> Offices have been asked to attach 'art' or 'rubbish' stickers after a contract cleaning firm disposed of a valuable work by the installation artist Michael Landy. Perhaps the mistake was understandable: Landy's installation, at the Karsten Schubert Gallery in West London, was a garbage can full of, well, rubbish.[6]

As the above example – one of many – indicates, the use of non-traditional materials and forms by living artists makes the task of identification difficult for the layperson *even when the art is displayed in an art gallery.*

It is not uncommon to hear the following questions asked by the general public: 'What is that abstracted image or totally abstract work supposed to be? What does it mean? Why are the colours so unnatural? Why are the figures so grotesque and distorted? Why has the artist used such peculiar or disgusting materials (blood, urine, dung, dead animal or body parts, and so on)? Why should this kind of art be imposed upon us by arts bureaucrats who do not share our tastes? Why should it despoil public spaces indoors in galleries or out of doors in the street? Why should we tolerate imagery and performances that are blasphemous, disgusting, morbid, pornographic, sexist or violent? Surely, such art deserves to be banned, prosecuted or even destroyed.'

A perennial complaint about new, shocking art funded to some degree by the public purse is: 'It is a waste of the taxpayer's or ratepayer's money.' By contrast, the irate taxpayers never seem to complain about the huge waste of money involved in the police's and court's time spent investigating and prosecuting artists for minor offences for which they are then acquitted or fined paltry sums. Nor do they ever seem to consider the money that the arts generate for the nation via industries such as tourism. What one would like to ask the complainers is: 'Do you support the principle of public subsidies for the arts or not? Are you prepared to abolish the Arts Council and the British Council and thus reverse 50 years of state policy? Should artists be allowed to experiment and take risks or not? Are you prepared to grant the right of freedom of expression to artists or not?'

Censorship

Unlike films and videos, contemporary art is not subject to control and censorship by a national, official body like the Board of Film Classification before it is exhibited. (However, entrances to some exhibitions have included warnings that the contents were disturbing and some galleries have operated an 'adults only' admissions policy.) Evidently, the British state regards visual fine art as much less dangerous and powerful in terms of its potential impact on the public than the mass media. Even so, authority figures such as Members of Parliament, local councillors, university/art college managers, and the top brass of the Arts Council often become agitated and embarrassed whenever artists produce work which challenges conventional artistic and moral values and which attracts adverse media coverage. Retrospective acts of censorship and suppression may then occur, such as the removal of a controversial painting from an exhibition after it has opened. There are also various Acts of Law that the police can resort to should they wish to arrest and charge artists.

The British, a Nation of Philistines?

The notion that there exists a homogeneous British people who have shared for several centuries a set of common characteristics and values is a highly problematic one, especially today when the population of a city such as London is so racially and culturally diverse. Nevertheless, there is a modicum of truth in some of the generalisations made about the British: they are more attracted to literature than to the visual arts; they prefer the rural landscape to the urban one (even though most of them live in towns or cities); they tend to be empirical and pragmatic rather than theoretical (some might think this is a strength rather than a weakness), hence they favour the concrete and the particular rather than abstractions and generalisations, and therefore display a preference for detailed, naturalistic representations showing evidence of long hours of hard work – when they buy art, they want value for money; they are anti-intellectual – they prefer to rely on something called 'common sense', even though the whole history of science has been a struggle to transcend common-sense conceptions of reality; they distrust extremes and therefore value compromise.

Some writers are convinced that the British are a nation of philistines and, certainly, there are many Britons who are. The Conceptual artist Michael Craig-Martin told David Lee in 1995: 'Art is central to the cultural life of other countries but not in England where most intellectuals are philistines when it comes to the visual arts.'[7] Given this situation, it is no wonder that Modern art from the continent of Europe has received a cold reception in Britain, and even those British architects and artists who were influenced by it before 1945 have tended to dilute it for home consumption. Leading Modernists such as Gabo, Moholy-Nagy and Mondrian who came to Britain soon moved on to the United States. After the Second World War John Heartfield left London for East Germany and Kurt Schwitters died in neglect and obscurity in Ambleside in the Lake District in 1948.

Modern Art in Britain 1940s–1960s

To celebrate the renewal of contact with European culture after the end of the Second World War, the Victoria and Albert Museum mounted, in December–January 1945–46, a display of the work of the School of Paris Modernists Picasso and Matisse. The derision this exhibition provoked in certain quarters was a measure of the opposition to Modern art which then existed in the art world and amongst the public at large.[8] In more recent decades, as a consequence of various factors – discussed below – the audience for the visual arts has become much larger, more knowledgeable and sophisticated.

The Arts Council of Great Britain was founded in 1946 and, in the decades that followed, its annual budget grew steadily and it succeeded, to a considerable extent, in fulfilling its brief to inform the people about the arts. The government found the institution – an unelected quango – convenient because it enabled art and artists to be kept at 'arm's length'. Should a scandal occur the Arts Council would take the flak. Bitter experience taught Arts Council officials to keep artists at a distance – they dealt with them via another layer of bureaucracy, that is, by dispensing money to smaller arts organisations rather than directly to the artists.

The Institute of Contemporary Arts in London, also established in the aftermath of the Second World War for the purpose of introducing the most advanced art to Londoners, was one such body. During the 1970s it was to be reproached several times by the Arts Council for its exhibition policies. Even the Royal Academy – a fortress of reaction in the 1940s – eventually accepted the need for change and allowed leading Modern artists to become members; for some time now it has also mounted major shows of Modern and contemporary art (culminating in the *Sensation* show of 1997).

The Tate Gallery, as well as its satellites in Liverpool and St Ives, and a network of other arts centres dispersed throughout the country, organised thousands of exhibitions of new art and issued almost as many catalogues. Although held back by the small size of its purchasing fund, the Tate also gradually increased its holdings of Modern art. Its acquisition of 120 American firebricks during the 1970s was to provoke a barrage of criticism.

In 1951 London's South Bank attracted millions of visitors to the main site of the Festival of Britain. On view were a range of artworks of varying degrees of Modernism including sculptures by Reg Butler, Siegfried Charoux, Jacob Epstein, Barbara Hepworth and Henry Moore, a fountain by Eduardo Paolozzi, and murals by Ben Nicholson, Victor Pasmore, John Piper, Graham Sutherland and Feliks Topolski. As its contribution to the 1951 celebrations, the Arts Council organised a travelling exhibition of new paintings entitled *60 Paintings for '51*. As we shall see, at least one work in this show – a semi-abstract painting by William Gear – proved highly controversial.

During the era of Welfare State Culture,[9] the London County Council and planners of new estates and new towns such as Harlow and Stevenage commissioned many new public sculptures from such artists as Ralph Brown, Butler, Hepworth, Moore and Olyfe Richmond.

During the 1950s, television became a mass medium in Britain. From then on, as the number of channels increased, British arts television programmes, series and strands brought the arts into millions of homes.[10] Most of the output of arts television was and is celebratory. One of the few programmes which questioned the art world's support for avant-garde art that was incomprehensible and 'fraudulent' in the eyes of the general public was a Fyfe Robertson report about the 1977 Hayward Annual exhibition. This show and documentary will be one of the case studies of the 1970s.

In addition to television, a mass of illustrated material on the visual arts was supplied by book, magazine, poster and postcard publishers. In the 1940s there was a dearth of art books and colour reproductions, whereas now there is a deluge of them. And, as a consequence of the expansion of the higher education system – universities and art colleges – successive generations studied and practised the arts and became more open-minded towards the most recent trends. Many art and design students did not manage to become professional artists and designers after finishing their education, but they did swell the ranks of informed consumers of visual culture. Art and design colleges also sustained hundreds of visual artists who could not live by the sale of their work alone by providing them with full- or part-time employment. In the view of some critics, it was this indirect form of public subsidy which encouraged artists to become inward-looking and self-indulgent, and to produce work which had little or no commercial or popular appeal.

Recalling the 'euphoric atmosphere' of the 1960s the critic Richard Cork wrote:

> The attractiveness of Pop Art, the explosion in art book publishing, the unprecedented spread of confidence in British artists, all this convinced me that this country was at last poised to disprove the hoary old adage about the inability of the English to sustain any great interest in visual art.[11]

Towards the end of the decade the police's closure of a show of erotic art by the American Pop artist Jim Dine, followed by the prosecution of Dine's dealer Robert Fraser and a wave of occupations in several art schools – most famously Hornsey – indicated that Cork's optimism was somewhat misguided.

The 1970s–1990s

The 1970s tend to be missing from history of art surveys. Some historians foolishly claim that nothing of significance happened during that decade or that there was no dominant style or tendency. Arguably, the distinctive features of 1970s' art were its re-politicisation and feminisation. In terms of the theme of this book, the 1970s – especially the year 1976 – was an exceptionally active and interesting decade. As Cork, writing at the end of 1976, put it: 'It is difficult to recall a period in recent history which produced the flurry of scandalised attacks we have witnessed over the past twelve months.' He was referring to the Carl Andre 'bricks' affair at the Tate, and the Mary Kelly 'nappies' show and Genesis P-Orridge's *Prostitution* exhibition held at the ICA. Gloomily, he predicted: 'The prospects for a genuine interrelationship between new art and its putative audience seem alarmingly remote.'[12]

During the 1980s – the principal slogan of which was 'greed is good' – a boom occurred in the British economy and the art market which grew in importance. There was also a resurgence in the art of painting to meet the demand of curators and collectors who had not liked the Conceptual and Political art of the 1970s. Charles Saatchi, one of the world's major collectors of new art, established a large collection/gallery in North London and opened it to the public.

In 1984 the Tate Gallery began to host an annual competition called the Turner Prize which is currently sponsored by Channel 4 Television. Even those who dislike the idea of making artists compete against one another for monetary reward acknowledge that the Turner Prize has provided considerable publicity for contemporary art via its associated exhibitions and Channel 4's coverage of the work of the contending artists and the award ceremonies. As we shall see, 1993 was a crucial year for the Turner Prize: Rachel Whiteread, that year's winner, had created a controversial public sculpture called *House* which attracted extensive media coverage. This was compounded by the attempt of the K Foundation to spoil the Tate's award ceremony. The K Foundation then went on to organise an event in which they claimed to have burnt one million pounds in the name of art.

So many visitors have tried to view the Turner Prize contenders' exhibitions at the Tate that at times the doors have had to be closed. Managers of art – like Nick Serota, director of the Tate Gallery – nowadays increasingly play the numbers game, that is, boast about attendance figures, even though many visits must be repeats by regular gallery-goers rather than by new customers. Like television executives, they have become obsessed by ratings. This development can be interpreted as a response to media attacks on contemporary art during earlier decades. Arts managers fear loss of government subsidies unless it can be shown that there is wide support for what they are doing.

In the 1990s interest in the art produced by yBas (young British artists) – the BritArt generation – reached unprecedented heights both here and abroad. What differentiated these artists from earlier genera- tions of avant-gardists (except the Pop artists) were their business/ media skills and the increased accessibility of their works. Sculptures may have been displayed in the Tate Gallery or the Saatchi Gallery and priced well beyond the reach of most visitors, but at least they were comprehensible. Even schoolchildren could enjoy walking between glass cases with the innards of animals, which had been chainsawed in half, on display.

The result of all these developments is that several million Britons are now keen gallery-, museum- and exhibition-goers, and are avid appreciators of new art. It has even been claimed that more Britons and tourists visit art galleries each year than attend football matches. Nevertheless, many more millions of people remain ignorant of, and indifferent to, visual art in general and recent art in particular. (When the police give evidence in court about a raid on a gallery it sometimes emerges that this was the first time the detectives had ever been inside an art gallery.) It is this 'lumpen' sector of the populace that the tabloids – newspapers like the *Sun*, *Mirror* and *Daily Mail* – address and depend upon when mounting their sporadic attacks on art.

Even among those who are educated and familiar with the arts, there are hardcore traditionalists and lukewarm Modernists who are either antagonistic towards, or sceptical of, the extreme avant-garde. (Some critics use the term 'neo-avant-garde' to distinguish more recent, inauthentic tendencies from the earlier, authentic avant-garde.) Thus, in the period under review, a repeated pattern can be discerned: time and time again new, radical art has managed to offend journalists and viewers and has stimulated heated public debates. This is in spite of the fact that Modern and avant-garde art have become increasingly institutionalised. David Lee has observed:

> ... the avant-garde is now institutionalised in education to the extent that it
> is taught and emerges fully-formed from art colleges ... [it] is now also

institutionalised in public funding such that it has become the endorsed style of the state ... [13]

So, Modern/avant-garde art has become the official culture of the ruling elite in Britain, Europe and the United States. But perhaps its higher visibility reveals more clearly than before the gap between the tastes and values of the specialised subculture of the art world acting on behalf of the elite and the tastes and values of the bulk of the population.

Some artists – like Genesis P-Orridge, Cosey Fanni Tutti and Rick Gibson – have deliberately set out to disturb viewers, patrons and arts bureaucrats, and they have often succeeded. Other artists have provoked scandals quite unintentionally. Negative reactions have included questions being asked in the House of Commons; contemptuous press headlines; the character assassination of artists; jokes and cartoons; vandalism (as we shall see, one such act resulted in the death of the vandal concerned); legal prosecutions and court cases on various charges resulting, in certain instances, in artists and performers being fined and imprisoned; dismissal from art school teaching posts; loss of support from dealers and the Arts Council; death threats to artists from irate strangers; and censorship, even within the art world itself.

The Role of the Mass Media

Mediating between art/artists and viewers are the press and other mass media such as radio, films and television. Today their power and pervasiveness are such that no artists can avoid having to come to terms with them.[14]

Magazines and newspapers developed into mass media during the nineteenth century and they began to employ critics to review exhibitions on behalf of readers, many of whom had not seen the exhibitions in question. Nowadays there are dozens of magazines which specialise in reviewing the visual arts but these can be regarded as the 'trade' journals of the art world; many of these are sustained by income from advertising paid for by galleries and museums. The kind of art criticism found in them is frequently as difficult and esoteric as the art being discussed.

Some critics feel close to artists and function like advocates or even press agents; others feel closer to their readers and see their duties as elucidating art as far as this is possible, reporting the art scene in a sceptical way and writing in plain English. Brian Sewell is an example of the latter kind of writer.

Anyone who scans a range of art magazines will soon discover that critics themselves are divided in the sense that they favour different artists and different styles/tendencies. Among them can be found writers like Sewell, Giles Auty and the late Peter Fuller who have all heavily criticised the pretensions of British, avant-garde art. During the 1990s Sewell even managed to outrage the British art world with his vituperative attacks published in the *Evening Standard*.[15] 'Philistines', therefore, have some allies inside the art world.

Arts news reporting and criticism in the quality broadsheets has provided reasonably serious discussion and informed evaluation of the visual arts, but the same cannot be said of the national, tabloid press. Its role has generally been a spoiling one, characterised by utterly predictable knee-jerk reactions and populist attacks on contemporary art and artists employing front page headlines such as 'What a Load of Rubbish'. The results have been trivialisation, misleading and inaccurate accounts of what artists had actually produced, manipulation of readers' emotions, and encouragement of philistine attitudes and aggressive feelings. It seems more than coincidence that acts of vandalism have repeatedly happened after the vilification of a work of art in the tabloid press.

Richard Hoggart has characterised the popular (or rather populist) press as follows:

> Popular journalism is of its nature predatory, ruthless, remorselessly hectic; but for most of those who feed it its processes are not sophisticated; they are rock-bottom vulgar. The industry needs rock-bottom vulgarians right up to and including the occupiers of the editors' chairs. Today's editors of such papers ... are not subtle string-pullers. Confident, loud-mouthed, quick on their feet, certainly; and also archetypal holders of the attitudes they assume in their readers or assume their readers most want to see expressed.[16]

At the same time, tabloid journalism is a crude form of the arts of writing and graphic design. This fact has been recognised by the fine artist Sarah Lucas (b. 1962) who has made works reproducing layouts from the *Sunday Sport*, a paper that wallows in tall stories and bad taste.

Many contemporary artists cannot complain about their treatment by the tabloids because they themselves have made strenuous efforts to attract the attention of journalists by mounting shows and issuing press releases designed to provoke a reaction. As we shall see, North American artists such as Rick Gibson and J.S.G. Boggs were particularly adept at such tactics. Coming from a society where selling, marketing, publicity and the mass media are even more prevalent than in Europe, these artists followed the maxim 'all publicity is good publicity'.

Today there are artists like Jeff Koons and Damien Hirst who take charge of their own publicity and marketing by designing and starring in their own advertisements. Photographs of artists are now commonplace and have played an important role in communicating specific images of the artist to the public. More and more artists issue 'self-portraits' intended to catch the eye of picture editors and readers: the British artist Sam Taylor-Wood (b. 1967), for example, has photographed herself with her legs and panties exposed while wearing a provocative T-shirt emblazoned with the invitational words 'Fuck, Suck, Spank, Wank'.

1. Sam Taylor-Wood, *Fuck, Suck, Spank, Wank*, 1993.
C-Type print, edition of 100, 145 x 106 cm.
Photo: courtesy of the artist and Jay Joplin, White Cube Gallery, London.

Some artists who succeed in becoming celebrities revel in all the media attention they receive and are able to cope with it: Warhol, Koons and Hirst are three examples of this. Others, however – those who are by nature more retiring – find it distressing. Rachel Whiteread, for instance, told the reporter Lynn Barber in 1996: 'It just drives me mad … I just don't want to know … I don't read the stuff – all it does is kind of paralyse you with worry and it just makes your job a lot harder.' [17]

While the reporting of art in the tabloids and other media does have some deleterious effects, it can also arouse the public's interest and curiosity. Fans of Hirst have argued that, because he is regularly featured in the tabloids, this is a sign that certain cultural barriers have been broken down. As we shall discover, the extensive media coverage of Whiteread's *House* in 1993 resulted in crowds of visitors making their way to the East End of London to view her concrete construction. Controversies about new art can and do generate intellectual excitement, as well as a sense that art matters. One has to admit that without periodic scandals and controversies, the art scene could be very dull.

One often has the impression that the tabloids report scandals and shocks where there are none or they blow them up out of all proportion. Sensational stories sell copies. Even when there is genuine outrage, a protest campaign may well backfire because, as Mark Lawson has pointed out:

> Public objection from a vociferous lobby guarantees greater visibility and profits for a work of art. A minority interest becomes a majority one … Every time a public controversy occurs in the arts, I am struck by the failure of the puritans and anti-modernists to understand that they are the best PR agents an artist could have … campaigns are now almost guaranteed to fail and to serve only to raise public awareness of a product on a scale which the original distributors could never have hoped to achieve through conventional advertising.[18]

Destruction and Vandalism

According to Freud, the intense stimuli or excitations associated with the experience of shock break through the protective shield erected by the psyche and produce traumas which are coped with by different people in various ways: flight or fight, anxiety, hysteria, expressions of anger, and so on. Cases of individuals who became so incensed that

they threatened artists with violence or physically attacked their art
will be expounded in further sections.[19] Destruction, therefore, is a
recurrent theme.

Acts of vandalism are usually perpetrated against art objects while
the artist is absent, but there are examples of live performances being
ruined by angry viewers. One of these is the case of the Ting Theatre of
Mistakes which performed a work entitled *Scenes at a Table* in the
Serpentine Gallery, Kensington Gardens, in the autumn of 1976. The
art critic Sarah Kent described it as 'an intense meaningless game in
which arbitrary rules are obeyed and gestures observed and repeated'.[20]
After two and a half hours, one member of the audience could stand it
no longer: he rushed forward, pushed the performers around and yelled,
'I'm sick of watching you, you pretentious creeps. I suppose you think
this is a contribution to theatre ...' and he was then joined in his
protest by a friend. The performers found this was a 'mistake' that they
could not absorb into their act and so they abandoned the performance.

When directed at images, destruction is termed 'iconoclasm'.
Iconoclasm has a long history and intense spells of it, usually as a
consequence of religious fanaticism, have resulted in the wholesale
defacement of churches, religious paintings and sculptures. As Andrew
Graham-Dixon, author of a history of British art, has explained, such
outbursts occurred in Britain during the sixteenth and seventeenth
centuries. 'Iconoclasm', he remarked, was once 'a tool of revolution'.[21]
During recent decades iconoclasm has been associated with lone, angry
or mentally disturbed individuals rather than with whole social
movements; however, such individuals may simply represent the tip of
an iceberg.

Graham-Dixon also argued that, compared to earlier periods of
image hatred, 'Iconophobia in the twentieth century, by word or deed,
is history replayed not as tragedy but as farce.' However, he added:
'Despite that, there is something impressive about the persistence of a
dislike so active that it requires the demolition of the object. In Britain,
it seems, the old emotions aroused by art – particularly the old negative
passions – have never quite gone away.'[22]

Destruction has also been a subject for artists and an artistic
technique – witness the events mounted during the Destruction in Art
Symposium (DIAS) of the mid-1960s. The case study in section 5
concerns the prosecution of two of the organisers of the DIAS. In the
case of graffiti, public opinion is sharply divided: there are those who
see it as a type of decoration and others who regard it as a type of

vandalism of public property. In 1996 one graffiti artist from Sheffield was sentenced to five years in prison for his 'crimes'.

As we shall discover, the destruction of art is not limited to crazed individuals or extreme avant-garde artists, it is also perpetrated by pillars of the community, such as, for instance, the wife of Sir Winston Churchill, the directors of Morgan Crucible (a multinational company) and Cambridge undergraduates. Destructive attacks on art have also been mounted by righteous feminists whose motives were ethical, political and rational, and whose actions, so they have claimed, were lawful. Some acts of vandalism are actually welcomed and applauded by the tabloid press and many members of the British public – witness their reaction to the defacement of Marcus Harvey's painting *Myra* when exhibited at the Royal Academy in 1997.

Art in Public Places

Place or display context is a key factor in the general public's response to contemporary art. A new sculpture located in the grounds of a sculpture park (unkindly defined by one wit as 'a museum with rain') – a semi-public space dedicated to art – may be accepted without demur, while the same sculpture located in a town square or a suburban open space may arouse intense hostility. Most people feel an attachment to the place where they live and work; consequently they develop a protective attitude towards 'their' territory. Elected representatives, such as local councillors in particular, are sensitive to any additions to the environment, especially when public expenditure is involved. Yet, in the case of Gateshead Metropolitan Council, local Labour councillors have pursued a policy of commissioning public sculptures as a means of improving the environment and raising the cultural profile of the region.

As the case studies concerning sculptures by Barry Flanagan and Antony Gormley reveal, local people often react negatively to the sudden appearance of a strange object made by an 'outsider' in their environment. To them, a familiar place has been violated. The public feel that yet again 'they' have imposed something on them without any consultation, without any regard to their opinions and wishes. Consequently, the fuss caused by public sculptures or murals is often greater in small provincial towns or in suburbs than in the centres of large cities. In the case of villages, the proposal to erect a new sculpture can divide the community into two, bitterly opposed camps.

If local feelings run very high, then the reviled object may have to be removed. However, the history of the Eiffel Tower (1889) in Paris shows that initial feelings of detestation can subside and be replaced by feelings of affection. Today it is virtually impossible to imagine the skyline of Paris without the Eiffel Tower because it has become a popular tourist attraction and a visual emblem of the city. It may be necessary, therefore, for the supporters and sponsors of a new public sculpture – such as Gormley's *Angel of the North* – to keep faith with the commissioned artist and ride out the storm of protest.

James Lingwood, a co-director of the Artangel Trust, a London organisation which commissions temporary public works of art, has written a thoughtful essay entitled 'The Limits of Consensus' which stresses the heterogeneity of reactions to public art.[23] It is an unspoken assumption of most writing about art that art should be universal in its appeal, and should interest and please everyone. Lingwood argues that this expectation is unrealistic. Citing several works of art commissioned by Artangel, he stated: 'Each created a substantial community of interest and each provoked indignation, media censure and political outrage, synthetic or otherwise ... They were not sculptures in search of a consensus.'

According to Lingwood, Whiteread's *House* provoked 'a multiplicity of convictions, a host of different thoughts and responses' which it was not possible to explain in terms of old battle formations or partisan blocs of opinion, such as the art world versus the general public or the middle versus the working classes, because 'differences were always *within* identifiable groups of people, rather than *between* them'. He concluded: '*House* laid bare the limits of consensus. It did not expect to be ring-fenced from the contingencies and passions of everyday life.'

Shock in the Media

Although people often complain that contemporary art is shocking, its shock value is surely much less than the bad news reported via the mass media virtually every day. (This was a point Francis Bacon used to make when interviewers informed him that people found his paintings shocking.) We are all exposed to news stories and images of wars, famines, disasters, genocide, torture, mass murder by deranged individuals, rape and other violent crimes, child and animal abuse. Compassion fatigue is a defensive reaction to such exposure.

Given the horrendous photos and films featured on the news, it is surprising the public can still be outraged by the images and activities of fine artists. One explanation may be the long-standing assumption that art is a positive cultural phenomenon: it is by nature good because it offers aesthetic, decorative and other pleasures, because it is celebratory and life-affirming. There is some truth in this view but it is not the whole truth because art too is implicated in the power structures of society and therefore contributes to repression and inequality. Furthermore, some of it has addressed the negative side of human behaviour; see for example, Goya's *Disasters of War* (1810–14), a series of etchings. There is something profoundly disturbing and contradictory about images of mutilated corpses which are also found to be beautiful and aesthetically pleasing. Some sculptures by Dinos and Jake Chapman play upon this contradiction.

The public is also exposed to shock from other quarters, namely, advertising and systems of mass entertainment. Oliviera Toscani of the Italian company Benetton has been responsible for billboard adverts showing such images as a naked, bloodstained baby straight from the womb, priests kissing nuns, a man dying of AIDs surrounded by sobbing relatives and a black woman suckling a white baby; these images created a furore and were subsequently banned. New films and television programmes which provoke headlines and censorship on the grounds of blasphemy, immorality and excessive sex or violence are constantly being produced. Secondary comment in the media is, of course, free publicity for the companies, films and so on, concerned. So they, like the tabloids, find sensation profitable.

Desire for, and Functions of, Shock

What many people seem reluctant to admit – because they are hypocrites – is that they have an appetite for sex and violence. Protecting the psyche from shock eventually becomes boring and, consequently, sooner or later, people will seek exciting stimulation. The fact is that many people enjoy being startled, thrilled, frightened and shocked. Big dipper rides, violent action/crime books, comics, films and television programmes, the London Dungeon, and gruesome horror movies would not be so popular if this were not the case. Furthermore, many people are curious about, and fascinated by, ugliness and deformity: witness the appeal of fairground freak shows and distorting mirrors, as well as films like *The Elephant Man* (directed by David Lynch, 1980). Similarly, there are those in the art world who crave novelty and the frisson of delight that shock brings. Artists such as the Chapman brothers, aware of this situation, make works of art which deliberately exploit people's ambiguous desires in relation to sex, violence and deformity.

Some theorists believe that the shocks of avant-garde art and mass entertainment are cathartic, that is, they enable fears and repressed emotions such as aggression and lust to be released in conditions of safety. (One of Damien Hirst's works – a tiger shark preserved in a tank – is entitled *The Physical Impossibility of Death in the Mind of Someone Living* (1991). This title alone draws the attention of viewers to an unpalatable truth that they normally avoid considering.) Morse Peckham, author of a biological and behavioural account of art, has even maintained that art performs an adaptive function: 'Art is the exposure to the tensions and problems of a false world so that man may endure exposing himself to the tensions and problems of the real world.'[24] David Mach, a Scottish sculptor featured in this book, has claimed that his work helps people to survive from day to day.

Other thinkers have argued against the values of originality and shock in art as, for example, a writer in the conservative weekly the *Spectator:*

> Artists are not lone, misunderstood creatures, destined to fight the prejudice of the philistines. Great art has always been profoundly conventional ... No great art has ever been produced starting from the premise that anything goes ... the desire to escape convention is futile. The frantic search for total originality, as though originality were a virtue in itself ... is a recipe for the production of bad, trivial art. The wish to disgust where no man has disgusted before is not an artistic, but a political impulse, and an adolescent one at that.[25]

Conclusion

Although this book is, on the whole, sympathetic to contemporary art, it does not shrink from expressing doubts about the value and quality of the art cited. Just because a work is new, radical and avant-garde does not make it profound in terms of content, or excellent from an aesthetic point of view, or progressive from the standpoints of ethics and politics. As Roger Kimball rightly observes: 'Offensiveness is ... not an index of artistic quality.' He adds: 'It is widely assumed that by baptising something as "art" we thereby exempt it from other kinds of criticism – as if an object's status as art rendered it invulnerable to extra-aesthetic censure.'[26] (Works of art should not be beyond ethics but, at the same time, since they are simulated rather than real, they ought not to be taken too literally: a picture of rape is not an act of rape.) Popular or 'philistine' negative reactions to examples of recent art, therefore, are not automatically invalid. As someone who came from a working-class family I have some understanding of, and residual sympathy for, proletarian 'philistinism' or scepticism.[27] Furthermore, the motives of the artists may be just as mercenary and publicity-orientated as those of tabloid journalists.

What the examples discussed reveal is that there are various warring factions even within the London-dominated British art world and that there are other divisions in British society, that is, the various classes and class fractions, and groupings which differ in terms of their gender, education, race, religion, and so on, and taste constituencies, that help to explain the differential reactions new, challenging works of art so often provoke. By discussing a sequence of specific, concrete examples, I hope to counter the tendency of writers on recent art and society to make sweeping, and therefore, misleading generalisations. And, by including some little known cases, I hope to provide a more original account of art in Britain since the 1940s.

Each controversy – a kind of snapshot – exposes some of the complex relations between art and British society. So many accounts of art simply discuss it as if it were an autonomous realm of formal innovation and stylistic development that had no impact on viewers and no social consequences. (Art often has an impact on society, which then has positive or negative consequences for the art and the artist.) This book, in contrast, is concerned with the interfaces between art and the public/arts institutions/the media/national and local government/the police/the law and the legal system. It is, therefore, a contribution to the reception history of art ('reception history' or 'reception aesthetics' is one kind of writing concerned with the psychological and social impact of works of art). In total, the controversies provide an oblique but illuminating perspective on the history of art and culture in Britain during the past half century.

One of the book's lessons is that a serious engagement with contemporary art is needed before it can be dismissed or condemned out of hand, but also that discrimination in terms of quality is essential, no matter what the age, character or notoriety of the art in question is. Of course, this begs a number of questions concerning who is making value judgements in whose interests, and whether or not the criteria underpinning evaluations are relative or absolute.

Some of the works of art discussed in this book are not of high aesthetic value because they were conceived in different terms, that is, the contents, themes and issues they addressed were considered by their creators to be more important than optical or tactile pleasures. Furthermore, it should become clear that in certain instances what the artists produced were 'social sculptures', that is, playful cultural or social experiments designed to challenge British institutions and to test the limits of tolerance.

1
1949: MUNNINGS AND MODERN ART

In April 1949 Sir Alfred Munnings created a national furore by attacking Modern art in strong language via a radio broadcast of a speech given at the Royal Academy. His reactionary views were shared by most academicians, the leader of the Conservative Party and a wide cross-section of the public. Struggling to counter these views were the supporters of Modernism within the British arts establishment.

During the late 1940s an unusual alliance was forged between the professional politician, Sir Winston Churchill (1874–1965), and the professional and commercially successful painter of horses, Sir Alfred Munnings (1878–1959). The former was a 'Sunday' painter who enjoyed painting landscapes out of doors in a manner indebted to Impressionism. The latter was notorious as a verbose, English eccentric of rural origins. (His favourite catchphrase was: 'What a go!') In terms of art, Munnings was a traditionalist and an empiricist: he believed artists should emulate masters such as Michelangelo, Rembrandt and Stubbs, and paint what they can see as accurately as possible; consequently, he hated Modern art because of its 'abnormal fooleries' and 'distortion' of reality. Paintings by Cézanne, Matisse and Picasso, according to Munnings, were the products of 'disgruntled, cunning, incompetent minds'. He also objected to the fact that Modern art seemed to require the support of pretentious art criticism and complex theory.

These opinions were identical to those that Adolf Hitler expressed in the 1930s when vilifying so-called 'degenerate' Modern art. Like Hitler, Munnings was also an anti-Semite who shared the Nazi opinion that Modern art was an evil Jewish conspiracy. In one 1930s' tirade against Modern Jewish artists he cited Picasso, only to be reminded by his listener that Picasso was Spanish, not Jewish. Undeterred by reason, Munnings switched his attack to the Jewish dealers and critics who were deceiving the public by promoting artists like Picasso. Later, in 1948, he caused a scene at the Garrick Club when he called Sir John Rothenstein, Director of the Tate Gallery, a bloody Jew and said this was the reason why another Jew – the Russian painter Marc Chagall – had been given a show at the Tate.

Munnings served as President of the Royal Academy from 1944 to 1949. The Academy at that time was a deeply conservative institution. No self-respecting Modern British artist would become a member or show work in its Piccadilly galleries even if they had been invited to do so. It was thanks to Munnings that Churchill's paintings were exhibited at the Royal Academy Summer Exhibition of 1947. He arranged for six paintings to be submitted to the Selection Committee under the pseudonym 'David Winter' and was delighted when they were accepted. He also made sure that Churchill was awarded a Diploma as a Royal Academician Extraordinary. In his final year as President, Munnings revived the practice of the annual Academy Banquet (held on 28 April 1949). This was an all-male affair – women members of the Academy were excluded – at which speeches were given. In 1949 Munnings's dinner speech reached a much wider audience by being broadcast on the Home Service of BBC radio.

With the Archbishop of Canterbury, Field Marshall Montgomery and Churchill present, Munnings chose to mount his most public attack on Modern art. With drunken glee he reported a question Churchill had supposedly put to him: 'Alfred, if you met Picasso coming down the street would you join me in kicking his something something ...? I said, "Yes Sir, I would."' (Churchill later wrote to Munnings to complain, 'This is not the sort of statement that should be attributed to me.')

Also criticised by Munnings were Matisse's *The Forest* in the Tate Gallery collection, the Arts Council, London County Council public sculpture shows in Battersea Park – 'bloated, monstrous nudes' – Henry Moore's *Madonna and Child* sculpture in the Church of St Matthew, Northampton, and Anthony Blunt, Surveyor of the King's pictures. (Blunt, later unmasked as a Soviet spy, was a target because he had maintained that Picasso was a better painter than Reynolds.) Most of the audience enjoyed Munnings's jibes and greeted them with laughter and cries of 'Hear, Hear'. A minority disagreed and interrupted Munnings saying that Matisse's painting was 'a beautiful work'.

Naturally the speech provoked a public furore: the BBC's switchboard was jammed with calls. Many listeners rang to complain about Munnings's bad language (he had used the word 'damned') and others to defend Modern art. At that time, of course, telephones in Britain were restricted to the middle class so working-class opinion was not heard. Subsequently, sacks of letters and telegrams arrived from around the world. Most writers supported Munnings. Popular opinion was thus anti-Modern art and welcomed its public denigration. Press reports and cartoons were numerous. In the *Evening Standard* (4 May) David Low's cartoon depicted Munnings on horseback leading a charge up the steps of the Tate Gallery towards its apprehensive director, Rothenstein. It was headed 'Art War News'.

It is clear that in 1949 powerful forces within the British establishment were mounting a rearguard defence of traditional art against the advance of Modern art. It should be acknowledged that other establishment figures – Sir Kenneth Clark (for a time head of the Arts Council and a patron of Moore, Victor Pasmore and other living artists), Herbert Read and Roland Penrose (founders of the Institute of Contemporary Arts, London) – were supporters of Modern art. Rothenstein and the trustees of the Tate Gallery were also trying to increase the gallery's holdings of Modern art despite the restriction of a tiny purchasing fund. Evidently, the British arts establishment was divided into two camps, the reactionaries and the progressives.

It seems clear that Churchill was somewhat embarrassed by being publicly associated with Munnings' views even though in private he shared them. The latter was confirmed a few years later when he reacted with loathing to the portrait that Graham Sutherland (1903–80) painted of him in 1954. This portrait was commissioned as a gift by both Houses of Parliament to mark Churchill's eightieth birthday. After its unveiling in Westminster Hall, Churchill made a short speech in which he sardonically observed: 'The portrait is a striking example of *Modern* art. It certainly combines force with candour.' In reality, compared to a Cubist head by Picasso or Braque, Sutherland's representation was traditional and conventional. On learning how much the portrait upset Winston, his wife Clementine promised him that it would 'never see the light of day'. Consequently, in 1955 or 1956 she had the painting destroyed by burning. The fate of the portrait only became known to the public after Clementine's death in January 1978.

Munnings continued to rage against Modern art until his death in 1959. On one occasion he turned aside from painting horses to make a pictorial satire on Modern art. The painting, executed in 1956 for display in the RA's annual Summer Exhibition, was entitled

2. Sir Alfred Munnings, *Does the Subject Matter?*, 1956.
Oil on canvas, 78.7 x 108 cm.
Photo: courtesy of The Sir Alfred Munnings Art Museum,
Castle House, Dedham, Colchester, Essex, CO7 6AZ

Does the Subject Matter?. It depicts a scene in an art gallery – the Tate presumably – in which six figures, and a dog, are shown reacting to examples of Modern paintings and sculptures. Three Picassos hang on the wall and various shapeless lumps are displayed on plinths. The viewers include several of Munnings's friends who naturally respond with scepticism and distaste. On the extreme left Munnings features the tense, unctuous figure of Rothenstein with Jewish facial characteristics.

As far as Munnings was concerned, the School of Paris and its British followers were the enemy. What he did not realise, apparently, was that by 1956 New York had replaced Paris as the world's art capital and a new, different kind of abstraction had become dominant, namely, Abstract Expressionism.

2

1951: GEAR AND ABSTRACTION

As part of the 1951 Festival of Britain an exhibition of paintings was organised which included a prizewinning 'abstract' by William Gear. It aroused much adverse comment in the British press and questions were asked about it on the BBC and in the House of Commons.

The incident in the career of William Gear (1915–97), a Scottish painter, demonstrates the antipathy felt by the majority of the British people towards Modern art, particularly the abstract variety, during the 1940s and 1950s. This was in spite of the historical precedent of Turner who produced highly abstracted landscapes, seascapes and interior scenes. In a 1996 television history of British art the critic/presenter Andrew Graham-Dixon claimed that Modern art was founded in Britain by Turner and Constable. However, there is a strong empirical strain in the British people and, consequently, they prefer artists who 'paint what they see, who make trees in pictures look like trees in reality'. This is why Constable is closer to the hearts of Britons than Turner.

Because of their empiricism and nationalism the British have been suspicious of theory and abstract ideas emanating from German, French and Russian philosophers and revolutionaries. Modern art met resistance partly because of its supposedly foreign origins and its avowed internationalism. For many people on the right of the political spectrum both in Britain and in the United States, Modern art was associated with left-wing political ideologies such as anarchism, communism and socialism. There was some basis in fact for this opinion: many Modern artists have held left convictions. Picasso, for instance, was a member of the French Communist Party.

Gear came from a miner's family and grew up in Fife. He studied art and art history at Edinburgh College of Art from 1932 to 1937 and then obtained a travel grant to France where he spent time in Fernand Léger's studio. After military service in the Middle East and Europe during the Second World War, he lived and worked in Paris for three years (1947–50) where he had contact with such School of Paris abstract and semi-abstract painters as Nicolas de Staël, Hans Hartung and Alfred Manessier. For a time he also associated with the European avant-garde group known as CoBrA (Copenhagen Brussels Amsterdam)

(1948–51) whose members thought of themselves as an International of experimental art and who were sympathetic to Expressionism and Surrealism but opposed to geometric abstraction. In 1949 he shared an exhibition with Jackson Pollock in New York (Betty Parsons Gallery, November–December 1949). From 1958 to 1964 Gear was curator of Eastbourne's Towner Art Gallery. He then taught painting at Birmingham College of Art where he was appointed Head of the Faculty of Fine Art. He retired from the Birmingham college in 1975 but continued to paint until his death in 1997 at the age of 81. It is clear from this summary that Gear's experience was far more international and 'foreign' than the majority of British artists.

To celebrate the achievements of living British artists at the time of the Festival of Britain, the Arts Council organised a show entitled *60*

3. William Gear, *Autumn Landscape*, 1950.
Oil on canvas, 183 x 127 cm.
Photo: courtesy of the artist and the Laing Art Gallery, Newcastle-
upon-Tyne.

Paintings for '51. Sixty artists were invited to contribute 'large' new pictures and they were supplied with canvas which was then a scarce material. The list of artists invited provoked a negative reaction from a lobby of academic artists (which included Augustus John and Dame Laura Knight) who thought the Arts Council was politically biased in favour of artists on the Left. Fifty-four paintings were eventually displayed in Manchester City Art Gallery in 1951 (May–June). The exhibition then moved to London (June–July) and subsequently toured England and Scotland. The paintings on display were overwhelmingly representational; there were only three examples of abstract art: works by Gear, Ben Nicholson and Victor Pasmore.

From the show five prizewinners were selected by a three-man international jury. The paintings were purchased by the Arts Council and some were then donated to municipal galleries. Gear's winning painting – *Autumn Landscape* (1950) – is now in the collection of the Laing Art Gallery in Newcastle-upon-Tyne. It was awarded one of the five prizes of £500 and proved to be the most controversial choice.

Autumn Landscape communicates a sense of energy and dynamism. Its background consists of a patchwork of organic shapes over which angular, jagged irregular forms with strong, heavy outlines are superimposed. The complex overlapping of these forms creates an ambiguous, shallow space. Gear's favoured dark tonalities and his colours – olive greens, dull yellows and oranges, ochres, browns and blacks – have been described as 'bruised'. A white-painted form resembling a lightning flash stands out from the surrounding autumnal hues. The forcefulness and dourness of some of Gear's abstracts do make them difficult to appreciate, even by those who are otherwise tolerant of abstraction.

Right-wing newspapers such as the *Daily Mail* and the *Daily Telegraph* carried the story of Gear's winning picture together with grey reproductions of it in April 1951. An article in the *Daily Mail* was headed: 'Arts Council pay £500 for "jam pot thrown on canvas".' The reports prompted a stream of angry letters. One in the *Daily Telegraph* described paintings such as Gear's as 'fooleries' and complained about the 'ugliness' of Modern art compared to the 'beauty' of past art. A second moaned about the squandering of public money on 'grotesque doodling'. A third called for the abolition of the Arts Council for 'wasting public money'. A fourth expressed disgust and claimed 'a child of three' could have done better. A fifth linked the painting to the scientific and technological developments of the period by describing it as an 'atomic composition'. Predictably, a long letter from Sir Alfred Munnings appeared headed 'Fine Art on the Dustheap'. Yet again he attacked the influence of the School of Paris, the Arts Council and the Director of the Tate Gallery. Furthermore, he claimed that the Moderns could not draw.

Although critical letters were the most numerous, Gear did have his defenders – they included the poetess Dame Edith Sitwell and the collector Howard Bliss – who pleaded for open-mindedness towards the new in art and warned against judging paintings from low-quality reproductions. On 26 April Gear responded to his critics in the pages of the *Daily Telegraph*. One of his concerns was the intimidating effect abuse and hostility was likely to have: it would deter those who might otherwise be willing to appreciate and buy avant-garde art.

The debate spread to other media when a question was asked about the painting's purchase on the popular radio show, *Any Questions*. MacDonald Hastings, one of the panellists, defended the Arts Council's expenditure and argued that 'the public were the last persons on earth to judge good or bad art' because 'the public's opinion about art had been consistently wrong for 2,000 years'. R.P. Winfrey disagreed and claimed the public did recognise good art but what they didn't like in pictures were 'ladies with triangular bodies'.

Feelings continued to run high and in May a Liberal Member of Parliament, Edgar Granville, put a question to Hugh Gaitskell, then Labour's Chancellor of the Exchequer, which suggested that Gear's painting was not a representative example of British art. The reply given sidestepped the specific question by claiming that, taken as a whole, the five prizewinning pictures were representative of various styles and aspects of contemporary British art. Colonel Alan Gomme-Duncan, a Tory MP, was not satisfied. In November he told the House of Commons that Gear's picture was 'the most appalling example of Modern art ever produced'.

The main reasons for the public hostility which greeted Gear's prizewinning painting have been summed up by the art and design historian, Anne Massey:

> ... it was the international, modern nature of the work which so many found objectionable. The exhibition attempted to integrate Festival of Britain policy with that of the Arts Council by promoting wholly British culture. None of the contributing artists had spent as much time abroad as Gear had done ... Gear's painting was uncompromising, aggressive and abstract ... It

was the foreign nature of Gear's work which distinguished it from most of the other exhibits and which countered the consensus of Welfare State culture.

Two questions about abstract art were and are repeatedly posed by the general public: 'What is it supposed to be?' and 'Is it the right way up?' In Gear's case, his art still retained a reference to nature, as indicated in the statement he made in 1983: 'Most of the paintings have a reference to landscape or gardens, rather statements of kinship with the natural visual world. The works are created with "both eyes on the canvas" but with an aesthetic card index of things seen, selected and stored in the visual memory.' Furthermore, many of his titles indicate connections to landscapes and seasons. *Autumn Landscape* is a case in point. It could be read as a close-up of leaves and branches in motion and dappled with light.

Of course, abstract works of art do provide fewer clues as to the way they should be hung than representational pictures, and curators of exhibitions sometimes make mistakes when hanging them. Unfortunately, Gear's *Autumn Landscape* was printed upside down in the Arts Council's 1951 catalogue. Although it was due to a printer's error, the fact that even professionals make mistakes was a source of amusement to the press and the public. In April 1952 the popular illustrated magazine *Picture Post* published a double-page spread in which they made fun of Gear and the issue of hanging abstractions: *Autumn Landscape* and a photograph of Gear were printed upside down, and a photograph of one of his paintings on an easel was printed on its side.

The article was prompted by the exhibition *Seventeen Collectors* organised by the Contemporary Art Society and held at the Tate Gallery, in which two of Gear's paintings were deliberately displayed sideways by Howard Bliss, a patron of his art. Bliss was trying to make the point that abstracts can work no matter which way up they are hung and that artists do not necessarily know how to show their paintings to best advantage. In interviews Gear indicated that he disagreed with Bliss's actions and opinions.

Since Gear's paintings were being collected and one had won a prize, it is clear that he had some influential supporters. British industrialists also found his art attractive and useful: during the 1950s Gear was commissioned to produce wallpaper and textile designs, and his style of abstraction influenced patterns belonging to what came to be known as the 'Contemporary Style'. So, although the British public may reject abstract art when it is presented to them in the form of paintings displayed in art galleries, they may happily accept and enjoy it when it appears as decorative patterns on carpets, fabrics, linoleum and wallpapers. Indeed, in one *Daily Telegraph* article, *Autumn Landscape* was reproduced next to a linoleum design in order to demonstrate similarities. Gear was not upset by the comparison. Indeed, in a letter of reply, he pointed out that this proved the beneficial effect that Modern, abstract art was having on industrial design.

3

1953: THE COLD WAR MONUMENT THAT WAS NEVER BUILT

In 1953 a model for a huge public sculpture by Reg Butler won the competition for a monument to *The Unknown Political Prisoner*. His models and designs aroused much public controversy and one of his maquettes was smashed by an angry visitor to the Tate Gallery. Later, it emerged that the competition had been funded by American right-wingers keen to use art for anti-communist, propaganda purposes.

At the British Pavilion of the 1952 Venice Biennale exhibition sculptures by Kenneth Armitage, Reg Butler, Lynn Chadwick and Bernard Meadows, selected by the critic Herbert Read, were displayed. The phrase 'Geometry of Fear' was applied to them because they were spiky, metal structures which seemed to reflect in their harshness the postwar cultural climate formed by awareness of the twisted corpses of the German extermination camps, the fear of atom bombs, and the angst-ridden philosophy of Existentialism. This new, linear, metal sculpture was influenced by the work of the European artists Picasso, Giacometti and Germaine Richier, and the American artist Alexander Calder.

Butler (1913–81) originally trained as an architect in the 1930s. Because he was a pacifist and conscientious objector, he refused to fight in the Second World War and instead worked as an agricultural engineer. He had made sculptures sporadically for a long time but did not become a full-time sculptor until around 1950 when he was in his late thirties. He had no formal training as a sculptor – though he had worked as an assistant to Henry Moore – but he made full use of his architectural knowledge, metal-forging and welding skills to produce open, linear, metal, insect-like figures which had a science-fiction quality.

In 1953 Butler became widely known as a result of winning the Grand Prize – £4,500 – of an international competition for a monument dedicated to *The Unknown Political Prisoner*. He had worked on the project for two years and produced a series of different designs. According to Read, the British representative on the ten-man International Jury, the monument had a very general brief, that is, to 'pay tribute to those individuals who, in many countries and diverse political situations, had dared to offer their liberty and lives for the cause of human freedom'.

The subject was a melancholy one and therefore Butler faced a difficult challenge: how to devise a sculpture that conveyed the horrors of imprisonment but which, at the same time, had something affirmative to say about humanity. He also had to adapt the idiom of contemporary sculpture – which had broken with naturalistic represen-tation – to the needs of a commemorative monument. Butler's final 18-inch high maquette (1951–52) for the monument consisted of three elements: (1) a rock or stone base; (2) three female figures (watchers) situated on the base with their heads straining upwards; (3) a three-legged, open, wire structure with a central platform made from a bronze sheet above which were various other metal forms. This structure was not a direct depiction of an existing tower but it reminded viewers of cages, scaffolds, guillotines, watchtowers and crosses.

A ladder linked the stone base to the platform and from the 'cage' a vertical metal rod soared as high as a church steeple. The latter feature implied the transcendence of the spirit of the political prisoner over captivity and death. A staircase inside the stone base was planned in order to give visitors access to the surface of the rock so that they could stand alongside the over-life size, bronze watchers.

Strangely, the prisoner of the monument's title was not represented. He or she existed as a memory in the minds of the three watchers. Butler's decision to leave out the prisoner was perhaps more effective than showing him or her, because so often political prisoners are hidden from sight, tortured and murdered in secret. The art historian Robert Burstow makes the further point that, 'By not representing a particular figure Butler assured the anonymity and potential universality of the principal

**4. Reg Butler, *Working Model for 'The Unknown Political Prisoner'*,
1955–56.**
Forged and painted steel, bronze and plaster, 223.8 x 88 x 85.5 cm.
London: Tate Gallery Collection.
Photo: courtesy of Tate Gallery Publications Ltd.

protagonist ... and effectively symbolised the triumph of the intellect or
spirit over material captivity.'

The maquette was first exhibited at the New Burlington Galleries in
January 1953 and then at the Tate Gallery in March. According to
Richard Calvocoressi, the work of 140 finalists from 54 countries was
displayed. The exhibition lasted six weeks and 30,000 visitors attended.
When, during 1955–56, it seemed to Butler that the monument was
going to be constructed he made a working model for it.

Much press coverage and controversy were prompted by the competition. In the case of Butler's winning entry, discussion falls into two

categories: (1) comment concerned with the sculpture's modern character and the appropriateness of the design to its subject; and (2) comment related to its politically motivated sponsorship and propaganda function.

As Burstow has explained, many factions normally opposed to each other – Conservatives, Marxists, academicians and Social Realists – were united in their negative reaction. Some thought the sculpture too abstract for its subject matter even though it was, in reality, a figurative/symbolic structure. In the early 1950s there was a fierce argument in the British art world about the relative merits of abstract and realist art. Butler's sculpture became entangled in this debate. John Berger, then an art critic who supported Social Realism, looked for a winning entry that was more specific in its iconography and political message. Read responded by saying that what Berger really wanted was illustration.

One critic dismissed the sculpture as 'a bundle of twisted wire'. An erroneous rumour that the monument was to be sited on the cliffs of Dover caused public protests and motions in the House of Commons. Winston Churchill (Tory) was critical of experimental art, while Michael Foot (Labour) defended it.

During the 1950s television became a mass medium in Britain. Urban skylines were rapidly defaced by a rash of 'H'- and 'X'-shaped, metal aerials. Inevitably some cartoonists depicted Butler's monument as a giant television aerial. This interpretation was not that far-fetched because Butler had studied and photographed radio and radar towers during the late 1940s while planning large monuments of his own.

A woman who had survived Auschwitz praised the sculpture but the day after the maquette appeared at the Tate Gallery it was attacked and damaged by László Szilvassy, a Hungarian refugee and artist who claimed that the sculpture 'reduced the memory of the dead and the suffering of the living ... to scrap metal'. As a consequence of his action, Szilvassy spent a month in jail and was fined ten guineas plus costs.

Since the monument's competition was sponsored by the Institute of Contemporary Arts (ICA), it appeared to be an all-British affair. However, the proposal for the competition came from Anthony Kloman, an American related to the Modernist architect Philip Johnson, who had been a cultural attaché in Sweden. In 1951 Kloman was appointed Director of Public Relations for the ICA. Furthermore, expenses for the competition and the total prize money of £11,500 were supplied by John Hay Whitney who was an American oil millionaire, publisher of the *International Herald Tribune* and trustee of New York's Museum of Modern Art. Some years later it emerged that a Whitney charitable trust had been used by the Central Intelligence Agency to support various kinds of cultural initiatives and organisations in a covert attempt to win the ideological battle against the communism of the Soviet bloc. Western left-wing intellectuals were one target group.

The so-called Cold War which had developed between Eastern and Western powers after their victory over Nazi Germany became hot in 1950 when a war broke out in Korea. In the United States Senator Joe McCarthy conducted his anti-communist witchhunt during the early 1950s. More liberal, internationally-minded Americans, who understood the importance of art and culture, favoured a more indirect approach to winning hearts and minds, hence their sponsorship of the monument to a political prisoner. It served to link the Nazi concentration camps, so fresh in the minds of Europeans, with the present-day ones of Joseph Stalin's Gulag. (Stalin died in March 1953.)

For some right-wing Americans Modern art was indelibly associated with communism or socialism, for others it was an emblem of the freedom individuals enjoyed in capitalist democracies. The anti-communist purpose of the sculpture was revealed by the site suggested for its erection: the Humboldt Hohe, Wedding, in West Berlin, which was then an island of the West inside East Germany. Since the monument was intended to be 400-feet high, it would have been clearly visible from East Berlin. The monument was never built because Whitney withdrew his financial support in 1955 and other sources of funding could not be found. During the mid-1950s there was a thaw in the relations between East and West. The construction of such a monument at that time, therefore, would have been an embarrassment. Burstow has also argued, in a 1997 article, that the hidden American sponsors of the competition were put off by the Modernism of Butler's design.

It is clear from the fact that Butler won *The Unknown Political Prisoner* competition that in the eyes of some members of the international arts establishment his adaptation of the new idiom of metal sculpture to the needs of a public, commemorative monument had been successful. In contrast, the critic Berger thought the monument 'an emblem of defeat'. Others thought Butler's monument too 'abstract', too 'politically unspecific' to serve the anti-communist propaganda purposes intended by the clandestine American patron.

The British people, of course, were blithely unaware of the latter's influence. As far as most of them were concerned, Butler's sculpture was yet another example of the craziness of contemporary art, that is, a farrago of twisted wire without any meaning or value.

4

1958: THE STRANGE CASE OF WILLIAM GREEN

In the late 1950s media coverage of the 'beat, brutalist' painter William Green made him notorious, but shortly afterwards he dropped out of sight and was not heard of again until the 1990s.

A tiny minority of contemporary artists achieve long-term fame, critical acclaim and financial success, but the majority do not. However, a proportion do manage to attract the attention of the art world and the mass media for a short while – Warhol's 15 minutes of fame – before they are consigned to oblivion. William Green (b. 1934) is a case in point.

Although a son of suburbia, Green was an independently-minded and determined young man – he went to prison rather than serve two years National Service in the military. His early enthusiasms included the music of Gustav Mahler and big American cars. Between 1952 and 1954 he attended Sidcup College of Art and then, from 1955 to 1958, he studied painting at the Royal College of Art (RCA). His early work was figurative and expressionistic, but he was soon converted to informal (that is, non-geometric) abstraction. At that time some British art students were influenced by American Abstract Expressionism – examples of which were displayed at the Tate Gallery in the 1956 exhibition *Modern Art in the United States* – and by European L'Art Informel/Tachisme and Matter art. Two other students, Richard Smith and Robyn Denny, pioneered gestural abstraction at the RCA and upset their tutors in the process. By all accounts there was great hostility towards this kind of painting from artist-tutors such as John Minton and Ruskin Spear because it rejected several hundred years of artistic skill and humanist values. It also, of course, made their kind of figurative painting seem stale and old-fashioned.

For Green, painting was essentially 'disturbing a surface' rather than being a medium for copying nature. It was about experiment and improvisation. Therefore he combined strange materials and techniques to see what accident would bring. (On a visit to London, John Cage, the American avant-garde composer who used chance as a way of making music, expressed interest in Green's work.). Like Jackson Pollock, Green often placed his supports – oblong sheets of hardboard – flat on the studio floor. He then spilled and poured black bitumen paint over the surface in a random manner. No doubt bitumen was selected because it was a pigment with negative connotations. (Victorian paintings made from it had cracked and discoloured.) Instead of brushes and palette knives, Green used a variety of bizarre methods to make marks and patterns in the wet paint: riding a bicycle across the support; manhandling the bicycle to produce striations from the tyres; wearing old plimsolls, he stamped, danced and shuffled around the painting. Sometimes he sprinkled sand or cement on his work or he used paraffin to set his paintings alight (Denny had used fire in 1957); he also made use of the dangerous liquid nitric acid to burn the surface.

The results were large, dark, monochrome abstractions with scorched and blistered surface textures evocative of the Earth's crust after a nuclear war. (1958 was the year of the first Campaign for Nuclear Disarmament march.) Despite their abstract character, the writer and curator David Mellor has discerned links between Green's paintings and the human body.

Although Green was not a Pop artist, American mass culture was of interest to him: references were made to famous film stars – such as Susan Hayward – in the titles of his paintings, and one of his shows was promoted as 'a medical dissection' of Errol Flynn. In the late 1950s he also created photostatic, negative images of rock idols such as Elvis Presley.

As a consequence of Harold Rosenberg's theory of Action painting and Hans Namuth's 1951 film of Pollock at work, the artist's act of creation had become as important as the final result. When Action painting became an 'event' it lent itself to theatrical performances in front of audiences and to recording/transmission by time-based media such as film and television. Following the example of Georges Mathieu, a French Tachiste who toured the world giving public painting performances (one of which took place at the Institute of Contemporary Arts, London, in July 1956), Green organised similar events. It was not long before these attracted the attention of the British media. For example, Ken Russell filmed Green bicycling over his pictures for *Tonight*, a BBC television current affairs programme (the film was entitled *Making an Action Painting*). Pathe News also filmed him – *Eye of the Artist,* black and white (January 1958) – and Pathe Pictorial, colour (1958). The latter was a magazine-type short screened between main features in cinemas throughout the country.

However, the verbal commentaries and musical soundtracks accompanying such cinematic reports about the visual arts tended to convey the impression, 'Look how weird and eccentric today's artists are; contemporary art is fatuous and fraudulent; amusing but not worth taking seriously.' In other words, as far as the mass media were concerned, Green was merely an entertaining spectacle. Popular press journalists took a similar line while at the same time stressing the large sums of money that they assumed could be made by radical artists.

Predictably, Green's strange methods of making paintings generated newspaper cartoons and sarcastic headlines such as: 'Asphyxiation – at 100 gns a Time', the *Star* (8 January 1958) and 'Take a Painting, Set Fire to it – Earn Yourself £100', *Daily Express* (29 July 1958). They also prompted parodies by leading radio and television comedians. In Tony Hancock's comic feature film *The Rebel* (1961), for instance, Green was referenced when Hancock – playing an inauthentic avant-garde artist – cycled across his Action painting canvas stretched out on the floor of a Parisian garret. The film's scriptwriters were clearly relying upon the audience's memory of the recent publicity about Green.

As indicated earlier, some RCA tutors were irritated by Green's brand of abstraction. The Royal Academician Ruskin Spear painted a portrait of Green hunched and grinning beneath one his black abstracts, entitled *Portrait of a Young Contemporary.* Spear's picture can be viewed simultaneously as a tribute and a criticism. In effect, Spear tried to reverse the trend towards abstraction by incorporating Green and his painting within one of his own figurative pictures.

Other members of staff were worried that all the publicity that Green was attracting might be to the detriment of the Royal College. Carol Weight, the RCA's Professor of Painting, feared that outraged politicians would respond by cutting art education funds and those critical of Green even wanted him to be expelled. In the end, however, he was awarded a first class diploma.

Given Green's celebrity, his future seemed assured. His work was exhibited in galleries; he held shows at the New Vision Centre Gallery, London in 1958 and 1959. In March 1959 he designed layouts for the RCA, student magazine *ARK.* His fame even spread to France when he was featured in *Libération* and *Paris-Match.* His work was praised by the critics Lawrence Alloway and Roger Coleman and a gallery in

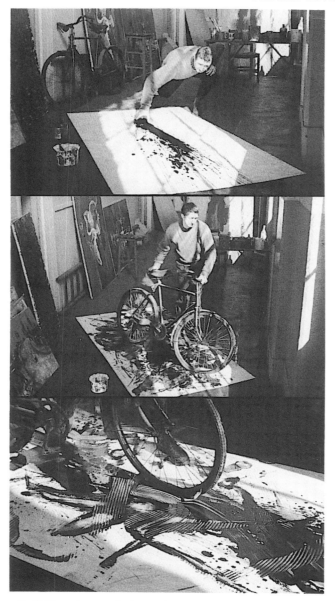

5. *William Green painting at the Royal College of Art*, 1958.
Three stills from a Pathe Pictorial film, 1958.
Photos: courtesy of British Pathe PLC.

Stuttgart expressed interest in mounting a show. But Green could not take advantage of this opportunity because earning a living was his first priority and a teaching post became available; for a while he taught Basic Design at Harrow and Ealing colleges of art, then in the 1960s he returned to Sidcup. Following an exhibition in 1966 at Sussex University he destroyed all his hardboard paintings and ceased to make art. So in the end, Green did not reap any long-term benefit, either financially or in terms of reputation, from all the media coverage he had received during the late 1950s.

Several reasons can be identified for Green's failure to fulfil his early promise as an artist:

1. the art market in Britain was underdeveloped compared to what it is now; there were few serious collectors or patrons and, therefore, most radical artists had to rely on art school teaching to earn a living;

2. abstract painting was not as accessible and attractive as figurative painting and there was considerable hostility to such art in Britain;

3. media attention made Green a celebrity but it also ridiculed and trivialised his work, making it difficult for others to take it seriously;

4. Green was not as adept at using the media as the later Pop artists – the David Hockney generation – were;

5. because much of the interest in his work depended upon witnessing the process of production, the final paintings were an anti-climax; compared to Pollock's, they were very limited in terms of their form and content;

6. gestural abstraction was a dead end in that it was not capable of further development;

7. although Green may have appeared original to English viewers, he was in fact a derivative artist, a follower of Mathieu and Pollock. Robyn Denny's verdict was more succinct: 'Green burnt himself out.'

For a quarter of a century Green took no interest in the art world and the art world and mass media took no interest in him. To all intents and purposes he had vanished and rumour had it that he was dead or had emigrated to Australia. Histories of British art made little or no mention of the vogue for Action painting in the late 1950s. For those who had known or remembered Green, he became a mythical figure comparable to the dead American film star, James Dean. Then, in the 1990s, he re-emerged in order to enjoy a second brief moment of media attention when he was rediscovered by Jane England (a Notting Hill Gate gallery owner) and Dr David Mellor (an academic lecturing at Sussex University).

In 1993 Mellor organised an exhibition at the Barbican Art Gallery about the British art of the late 1950s and the 1960s which included paintings by Green, similar to those of the 1950s, specially recreated for the exhibition. At the same time new works were displayed at the England & Co Gallery, West London (March 1993). BBC television also reviewed Green's abortive career when he was featured on an edition of *The Late Show*.

Green re-emerged as if from a time capsule. He was quite willing to repeat and resume his RCA painting as if nothing had changed in British society and in art in the meantime. The idea that Green could pick up in 1993 where he had left off in the 1950s was surely absurd, a dealer's and curator's dream. What it resembled, of course, was the media manipulation and marketing associated with the Pop music business: long-forgotten stars and musical styles are regularly revived for reasons of nostalgia and profit.

Histories of British art did need to be revised to include Green, if only to warn young artists that media coverage is not automatically the prelude to artistic and monetary success. It is a law of the media that the spotlight of publicity never dwells in one place for long. And such is the turnover of news and personalities that within a few months or years most celebrities are forgotten. Although some ex-film and Pop stars do make comebacks, it is far less common in the world of fine art.

5

1966: ART AND DESTRUCTION

In 1966 Gustav Metzger was one of the main organisers of the Destruction in Art Symposium (DIAS) held in London. The various events aroused much press coverage and public concern. Metzger was arrested and charged with presenting an 'indecent' exhibition.

Metzger is a small, intense man who has been described as 'the conscience of the art world'. He is a survivor, an itinerant intellectual-agitator who has lived in various European countries, including Britain. Metzger was born in 1926 into a Polish-Jewish family that lived in Nuremberg, Germany, a town infamous for its annual Nazi rallies. In 1939 Metzger and his elder brother came to England to escape Nazi persecution. Other members of his family were not so fortunate – they perished in the Holocaust during the Second World War. Naturally this loss contributed to Metzger's view that humanity is brutal, dangerous and self-destructive.

After trying his hand at various kinds of work, Metzger became interested in painting and sculpture. By 1959 he was living in London and writing manifestos about, and giving demonstrations of, Auto-Destructive/Creative art. He developed a form of Action painting that involved applying acid with brushes to nylon sheets stretched over glass. Auto-Destructive/Creative art was conceived 'as a desperate, last-minute subversive political weapon ... an attack on the capitalist system ... It is committed to nuclear disarmament ... It is an attack also on art dealers and collectors who manipulate modern art for profit.'

Although Metzger did not become a member of the Campaign for Nuclear Disarmament when it was founded in 1958, he shared its concerns. In 1960, along with the philosopher Bertrand Russell, he supported the Committee of 100, that is, people willing to commit acts of civil disobedience in order to provoke and overwhelm the authorities. The following year Metzger was arrested and jailed for a month for his participation in acts of protest. In 1961 he mounted a public event at the South Bank, London, where hydrochloric acid was sprayed on to three sheets of nylon (coloured white, black and red) stretched across a metal frame. As the acid hit the sheets, rents and holes appeared until the support disintegrated – the work was creative but, at the same moment, destructive.

Five years later Metzger, along with the Irish poet and playwright John Sharkey and others, organised a key cultural event of the 1960s: the DIAS held at various London venues and open spaces from 31 August to 30 September. (A second DIAS was held in the United States in 1968.) The London DIAS was an international gathering of artists, some of whom were worried by humanity's growing capacity for violence and destruction, and whose work was about destruction and/or used destruction as an artistic technique, literally in order to exemplify the point being made. More than twenty artists from ten countries attended and the events they mounted created a furore in the press and resulted in a prosecution.

Artists who participated included Al Hansen, John Latham, Yoko Ono, Ivor Davies, Werner Schreib, Raphael Montañez Ortiz, and Hermann Nitsch. Ortiz (an American of Puerto Rican origin, b. 1934) was noted for his demolition of chairs and pianos using an axe. At the DIAS press conference held on 31 August Ortiz announced that he would be presenting a Chicken Destruction Ritual. This news provoked a media outcry and animal rights protesters responded by picketing his events. Metzger and the rest of the DIAS Honorary Committee then forbade the killing of any live animals. Later, in the United States, Ortiz went on to mount events that did involve the ritualistic sacrifice of live chickens and mice.

Latham (British, b. 1921) had already caused something of a scandal in Britain because of his assemblages constructed from mutilated and scorched second-hand books. For the DIAS he built *Skoob Towers* ('skoob' equals 'books' spelt backwards) and then set fire to them in a street outside the British Museum and Library. Latham's motives were different from Metzger's. He was seeking to demonstrate that 'the cultural base' was burnt out and to call attention to his own alternative, cosmological theory of time and 'structure in events'. Firefighters and police were called to the burning towers but Latham avoided arrest by not admitting authorship. Some time later Latham was sacked from his part-time teaching post at St Martin's School of Art because of a performance which involved the chewing and distillation of a library copy of Clement Greenberg's famous 1961 collection of essays, *Art and Culture*.

Despite such figures as Latham, Francis Bacon, Stuart Brisley and Genesis P-Orridge, British art has not produced anything as extreme and disturbing as the performances and films of the Austrian artists known as the Wiener Aktionismus or Vienna Institute for Direct Art. It was one of these artists, Hermann Nitsch (b. 1938), who was responsible for the event which resulted in a court case. Nitsch's *Abreaktionsspiel no. 5* (Fifth Abreaction Play) was performed at the St Bride Institute (off Fleet Street) on 16 September. The carcass of a dead lamb was strung up in front of a white canvas and eviscerated while a film showing male genitalia being manipulated by strings and immersed in liquids was projected over it. Loud sounds made by whistles, rattles and other instruments accompanied the brutal display. A young man stuffed the animal's lungs down the top of his trousers and then a raffle was held for the carcass. Two journalists were so affronted they telephoned the police who arrived towards the end of the event and seized the 'obscene' film and other equipment.

Barry Farrel, reporting for *Life Magazine*, described Nitsch as 'small and round and monotone in black shirt, black suit and black humour'.

Jay Landesman, an *International Times* correspondent, was impressed by the way he 'worked over a skinned lamb like there was no tomorrow'. Nitsch had begun his career in a conventional manner by studying the applied arts at art school during the 1950s. His early paintings were dominated by Christian religious themes and the crucified Christ was, of course, called the Lamb of God. He was then attracted to poetic drama and eventually conceived of an Orgies-Mysteries (O-M) type of theatre which would unite all the arts, stimulate the different senses via real rituals rather than plays with actors playing fictional parts. Nitsch pointed out that most of us eat animals but are unwilling to face up to the reality of slaughtering them. In 1959 he became aware of Action painting and Tachisme. They encouraged him 'to pour, splatter and splash liquids' (paint and blood) during his O-M theatricals.

6. Hermann Nitsch, *Aktion 4*, November 1963.
The event took place privately in Nitsch's studio, Vienna and was recorded on film. Photo: courtesy of H. Nitsch.

The psychoanalytic concept 'abreaction' – release of mental tension due to an unpleasant experience – became important to him and he went on to design events with 'sado-masochistic excess' that would initially shock, repel and disturb audiences but which would ultimately provide them with rewarding, cathartic experiences.

It is clear from the above that Nitsch's events were not examples of gratuitous violence or pornography, but since he aimed to shock he could hardly complain when he succeeded in doing so. (In Austria he and his collaborators have been subject to many prosecutions and prison sentences.) However, it was not Nitsch but Metzger and Sharkey whom the British police charged with presenting an 'indecent exhibition'. Metzger had to spend months preparing a defence and, eventually, in July 1967, a trial lasting several days took place at the Old Bailey. Photographs of the Nitsch 'action' provided visual evidence. Metzger defended himself by arguing that Nitsch's performance 'symbolised events in wartime Germany'. The jury found the two defendants guilty but made a strong plea to Judge Rogers for leniency. Sharkey was given a conditional discharge while Metzger was fined £100. According to one account, this sum was immediately donated by visitors to the court but Metzger recalls it being paid by the British patron of Modern art, Roland Penrose.

The DIAS was widely reported in both the national and the international press; discussions and interviews were also broadcast on the radio. It was previewed and covered by such British art magazines as *Art & Artists* and *Studio International* whose editors and reviewers were more sympathetic than newspaper reporters. The artists had argued that human aggression could be sublimated through Destructive art, but their critics disagreed. The *Guardian*'s reporter, for instance, thought that 'violence makes violence' and concluded 'destruction-in-art is mainly perverse, ugly and anti-social'. A writer in *Peace News* claimed that Destructive art was 'guilty of complicity in the general drift towards catastrophe' and *The Times*'s critic declared that 'The visual arts today are a kind of brothel of the intellect.' The verdict of the *Evening News* was simply 'Sick Art'.

Violence and destruction in art are regularly a cause of disquiet. Given the predominant orientation of the arts towards affirming the status quo and providing aesthetic pleasure, Metzger's 'aesthetic of revulsion' clearly worked against the grain. Journalists covering the DIAS events of the 1960s complained about the dubious morality of using destruction to protest about destruction, but was not the

Nietzschean tactic comparable to a vaccine – using a small dose of a disease in order to immunise the body against it? The press ignored the cathartic and therapeutic effects of witnessing bloody violent events. (Is this not the social function of crime and horror movies?) Metzger later insisted that the DIAS provided an opportunity to enquire into the sources of violence in human behaviour and that destruction *in* art did not mean the destruction *of* art.

6

1967: SWINGEING LONDON

In 1966 and 1967 the art dealer Robert Fraser appeared in court to answer charges of displaying 'indecent' drawings by Jim Dine and possessing drugs. He was sent to prison for the second offence. An outraged Richard Hamilton produced a series of artworks as a record and as a critical comment.

During the 1960s Robert Fraser (1937–86), the Eton-educated son of the wealthy banker and art lover, Sir Lionel Fraser, ran a gallery at 69 Duke Street, in London's Mayfair. He specialised in Pop art, both British and American. Fraser was a homosexual and drug addict who had a wide circle of friends in London's artistic and musical circles. For instance, he knew the singer Marianne Faithfull and members of the Beatles and the Rolling Stones. Indeed, he was instrumental in obtaining Beatles' record cover commissions for the fine artists Peter Blake and Richard Hamilton.

In September 1966 Fraser mounted a show of new works by the American Pop artist Jim Dine who was then living in London. Dine's subject matter was genitalia: on one wall drawings of the male penis in various stages of erection appeared; on the opposite wall drawings of the female organ; one image was deemed to show copulation in progress. A series of collage/drawings entitled *Dine–Paolozzi* because some of the source material had been supplied by the British sculptor Eduardo Paolozzi, included explicit representations of the female genitals and pubic hair. Despite this, Dine claimed – somewhat disingenuously – that the collages were 'asexual'. He later told Constance Glenn:

> I did a series of drawings depicting male and female sex organs, but I don't
> see these as pornography. I see them as objects. They represent a very
> natural part of my style. The object fascinates me. I think of the foot as an
> object ... To me, sex organs are objects. Powerful objects.

Since Fraser's gallery had a large, plate glass window, it was alleged by
the Metropolitan Police that the drawings could be seen from the
street. (Fraser claimed they could not.) A retired general from Wey-
bridge made a complaint, the police investigated and, as a consequence,
Dine's work was seized and Fraser was charged under an indecency
clause of the Vagrancy Act of 1836. At the conclusion of a trial held in
November at the Marlborough Street Magistrates' court, Fraser was
found guilty and fined £20 plus 50 guineas costs. Although this time
Fraser was punished lightly, the authorities were to retain an interest
in him and his social circle.

On 12 February 1967 Fraser was arrested again, along with Mick
Jagger and Keith Richards, following a drugs raid on Richards's home,
Redlands in West Wittering, Sussex. Accompanying Fraser at the house
party was his Moroccan manservant, Ali. According to Sue Miles,
Fraser attempted to flee and was rugby-tackled in the garden by two
women police constables. The press and other media had a field day:
this was the famous 'Naked Girl (Marianne Faithfull) on a Fur Rug'
incident. Jagger was found to be in possession of amphetamine pills
while Fraser had a quantity of heroin on him. Cannabis and LSD were
also reported to be present. Jagger's biographer Christopher Anderson
describes Fraser as: 'A handsome adventure-seeker with a taste for
high-stakes gambling and high-quality cocaine.' (The cost of Fraser's
hard drugs habit meant that his artists were often not paid monies due
to them.)

At their trial at Chichester Crown Court in June, Fraser pleaded guilty
and a jury found Jagger guilty. Judge Block observed that there were times
when 'a swingeing sentence' was needed to act as a deterrent. Both men
were sent to prison in Lewes, Sussex, but Jagger was released on bail
almost immediately. Following a *Times* editorial in which William Rees-
Mogg asked, 'Who breaks a butterfly on a wheel?', his three-month
sentence was later commuted to one year's probation. Fraser was not so
fortunate: he was fined £200 and sentenced to six months in prison,
which he served in Wormwood Scrubs, London.

The British Pop artist Richard Hamilton (b. 1922) was angered by
what he saw as the unjust treatment of his friend and dealer. He thought

that if Fraser wanted to harm himself by taking drugs then that was his private concern. Prison was not the appropriate place, he considered, to cure Fraser's 'sickness'. While Fraser was inside, Hamilton helped to organise a group show of the work of 29 artists in the Duke Street gallery (summer 1967) as an expression of solidarity and support. He also signed a letter, along with others, which was published as an advert in *The Times* (24 July 1967) which argued that the law against marijuana was 'immoral in principle and unworkable in practice'.

Fraser's and Jagger's arrest preoccupied Hamilton throughout 1968 and 1969 when he produced a series of artworks entitled *Swingeing London '67*. (Another work was made in 1972 in collaboration with the German artist Dieter Roth.) It consisted of seven silk-screen paintings, a watercolour study, an etching and a poster based on a collage of newspaper cuttings/photographs. Its title was a sardonic pun on the label 'swinging London' which had been given currency by a *Time* magazine article dated 15 April 1966 in which Fraser and his gallery had been mentioned.

Although Fraser's gallery was closed for a time, press cuttings continued to arrive. The collage Hamilton made from them – a vivid relic of the feeding frenzy of the press – was converted into a photo-offset lithograph and published as a poster, in an edition of 2,000, by the Milan company ED 912 in 1968. This 'newsposter' demands to be read in the literal sense. What Hamilton's juxtapositions of cuttings revealed was that much of the 'factual' information provided by the press was sensational, trivial and inaccurate. Where certain items were mentioned Hamilton added samples, for example, a fragment of a Mars Bar wrapper. A Mars Bar was rumoured to have been used in sexual relations between Faithfull and Jagger. In her memoirs Faithfull claims this story was a complete fabrication.

Hamilton's paintings were based on a press photograph by John Twine taken on 28 June 1967 showing Jagger and Fraser handcuffed together inside a police van. The image was a kind of visual pun: the prisoners were captured in a double sense, by the law and by the camera. Several pictures were planned because Hamilton was unsure about how his decision to combine painting and photography would turn out. In accordance with previous practice, he explored the mass media as a subject while simultaneously experimenting with artistic media and processes.

Canvases were painted with either oil, enamel or acrylic and then a silkscreened image in black was superimposed. In one version – now

7. Richard Hamilton, *Swingeing London '67*, 1968.
'Newsposter', photo-offset lithograph, 70.5 x 50.2 cm.
Publisher: ED 912, Milan.

owned by the Tate Gallery – the image was silkscreened on to a white background and then paint applied. To capture the glint of the metallic handcuffs, these were made from aluminium sculpted into a low relief. Inadvertently, they symbolised the intimate relationship that had developed between the worlds of Pop art and rock music in London during the 1960s. The seventh variation employs a smooth, primed, hardboard surface. This work also has a relief element consisting of a plywood simulation of the window of the police van which serves to frame the two prisoners.

The paintings differ in terms of their colours, textures, sharpness of focus, detail, lightness and darkness (one is so dark that it seems to represent a night scene). Both prisoners raise their hands to shield their faces from the photographer and the flashlight of the camera illuminates and freezes their defensive gesture. Hamilton was clearly fascinated by the complex form – reminiscent of the wings of a fluttering bird – produced by the two hands partially concealing both heads. Jagger and Fraser appear vulnerable, like sitting ducks for the press photographers. Viewed as whole, the series has a cinematic feel because it resembles the successive frames of a film.

In May 1969 Hamilton held a one-man show at the Fraser gallery. Nearly half this exhibition consisted, aptly enough, of the *Swingeing London '67* works. The architectural and design critic, Reyner Banham, a friend of Hamilton's from the days of the Independent Group meetings held at the ICA in the 1950s, reviewed the show for *New Society*. He commented:

> ... their quality grows with revisiting. They have a slow burn, rather than an immediate impact, because they are not simple mechanical transformations of news images into protest icons, but have a whole unique biography behind them, and learned awareness of the illusionistic techniques that have been the craft of Western art since the Renaissance.

As an indication of the later monetary value of Hamilton's paintings, one of the series was sold for £86,900 at Sotheby's in June 1991.

Swingeing London '67 memorialises a minor but highly publicised event of 1967. It also serves as a corrective to the myth of the 1960s as a fully liberated, permissive decade. While British politicians such as Prime Minister Harold Wilson were happy to be photographed with the Beatles and were prepared to give them honours for their foreign earnings, they were at the same time afraid of the power rock stars had over the young. Part of the establishment, therefore, fought a rearguard action against the youth and Pop culture of the 1960s.

Mick Jagger emerged from the events of 1967 more notorious than ever and he went on to become one of rock music's wealthiest megastars. Fraser's fate was very different. Faithfull recalls: 'He was never the same after he came out of prison. He got incredibly disillusioned by the whole thing. He came out with black vengeance in his heart and, after that, it all went against him.' After a series of shows, one of which was by John Lennon, Fraser closed his gallery in 1969 and lived for a time in Morocco and India. In 1983–85 he tried his hand at dealing in art again by opening a gallery in Cork Street but this proved to be a financial disaster. In 1985 he became ill while in New York and returned to London to live with his mother. To help him get around Paul and Linda McCartney provided him with a car and driver. Barry Miles, McCartney's biographer, reports that 'Robert died of an AIDs-related pneumonia and meningitis in January 1986' at the age of 49.

7

1971: THE CATFISH CONTROVERSY

In 1971 Spike Milligan, a leading British comedian and animal lover, broke a glass panel in the entrance door of the Hayward Gallery as a protest against the planned electrocution of catfish by the American artist Newton Harrison as part of an art exhibition. The Arts Council reacted quickly to allay public concern.

During the autumn of 1971 the Arts Council of Great Britain mounted an exhibition, curated by Maurice Tuchman and Jane Livingston, at the Hayward Gallery, London, entitled *11 Los Angeles Artists*. The most controversial contributor proved to be Newton Harrison (b. 1932), a professor from the University of California in San Diego. Harrison grew up on the East Coast where he first trained as a sculptor and then switched to painting. However, towards the end of the 1960s Harrison, along with other artists, became interested in the relation between art and technology with particular reference to the environment. Fine art, Harrison became convinced, had become 'sterile, a closed system ... stiflingly cross-referential' and he concluded that 'its whole ground must be redefined'. In the Earth or Land art movement of the period, artists began to work directly with nature far from museums, thus the word 'ground' was taken literally.

During the 1960s the Green or Ecological movement emerged as increasing numbers of people worried about the future survival of the human species given the damage and pollution humanity was causing to planet Earth. Harrison began to study ecosystems obsessively and to generate drawings for earth or aquatic-based farming systems such as portable orchards and fish or shrimp farms. If, in the future, the soil and the sea became polluted, such farms – Harrison reasoned – could produce food. His drawings, like those of engineers, were diagrammatic, technical and included explanatory texts and instructions. Harrison's interest in the visual, aesthetic dimension of drawings decreased as he emphasised their functional ability to communicate vital information.

Harrison's Hayward show exhibit was entitled *Portable Fish Farm: Survival Piece 3* and consisted of six, rectangular, sea-water tanks or 'pastures' containing catfish, oysters, shrimps and lobsters. (A British fish specialist flew out to California to obtain the catfish.) Two dozen catfish were bred in a special spawning container. The exhibit, with its

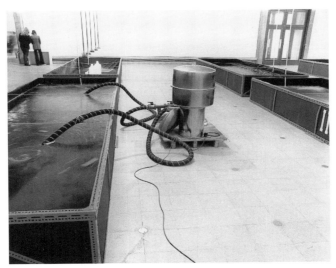

8. Newton Harrison, *Portable Fish Farm*, 1971.
Installation shot, *11 Los Angeles Artists* exhibition, Hayward Gallery, London. Photo: John Webb, reproduced courtesy of the artist and the Hayward Gallery, South Bank Centre.

live creatures and sounds of splashing water and machines, was
nothing like a traditional work of art. Many visitors must have thought
they had stumbled upon an agricultural installation by mistake.
Harrison believed that 'art is relational' and that, eventually, 'All its
relationships hark back to nature.' In this case, the fish farm was an
'analogue' or model of natural processes. In other words, Harrison
provided a practical demonstration of how humanity could rely on
nature but in a sustainable way.

Associated with the farming operation was a ritual event, that is, a
harvest feast. The catfish were to be reared, killed – by electrocution –
cooked and eaten. Instructions for feeding the fish and recipes for
cooking them were supplied by Harrison in his drawings. About this
time Harrison commenced an artistic collaboration with his wife Helen
(b. 1929) (they had married in 1953). She helped with the feast event.
As New Yorkers, both she and Newton had participated in the
Happenings of Allan Kaprow and performance was to become an
important element in their future work.

Unfortunately for the Harrisons, the plan to kill and eat fish as part
of an art exhibition fell foul of the British sentimental attachment to
animals. Despite the fact that most Britons eat fish and meat, and
exploit animals for all kinds of purposes, they purport to love them, or
at least certain kinds of animals – dogs, cats, horses and hamsters in
particular. However, although Britons are in the vanguard of protests
against the ill treatment of animals in any form, many of them enjoy
fishing and hunting. Many animal lovers do not seem to realise that if
farm animals were not killed to be eaten farmers would stop rearing
them altogether.

Newspapers such as the *Evening News*, *The Times* and the *Daily
Mail* carried the story and the latter featured a leading article addressed
to the Arts Council which stated: 'We don't care what ludicrous
happenings you care to promote, just so long as we don't have to pay.'
Protests against the proposed killing of catfish were made by the Royal
Society for the Prevention of Cruelty to Animals (RSPCA) and by
individuals such as Jon Bird (an artist/lecturer) and Spike Milligan (a
brilliant, zany comedian).

Terence Alan Milligan was born in 1918 and brought up in India
where he witnessed many acts of cruelty against animals. Later on he
became a passionate defender of animals, a conservationist and an
amateur painter who exhibited in Royal Academy Summer Exhibitions.
Milligan became famous in Britain during the 1950s when he played

Eccles, a character in *The Goon Show*, a popular radio series. Besides being a highly original humorist, Milligan was also a manic-depressive. He found nothing amusing about the planned fish cull and feast.

On 29 September Milligan telephoned Norbert Lynton, the Arts Council's director of exhibitions, and announced his intention to smash a plate glass panel at the Hayward. Lynton tried to explain the ecological aim of the work and invited Milligan to meet the artist. Milligan refused and, the next morning, after waiting two hours for the arrival of a film crew and reporters, he shattered a door panel with a small hammer. (Lynton had already prepared an invoice for the cost of the repair and ordered a temporary replacement sheet of plastic.) Milligan then gave an interview in which he expressed his anger and revulsion at the proposed killing of catfish and called for the introduction of a law to prevent it happening.

Su Braden, art critic of *Time Out*, wrote an open letter to Milligan in which she accused him of confusion and narrow-mindedness. She defended Harrison's work and argued that his 'cruelty' to fish was no worse than that inflicted by fishermen and fishmongers. She then asked Milligan: 'How many fishmongers' windows have you broken today?' Braden was worried that the adverse publicity might make the Arts Council's exhibitions policy less adventurous in the future. The Harrison exhibit, she claimed, was the first 'installation' show they had mounted.

Jonathan Benthall thought the protesters had a point because Harrison was proposing to 'take life *in a symbolic way* ... he seemed naively unaware of the very powerful literary symbolism of electrocution, which surely evokes judicial execution, whether just or unjust'. Furthermore, there was something distasteful about a feast for 'a group of rather precious art-lovers' rather than for 'the poor and undernourished'. Since the killing 'was an unnecessary indulgence', it was morally wrong.

Hugh Willatt, secretary-general of the Arts Council, declared that because the Council was a public body responsible for public funds, it had to take account of the attitude of the public as whole; consequently it was not willing to permit the killing of fish as part of an exhibition. According to Andrew Sinclair, Lord Goodman, then chairman of the Arts Council, told Harrison that British viewers would be upset at the slaughter of fish with moustaches which reminded them of their uncles. To which Harrison replied: 'People should learn by example that life is cruel.' Goodman riposted: 'It is for a catfish which falls into the hands of a demented American artist.' Harrison has disputed the accuracy of these reports of his conversation with Goodman.

Lord Goodman convened an emergency meeting of the Arts Council at his flat. Tuchman warned that all the American artists would withdraw their work if Harrison's was censored. Lady Antonia Fraser observed: 'Nothing is happening which a woman doesn't do all week.' It was decided to ask the RSPCA to find a humane way of killing the catfish in private because the crux of the objections seemed to be their public execution. (In contrast, Harrison thought it wrong for humans to close their eyes to death and advocated that slaughterhouses should be open to the public.) Sinclair reports that the RSPCA discovered that the electrical device Harrison had intended to use would have electrocuted him as well because he had not allowed for the UK voltage. (Harrison denies this was the case.) After initial doubts, Lord Goodman backed the continuation of the exhibition.

John Russell, London correspondent of the New York magazine *Art News*, reported to America: 'To anyone who had even glanced at the news from Vietnam, or Belfast, there was something signally fatuous about high-level committee meetings that were held day after day, to resolve the Catfish Deadlock.'

According to some accounts, the protests and adverse publicity caused the cancellation of the opening party/feast for members of the Contemporary Art Society scheduled for 30 September and the temporary closure of the Hayward. However, Lynton's recollection is that the exhibition opened as planned and 'there was a catfish feast that evening or the next. Subsequent feasts happened at intervals, without previous announcement, with eminent people doing the cooking and any visitor to the gallery invited to participate – which they did with gusto.'

Aside from the issue of cruelty to fish, the question of exhibit's status and quality as art was raised by a number of observers. For instance, Lord Goodman remarked: 'It may be tasty, but is it art?' Since it was not art in the traditional sense, it proved difficult to estimate its artistic quality and aesthetic value. Arguably, the exhibit marked a shift from artists *depicting* nature to *using* nature in order to explore the crucial interrelationship between human beings and nature. The exhibit took on some of the aura of art by being displayed in an art gallery context and via the performance aspect of the fish banquet. In exhibitions that the Harrisons mounted subsequently, they employed a variety of media – maps, photographs, texts, performances, video – in order to get their message across, thereby placing the emphasis again on visual representation and aesthetic qualities.

Benthall, a science and technology expert, was one of the few reviewers to consider Harrison's exhibit from an ecological perspective. He argued that no complete 'cycle of production and consumption' was presented and that the fish farm depended upon 'an elaborate support system of water-heaters, agitators, syphons etc., powered by electric current' from London's power stations. In short, it was not self-sufficient. Harrison has replied that the exhibit was never designed to be completely self-sufficient.

Writing in 1972, Benthall predicted that the Hayward exhibit would be remembered 'more as a news story rather than as a work of art'. At least the fuss created by the animal rights lobby did result in Harrison's ideas reaching more people than those who visited the Hayward. Harrison and his wife may have been surprised and disappointed by the antagonism they aroused in Britain, but this did not dissuade them from the path they had chosen. In the United States the Harrisons were to become highly regarded ecological artists.

8

1972: MODERN SCULPTURE VANDALISED TO DESTRUCTION

In 1972 an abstract sculpture by Barry Flanagan located in a university town prompted such negative feelings that it was repeatedly attacked until the remains had to be removed by council workers.

On Laundress Green, a flat area of grass near the River Cam, an old mill and Darwin College, in the university town of Cambridge, a sculpture by Barry Flanagan entitled *Vertical Judicial Grouping* was erected in April 1972. It was part of the 'City Sculpture Project '72' funded by the Peter Stuyvesant Foundation (an arts sponsorship initiative taken by an international tobacco company). The project was the brainchild of Jeremy Rees, director of the Arnolfini Gallery, Bristol, and coordination on behalf of Stuyvesant was undertaken by Anthony Stokes.

The project's basic premise was to commission leading sculptors – selected by Stewart Mason and Philip King – to make works for sites in eight British towns and cities and leave them up for six months to allow the public to get used to them. Documentary-type exhibitions, financed by the Arts Council, were also to be mounted to provide viewers with contextual information. No local government funding was to be involved to avoid the common accusation, 'This is a waste of the ratepayers' money.' The organisers hoped, by these methods, to 'promote a dialogue between the artist and the public' and thereby to increase the popularity of modern sculpture. In the case of Cambridge, their good intentions were quickly dashed.

Flanagan, a droll and quirky individual, was born in Wales in 1941. After being privately educated, he studied architecture and sculpture in Birmingham for two years (1957–58), and then attended St Martin's School of Art, London, from 1964 to 1966. Reacting against the Modernist, painted-metal constructions of Anthony Caro and the 'New Generation' sculptures of tutors Isaac Witkin and Phillip King, he produced work in a variety of materials and media such as films, furniture, concrete poetry, projected light, drawing, and he made sculptures from rope, plaster, sticks, stones, canvas, glass and sand encased in resin-impregnated bags. Certain sculptures even incorporated real objects such as cellos, mirrors and settees. The biomorphic imagery of the Spanish Surrealist painter Joan Miró was an important, early influence on Flanagan. In relation to materials another influence was the labouring work which he undertook on building sites.

In some instances he devised temporary, mixed-media installations – playful, seemingly casual arrangements of disparate items – for art galleries. Although the term 'abstract' was applied to his sculptures, many had metaphoric and anthropomorphic overtones or made sly comments on recent trends in contemporary art. In the mid-1970s he gained public notoriety – at the same time as Carl Andre – for a Minimal, 'soft' sculpture entitled *Pile 3* (1968, Tate Gallery Collection), which consisted of five pieces of hessian, dyed in different colours, folded and stacked like a pile of towels.

The most eye-catching features of Flanagan's Cambridge sculpture were four pillars or 'totem poles' made from fibre-glass which twisted and tapered 5.5 metres into the air. (Locals described them as 'worms' and 'spiky things'.) They were placed on either side of a metal structure that was, in contrast to the poles, geometric – half a rectangle – with

9. Barry Flanagan, *Vertical Judicial Grouping*, 1972.
Fibreglass pillars 550 cm high, plus metal 'goalpost'. Laundress Green,
Cambridge. Photo: *Cambridge Evening News*.

two ends anchored in the earth. (It resembled a football goalpost.) The
poles and the metal form thus constituted a kind of organic/non-
organic juxtaposition.

Laundress Green appealed to Flanagan as a location for sculpture
and he declared that the work was 'manifestly visual, very much to
do with the eye, the site and the seasonal scenario'. It seems that he
was looking forward to the part played by shadows cast by the
sculpture during the coming summer because he remarked: 'The
shadows' abstraction upon the meadow carries some mathematical
sense.'

Local reaction to Flanagan's sculpture was mainly anger and disgust.
The *Cambridge Evening News* published articles and letters about it for
two months. A local vicar, the Reverend Arthur Phillips, told one
reporter, 'I think the thing is quite revolting. It made me feel quite sick
when I saw it.' He claimed it spoilt the view and added, 'Perhaps
someone should come along and blow it up.' Some citizens of
Cambridge duly answered the vicar's call for iconoclasts: within a few

days of erection one of the poles had been pushed over; within a fortnight the sculpture had been attacked four times. The poles were used as a hoop-la for lavatory seats; dirty washing was hung between them; an attempt was made to burn them and one was chopped in half. Mothers complained of the danger the sculpture posed to their children should they happen to play on the metal part.

The sculpture was soon reduced to the 'goalpost' and the stump of one pole. The decapitated top half of the pole was later discovered in the junior common room of Peterhouse, the oldest college in Cambridge (founded in 1284). On 10 May the sad remains of the sculpture were removed by Cambridge Council workmen at the request of the Stuyvesant Foundation. When Flanagan was informed, he remarked: 'An artist can expect a few tomatoes, but this is ridiculous!' He then pointed out that the work was underinsured (the implication being that he was going to be out of pocket). At the Rowan Gallery in London in November 1972, Flanagan showed a model of the piece destroyed in Cambridge with various landscapes and townscapes projected behind it to show its relation to different physical contexts.

Flanagan, in fact, was no stranger to vandalism: in 1969 he visited the Hayward Gallery in London where one of his installations of rope and sandbags was on display, only to find it was being tossed around by some children, egged on by their mother, who turned out to be a well-known British novelist. No apology was forthcoming. But Flanagan also disdained the public: he told one critic that his art was produced firstly for his peer group and only secondly for the public. The general arrogance of modern sculptors in relation to the lay audience was summed up in William Turnbull's comment: 'The problem of public sculpture is largely with the public – not with the sculpture.'

The vandals who attacked Flanagan's Cambridge sculpture did not single out his work in particular but also savaged another sculpture called *Burning Bush* by L. Brower Hatcher. A mass of tangled wire somewhat resembling a huge hedgehog, made from spray-painted, high-tensile, steel wire, it was about 1.5 metres high and 2.4 metres long and was situated at Christ's Pieces, a green with trees close by Christ's College.

Rodney Tibbs, the art critic of the local paper, was not prepared to praise the vandalised sculptures as art, but he was highly critical of the intolerance manifested in Cambridge towards Modern art, especially when the populace considered itself to be 'a liberal and enlightened community'. A Labour councillor who had expressed criticism of the sculptures from the outset, offered the explanation that vandalism had occurred because the residents of Cambridge cared more about the environment than people elsewhere, and consequently they were not prepared to see local beauty spots disfigured by ugly, modern sculptures.

Some of the vandals turned out to be Cambridge undergraduates, the intellectual cream of the nation's youth. Three men and one women were arrested by police in the middle of the night on 30 April in the act of dismantling Flanagan's sculpture. They had arrived by punt along the River Cam in order to transport the sculpture to Trinity College. In court, in June, they attempted to justify their action by telling the magistrate, 'Nobody likes it at all.' They were fined £20 each and bound over for six months.

This incident vividly demonstrated the problems attendant upon placing modern, abstract sculptures in sensitive public spaces. For such a project to work, there has to be consultation with local residents – not just local councillors – and their assent needs to be obtained beforehand. The sculpture too has to be couched in a comprehensible language, it has to suit the site and relate to the lives of local people in some way, otherwise its fate is likely to be vandalism and destruction.

Flanagan did seem to learn some lessons from the experience because after the Cambridge event he switched to traditional sculptural materials and techniques such as modelling in clay, casting in bronze and stone carving. Furthermore, during the late 1970s, his sculptures became quite clearly representational. For example, he modelled animal sculptures – leaping, dancing, boxing hares – in clay and wax for casting in bronze. Animal representation, of course, is a hallowed genre of British art. Although Flanagan's hares are not naturalistic like those of academic artists, they have proved very popular with collectors, dealers and museums. They are also accessible to the general public and have lent themselves to display out of doors: hares have appeared outside the *Economist* building in London and also in front of a hotel in Osaka, Japan, where they were mounted on the top of tall poles – well out of reach of potential thieves and vandals.

9

1973: WOMANPOWER EXHIBITION PROVOKES
STRONG REACTIONS

In 1973 an important Feminist art show was held in a London public
library. It mounted a challenge to entrenched patriarchal power
structures and gender divisions. It prompted much public controversy and press coverage; even the police became involved.

Feminism revived during the radical ferment of the 1960s both in the
United States and Europe. But women discovered that even revolutionary groups were dominated by men who expected women to serve them
in traditional ways. This led to separatism: women-only meetings and
groups, magazines written by women for women, art galleries run by
women showing art by women that addressed issues and subjects of
special concern to women, and so on. One of the early manifestations
of this tendency on the fringes of the British art world was *Exhibition
on Womanpower: Women's Art*, which took place in the London
Borough of Camden during April 1973. Over 90 paintings, drawings
and posters were displayed.

Approval for the exhibition was given by the Camden Arts and
Libraries Subcommittee on the advice of visual arts manager Peter
Carey who was himself an artist. At that time Camden – which
stretched from Hampstead Heath in the north to Holborn in the south
– was one of the wealthiest London boroughs and it had an active,
progressive and liberal policy towards the arts.

The exhibition space was the first floor hall of a large, well-
appointed, public library at Swiss Cottage, near swimming baths and a
children's playground. (The building had been designed by Basil Spence
and opened in 1964.) Visitors had to pass through this hall in order to
reach the lending and reference libraries, so the exhibition was seen by
a wide cross-section of the public, many of whom would not have
visited such a show had it been held in an art gallery.

The show was organised by the five exhibitors: Anne Berg and
Elizabeth Moore (both Britons), Monica Sjöö (of Swedish origin),
Beverly Skinner (American) and Rosalyn Smythe (Canadian). These
artists had formed a group in 1971 even though they lived in different
places – London, Bristol and Manchester. Despite the issues that
united them, there was no common pictorial style. They had little

money and were living on welfare or earnings from odd jobs. Three of them had children and so were faced by the problem of trying to be both mothers and artists.

A cheaply-produced document was issued to accompany the show which contained statements and poems by the contributors inspired by righteous anger. The introduction stated:

> We are all committed to the idea of art as political action. We all operate outside the capitalist art institutions. We are all interested in the magic aspect of picture making. We are interested in exploring women's culture, history and women's experience through our images. We have planned this as an ideological show.

Moore had spent time in New York where she had participated in the militant group W.A.R. (Women Artists in Revolution, 1969). One of her paintings was later widely reproduced; it shows two women in conversation, one of them saying, 'Some of my best friends are men ...', and the other replying: 'Yes, but would you want your sister to marry one ...' Nigel Gosling, art critic for the *Observer*, thought Moore 'the most technically assured, a traditional painter whose portrait of Jimi Hendrix draws all eyes'.

Sjöö was born in Sweden in 1938. Both her parents were landscape artists but while her father achieved art world success her mother did not. Sjöö left school at 16 and is largely self-educated in terms of her painting, poetry and knowledge. During the 1950s she worked as an artist's model in Paris and Rome and then, having had a child by a man from Bristol, she settled in England. In the 1960s she studied theatre design and was influenced by the ideas of Bertolt Brecht. Sjöö was the principal theorist of the group and in her manifestos she criticised the male-dominated art world. In Britain 50 per cent of art students were women but female tutors were rare and few women students managed to succeed once they had left college. Doors were closed to them by men who thought they should be at home looking after babies. While a few abstract artists like Bridget Riley – who did not want her gender to enter the equation – were accepted, those who actively challenged the patriarchal art system were either ignored or rejected. Consequently, Feminist artists had to find alternative sources of support, alternative exhibition venues, and so on. They had to make paintings, drawings and posters based on the reality of their daily lives, produce self-images that would be different from the exploitative and degrading images of women found in so much advertising.

10. **Beverly Skinner, with her painting** *A Daughter of the Moon Goddess,*
Arriving in the 20th Century on a Unicorn, **1972.**
Oil on hardboard, 122 x 122 cm, artist's collection, photographed during the
Sistershow (1973) at Bower Ashton Art College, Bristol.
Photo: *Evening Post* and *Western Daily Press,* courtesy of the artist.

Sjöö's pictures consisted of simplified representations of women
from many races drawn in thick outlines. In some instances the faces
were based on tribal masks and ancient European art. Her iconography
included women's work, childbirth, abortion, and male doctors, priests
and lawyers. The latter appeared in a painting entitled *Destroyers of
Women.*

Skinner was born in New York in 1938. Her work and ideas
stemmed in part from the hippie counterculture. She was preoccupied
with 'inner paradise, ecstasy, love, truth, beauty, wisdom, the union of
solar and lunar consciousness'. Her highly decorative paintings executed in a naive style were full of ancient goddesses, high priestesses,
mythical animals such as dragons and unicorns, yin and yang designs,
pentagrams, starry nights and crescent moons. Like several members of
the group she looked back to ancient, matriarchal societies in which
women had been more powerful.

Anne Berg had attended a university art department at Newcastle-upon-Tyne during the 1960s and while there had given birth to a child. She then found it very difficult to continue with her painting. Furthermore, she discovered that the 'Basic Course' exercises taught by Victor Pasmore had no relation to her daily life. Abstraction was thus rejected. As Sjöö, who also had two children and had spent years producing non-figurative art, put it later: 'How does one communicate childbirth, sisterhood, blood, sexuality, work and struggle in stripes, dots and triangles?' Berg's images depicted highly generalised and stylised female figures, some with children, integrated into rhythmical and symmetrical patterns. Other drawings showed women contemplating the heavens above or rows of houses below.

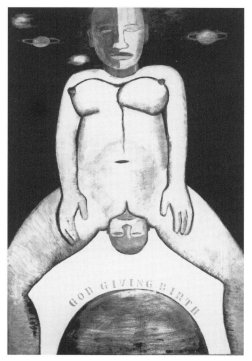

11. Monica Sjöö, *God Giving Birth*, 1968.
Oil on hardboard, 183 x 122 cm.
Skelleftea, Sweden: Museum Anna Nordlander Collection.
Photo: Nino Monastra, courtesy of the artist and Museum Anna Nordlander.

Predictably, reactions to the show were mixed and strongly emotional. Many women visitors responded positively to the exhibits but there were also negative reactions especially to Sjöö's painting *God Giving Birth* (1968) which depicted God as a non-white woman, legs apart, with the head of a child just emerging from her womb. (Sjöö has explained this picture was based on her experience of natural childbirth when her second son was born in 1961 and on her 'belief in the Cosmic Mother'.) One small boy was heard saying to his mum, 'But God was a man, wasn't He?' Some women visitors complained that such paintings were not suitable for the eyes of children. Sjöö had previously shown this painting at the 1970 St Ives Festival, Cornwall, where local councillors had ordered its removal on the grounds that it was 'sacrilegious and obscene'.

Some viewers were also irritated by the stencilled lettering which appeared in Sjöö's pictures. For example, one featuring women of many nations engaged in marching, domestic chores and childcare contained the slogan: 'House-workers of the World Unite', plus the demand: 'Wages for Housework'. Another incorporated the title: *Sisterhood is Powerful*. The addition of words, it seems, was thought to sully the purity of the medium of painting.

A comments book was provided and it was quickly filled. Some male visitors wrote angry, insulting remarks such as: 'When you have finished burning your bras why not burn your paintings too ... These are obviously five confirmed lesbians and very unattractive women who cannot get any man and this is why they do these ugly and aggressive paintings.' Another writer described the display as 'a conglomeration of spite towards humanity'.

Complaints were made by the local Festival of Light to the police about 'indecent' images showing full frontal nudity, couples making love and women giving birth. As a result, Scotland Yard's anti-pornography squad was called to investigate the potential obscenity of the show. They submitted a report to the Director of Public Prosecutions but he decided no action was necessary.

A tense public meeting attended by about 200 people was held on 27 April to discuss the issues raised by the exhibition. A Marxist female speaker argued that women's oppression was simply one facet of a general condition caused by capitalism and that no progress would be made until that economic system had been overthrown. A motion to forbid men from speaking was defeated but, according to Su Braden, the debate lacked direction and structure and was marred by 'vindictive abuse, uproar and screaming'; a woman with a baby kept shouting: 'I'm angry, I'm angry.' Margaret Harrison reports that the meeting degenerated into chaos when one man pulled up his shirt and declared: 'I may have a man's body, but I have a woman's soul.'

A great number of articles about the exhibition appeared in national and local newspapers and most of them labelled it a 'Women's Lib' show. One shrill headline stated: 'Yard Swoop on Women's Lib Art Show'. A reader's letter was headed: 'This Kinky Minority'. One daily paper commissioned photographs of the show but then refused to publish them on the grounds that 'too many black faces appeared in the pictures'. Carey manfully defended the exhibition and told reporters that he had received phone calls in which threats had been made to deface the paintings. He began to work daily in the exhibition space, ready to defend the paintings 'to the death'. All the publicity had some positive effects: attendance increased and eleven works were sold, one of them – *Being* by Anne Berg – to the Camden councillor David Offenbach.

Caroline Tisdall, art critic of the *Guardian*, defended the feminist artists' right of freedom of expression and rejected the accusations of obscenity, but she was not impressed by the quality of the art. In particular, she disliked Berg's 'whimsy' and Sjöö's 'dogmatic approach'. As far as the participants' 'artistic careers' were concerned, the exhibition was not a stepping stone to success: they no longer function as a group and have developed in different directions; none of them has become as internationally famous as Mary Kelly, Judy Chicago, Barbara Kruger or the Guerrilla Girls.

Arguably, this was inevitable given the group's alternative and marginal status, their art's lack of appeal to dealers, art councils' officers and art world intellectuals, and the artists' own rejection of 'the trendy art scene'. Nevertheless, as individuals they have continued to be creative. Since 1973, working in other groups, they have mounted exhibitions that toured Europe, they have continued to write and to publish and to participate in New Age and Goddess Festivals. Their work has been discussed in the regional media and Sjöö in particular has been featured in feminist art anthologies.

Despite the crudity and amateurism of much of the art on display, the Swiss Cottage exhibition was a bold initiative which succeeded in its aim of demonstrating the power of women when they band together in pursuit of their emancipation. It also raised issues that were to be keenly debated in the years to come; it empowered many of the women who saw it and served to educate some male viewers.

10

1974: THE OAK TREE THAT LOOKED LIKE A GLASS OF WATER

During the 1970s *An Oak Tree*, a work by Michael Craig-Martin, became notorious as an example of the absurdity of Conceptual art. The latter was dubbed by its enemies 'con art'.

Craig-Martin was born in Dublin in 1941. From 1945 to 1966 he lived mainly in the United States where, during the 1960s, he studied painting at Yale University at both undergraduate and postgraduate levels. He obtained a teaching post in Britain in 1966 and took up permanent residence in London a few years later. He is an artist who shows in upmarket Cork Street galleries and whose works are to be found in the collections of the world's major museums.

He is also an influential tutor at Goldsmiths College, an art school that trained many of the young turks of the British art world during the 1980s. (In 1994 he was appointed to the Millard Chair of Fine Art.) In addition, Craig-Martin has curated exhibitions and written articles for art magazines. Although some critics claim he is a 'radical, subversive' artist, he is in fact a valued member of the arts/media establishment: he regularly appears as a pundit on television arts programmes, serves as a trustee of the Tate Gallery and is a friend of the powerful collector Charles Saatchi.

While an art student in the United States Craig-Martin was influenced by Minimal art, particularly that of Robert Morris. Like so many others he developed from Minimalism into Conceptualism but his approach differed from that of Victor Burgin and the Art & Language Group. (Craig-Martin continued to use objects and to produce paintings while Burgin employed texts and photographs, and early Art & Language issued journals of their writings.) Writing in 1995, David Lee described Craig-Martin as follows: 'He is a figurehead and defender of the faith for Conceptual Art, its most lucid apologist and its most persuasive proponent.'

Craig-Martin has worked in Britain for many years but still speaks with an American accent. Some critics regard his work as American but inflected by British politeness; others characterise him as 'a wit' and 'a maverick'. He prefers to be called 'an artist' rather than a painter or sculptor because, although he has produced paintings and sculptures,

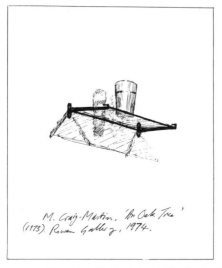

M. Craig-Martin, 'An Oak Tree'
(1973). Rowan Gallery, 1974.

12. John A. Walker, *Sketch of Michael Craig-Martins's 'An Oak Tree'*
(1973) London: Rowan Gallery, April 1974.
Pen and ink on paper, 19.8 x 15.5 cm.

his work extends well beyond these art forms. Over the years he has employed many diverse materials and everyday objects: plywood boxes, mirrors, milk bottles, buckets, venetian blinds, housepaints, clipboards, neon lights, and so on. All his works are extremely precise, clearly delineated and professionally presented. Obscurity, blurs, blood and guts have no place in his art. He draws the outlines of such mundane things as lightbulbs, chairs and ladders in coloured tape on walls but not scenes of human suffering, torture or war.

Since his art is cerebral and clinical it does not have the popular appeal of David Hockney's nor the sensuous attraction of Howard Hodgkin's. Conceptual art is appreciated primarily by art world intellectuals. If Craig-Martin is known to people beyond the art world, then it is for his thought-experiment *An Oak Tree* (1973) which was first exhibited at the Rowan Gallery, London, in April–May 1974. (The piece had the whole gallery to itself.) It was shown again in a one-man exhibition that toured Britain during 1976–77 and in his retrospective at the Whitechapel Art Gallery in 1989. A version of it is now owned by the National Gallery of Australia in Canberra.

According to the critic John Roberts, *An Oak Tree* 'is a charming work' which 'takes its place alongside other object-pieces of the same period which test the limits of the real'. During the 1970s it was scorned by such figures as Fyfe Robertson and Giles Auty as the epitome of charlatanism. Unlike these populist critics, I will pay close attention to the four, constituent elements of the piece: (1) a small shelf, made from glass, attached to a wall by metal brackets nine feet from the ground; (2) upon which stands, in the centre, a plain drinking glass two-thirds full of water; (3) a printed text, red in colour, in leaflet form (designed by Malcolm Lauder) entitled *An Interview with Michael Craig-Martin*; and (4), the title *An Oak Tree*.

Elements one and two, therefore, are both transparent, everyday objects which the artist has purchased and chosen to present rather than to create. These banal objects have been displaced from their usual bathroom setting to an art gallery. The fact that they are displayed so high up means they are out of reach, thus endowing the works with a tantalising, teasing character. Element four, the title, is puzzling because of the discrepancy between its natural referent – oak tree – and the actual, man-made objects on the wall. One is reminded of Magritte's famous caption 'Ceci N'est Pas Une Pipe' inscribed beneath an image of a pipe (*The Use of Words 1*, [1928–29]).

Element three, the text consisting of questions and answers, is written in a manner reminiscent of Wittgenstein's philosophical discourse. Since the interview was generated by Craig-Martin, he performed both the role of the artist and the role of the questioner, that is, the one who claims to perform miracles and the sceptical viewer. Specifically, the artist asserts that the physical substance of the glass of water has been changed into that of an oak tree; the change took place when he put the water in the glass. But of course the viewer's eyes do not confirm this assertion – though with some effort of will a degree of resemblance can be detected between the vertical glass standing on the horizontal shelf and the disposition of the trunk of a tree rising from the ground (the water would thus equal sap).

On being shipped to Brisbane in 1976 for an exhibition, *An Oak Tree* was impounded for a time by the Agricultural Division of the Customs because they thought, quite reasonably given the title on the bill of lading, that the crate contained a living plant. So, when Craig-Martin retrieved the crate, he presumably had to confess to Customs that there was no oak tree inside.

The miracle of the oak tree appears to belong to the category of artists' assertions familiar from Duchamp onwards: 'I am an artist, therefore if I say something's art then it is art ... ergo, if I say a glass of water is an oak tree then it is an oak tree.' (This attitude fails to take into account the fact that art is a social institution. More people than artists are involved in the definition and recognition of art.) Craig-Martin has stated: 'If *An Oak Tree* is true, which of course it is, then I can do anything I want.' (For him it was a way of leaping over self-imposed artistic limitations.) But he also told Rod Stoneman: 'The *Oak Tree* ... is clearly a lie, it depends on a lie. It also depends on cooperation in playing along with that lie in order for it to arrive at some kind of understanding about the truth.' He is an admirer of Oscar Wilde's 1889 essay on the value and art of lying. Picasso also characterised art as a lie which, nevertheless, gave access to truth.

It is pointless to refute the oak tree miracle by logical means because it defies sense impressions, reason and the laws of science. In theory Catholics should be sympathetic to *An Oak Tree* because they believe in miracles and accept that God took on the form of a Jewish man and that the application of *water* to babies' heads transforms them into Christians; when the faithful attend Mass they accept that the wafers and wine they consume are, in reality, the body and blood of Christ.

Craig-Martin was brought up as a Catholic and he was well aware that his piece was an instance of God-like transubstantiation. Lynne Cooke comments: 'Whereas the act of apprehension is normally considered to involve conceptual and perceptual activity, they are, Craig-Martin implies, insufficient in themselves: what is crucial is faith.' Certainly, some faith is inherent in the appreciation of art: the 'willing suspension of disbelief' during the illusionistic narratives of the theatre or cinema; 'seeing as' in painting, that is, seeing configurations of brushstrokes of pigment on canvas as the face of van Gogh, or clouds, and so on.

One would be tempted to conclude that Craig-Martin is an extremely arrogant artist were it not for the fact that he undermines his own position by also playing the part of the sceptical viewer. Faith is thus counterbalanced by doubt.

However, apart from the modicum of literary skill involved in composing and writing the text and the brainwork involved in conceiving the piece and taking the decisions to select shelf, glass and water, *An Oak Tree* evinces virtually no artistic skill of the kind traditionally associated with the plastic arts. This is because Craig-Martin's declared ambition at the time was to make art without any

13. Leeds United, *Felled 1996*, 1996.
Installation shot of display of thirty shelves and different glasses
containing six, different, clear liquids. Camden Arts Centre, London.
Photo: courtesy of Leeds United.

physical transformation of the material. His title and text ensure that
any transformation only occurs in the mind of the reader, and it offers
little either in the way of aesthetic pleasure. (These were the main
reasons it was rejected by those outside the art world.) If one agrees
that it is Conceptual rather than visual/plastic art, what cognitive
insights does it provide? Again the answer is: apart from the observation that faith can override the evidence of the senses, precious little. It
is a mild critique of religion, a minor mind game. Yoko Ono played the
latter with more zest during the 1960s.

As far as the younger generation of British artists are concerned, Craig-Martin's Conceptual 'masterpiece' is a suitable subject for art world in-jokes. At the New Contemporaries exhibition, held at the Camden Arts Centre, London, in July 1996, a group of Northern artists calling themselves Leeds United (after the football team of that name) parodied *An Oak Tree* by exhibiting 30 glass shelves with different kinds of drinking glasses resting on them, placed at various heights on the wall. The glasses contained six different kinds of clear liquid. Scattered on the floor below were a number of empty spirit bottles – the remains of an opening night drinking bout/performance. According to Leeds United, as a result of an alcohol-induced change of state, both participants and concepts were 'felled', hence the installation's title *Felled 1996* or *Ancient Deciduous Forest – Felled.*

11
1976: BRICKS AND BRICKBATS

On 16 February 1976 the front page of the *Daily Mirror* attacked a 1966 sculpture made from bricks by the American artist Carl Andre. The main heading was: 'What a Load of Rubbish'. Subsequently, media coverage was intense and the sculpture was vandalised while on display in the Tate Gallery.

Carl Andre (b. 1935), an American sculptor or 'artworker', became known to the art worlds of the United States and Europe during the 1960s as a leading exponent of the tendency known as Minimal art. During the following decade, he became famous in Britain as a consequence of press outrage at the purchase, in 1972, by Sir Norman Reid, director of the Tate Gallery – a somewhat belated purchase – of one of Andre's 1960s' works from the John Weber Gallery, New York, for an undeclared sum (rumoured to be between £4,000 and £6,000). The sculpture in question was called *Equivalent VIII* (1966) (the opaque title *Untitled* was also used in a Tate report) and consisted of 120 cream-coloured, American fire-bricks arranged on the floor in two layers of 60 to form an oblong. (Therefore, like a fractal, parts and whole were self-similar.) The bricks were not joined or cemented together in any way. Incidentally, the bricks did not date from the 1966 version of the sculpture – they had been of a different type and had been returned to a brickworks which subsequently closed. The Tate bricks were more recent purchases.

14. Carl Andre, *Equivalent VIII*, 1966.
120 Firebricks. London: Tate Gallery collection.
Photo: Tate Gallery Publications Ltd.
© Carl Andre/VAGA, New York and DACS, London 1998.

In his youth Andre had been influenced by the art of Constantin
Brancusi, a Modern sculptor who constructed certain works from
blocks of stone and wood. Andre also drew upon his experience of
working with standardised units as a brakeman in a railway yard. He
came to the conclusion that carving and modelling were unnecessary
because ready-made objects such as bricks were already 'cuts in space'.
Therefore, all he needed to do was to order them into geometric forms
or lines. After use, if a work remained unsold, it could be dismantled
and the objects returned to their place of origin.

Andre, a Marxist of sorts, claimed that his sculpture had proletarian
roots because it was related to working-class crafts such as bricklaying
and tilesetting. (His grandfather had been a bricklayer.) His use of
plain, common materials supposedly signified a connection with the
common people. Unfortunately, such connotations were not discerned
or appreciated by the common people of Britain.

While Brancusi stressed the vertical, Andre stressed the horizontal.
In so doing he rid sculpture of its pedestal. Canoeing experiences of the
flatness of still water surfaces persuaded him that sculptures should be

'level' and 'low'. In 1966 Andre held an exhibition called *Equivalents* at the Tibor de Nagy Gallery, New York. The wooden floor of the gallery became a plain ground against which a configuration of eight 'islands' of rectangular sculptures made from various combinations of sand-lime bricks were set. From above the installation resembled an abstract

**15. 'What a Load of Rubbish', front page of the *Daily Mirror*,
16 February 1976.**
Photo: courtesy of Mirror Group Newspapers.

painting or relief. Since the Tate's sculpture is a single, self-contained form, an 'outtake' from *Equivalents*, it lacks even the relational complexity of Andre's 1966 floorpiece.

Normally the cultural divide between the popular press and avant-garde art circles is so wide that neither pays attention to the other. However, in 1976 a significant exception to this rule occurred. A recession in the British economy alerted the *Daily Mirror* to the news-value of stories exposing wasteful public expenditure. (The purchase of Andre's 'bricks' by the Tate Gallery some years before was first reported in the Business Section of the *Sunday Times* on 15 February 1976.) By condemning the Andre sculpture the paper was able to pander to the presumed philistinism of its readers in respect of Modern art, while simultaneously gaining kudos as the watchdog of the public purse. The British art establishment, used to a condition of autonomy and superiority, was disturbed to find itself subjected to public ridicule from such an unexpected quarter.

Even the *Burlington Magazine*, a specialist, art-historical journal, carried a critical editorial. Richard Morphet, a deputy keeper of the Tate's modern collection, later defended the sculpture in the pages of the same journal. He justified the Tate's purchase by saying that art constantly evolved in terms of a series of distinctive, new movements and that, therefore, the gallery had a duty to keep abreast of them. He went on to praise Andre's sculpture because of its 'sense of human proportion, naturalness and limpid clarity'. It was, he declared, a positive statement of 'general relevance to modern society'. Morphet's apology was unconvincing: the public's perception that the emperor had no clothes was difficult to refute in this instance.

In regard to materials, Andre's aim was not to 'impose properties on materials' but to 'reveal the properties of materials'. His choice and use of mundane products such as bricks provoked much adverse reaction. (Yet, strangely, the general public does not condemn the ancient monument, *Stonehenge*, on the grounds that 'it is simply an arrangement of stones'.) To many lay people the material out of which art is made is highly significant and they have great difficulty in understanding that art can be made from any kind of material including, in the case of a self-portrait head by Marc Quinn, frozen human blood. As the critic Michael McNay noted, the very brickiness of the bricks seemed to upset people despite the fact that, in the field of architecture, bricks can be used to construct complex and interesting structures. Perhaps the real reason for the negative responses to Andre's sculpture was the fact that he did so little with the bricks.

Paul Johnson, a conservative journalist, began to refer to supporters of contemporary art as 'brickies'. In the mass media brick cartoons and puns proliferated and then the sculpture was vandalised. Peter Stowell-Phillips – a 21-year-old chef and amateur artist from Clapham – emptied a bottle of blue vegetable dye over it. According to the vandal, his action was popular with visitors to the Tate who 'all clapped and cheered me and patted me on the back'. As usual, his declared motive was anger at 'the wasted taxpayer's money' on such poor art. Since no permanent damage had been caused, the Tate curators did not press charges but they did ban him from the gallery. The work itself was removed for cleaning and to allow hot tempers to cool.

Andre himself responded to the media comment by publishing a collection of quotes in the magazine *Art Monthly* (October 1976) arranged on the page in a grid which resembled bricks seen from above. It was reprinted in *Art Monthly* in March 1993 with a commentary explaining that the sculpture had been exhibited seven times since 1976 and that each time it had received a bad press.

The emergence of Minimal art cannot be understood except in relation to a 'Less is More' aesthetic philosophy, a long history of simplification and abstraction on the part of some Modern artists whose objective was to eliminate 'unnecessary' artistic conventions in order to attain some pure essence. The British critic Peter Fuller named this emptying process 'Kenosis'. (Some critics believe the reductive programme was a desperate response on the part of fine art to the growth of powerful rivals, namely, the entertainment media.) Knowledge of this history is generally limited to the educated class faction familiar with the succession of moves that constitutes the 'development' or 'game' of avant-garde art. (The art world increasingly resembles the fashion business in that it has become a sequence of short-lived styles; the 'look' of each new style is usually a reaction to or inversion of the preceding style.) It is not surprising that people without the benefit of this education could not fathom why the art offered nothing in terms of figuration, colour, significant subject matter, imagination and technical skill. They were right to complain that Minimal art offered an impoverished aesthetic experience; after all, the very adjective 'minimal' admitted as much. With the advent of Post-Modernism, the slogan 'Less is More' became 'Less is a Bore'.

Politically-conscious critics of Minimalism objected to its lack of socio-political content and its avoidance of important historical events. For example, they pointed out that American Minimal art was produced at a time when the United States was engaged in a vicious war in Vietnam and apparently, the Minimalists had nothing to say about it. Andre had been involved in protest movements in the late 1960s but his political commitment was not visible in the content of his art.

Minimalist artists wanted to deny that art is part of culture by reducing it to nature. Andre once remarked: 'My work has no more idea than a tree, rock, or a mountain.' In which case, the layperson's view – 'It's not art' – seems perfectly justified. Since Minimal art rejected art's traditional characteristics, it was only the artist's tautological assertions – 'I am an artist, therefore, what I make is art. If I say it's art, it's art' – and the art display context – galleries, museums – which endowed it with the aura of art. Outside the gallery stacks of bricks ceased to be art or were not recognised as such by the vast majority of people. Bernard Levin, writing in *The Times*, refused to accept that art was simply what artists or art bureaucrats declared it to be: 'I know better than the people at the Tate who bought a pile of bricks and called it art. *I* call it a pile of bricks; and that is what it is.' Such disagreements reveal that art is a contested concept and that the definition of art in our society involves a power struggle between contending factions.

Paradoxically, despite its heavy reliance on art institutions, Minimal art had a tremendous democratic potential. Like food recipes or musical scores, many pieces were generated from sets of instructions: if someone paid the artist a small fee for a copy of the instructions and then followed them exactly they would obtain a piece of work. In other words, because Minimal art involved no skilled handwork, there was no need to pay large sums of money to obtain an 'original' or to insist on the artist's signature and evidence of provenance. What the Tate Gallery curators failed to perceive was that they could have established a large collection of Minimal (and Conceptual) art for virtually nothing. If they had done so, the charge of wasting public money would have been much easier to refute.

All the publicity aroused by Andre's 'bricks' piece resulted in it becoming famous and virtually every new visitor to the Tate now wishes to see it. This has enabled the Tate to claim that it has become a 'popular' work of art, but surely, it is a notorious tourist attraction rather than a truly popular work of art. What can be said in its favour is that it raised the issue of the identity of art in an acute form and thus prompted many people to ponder the questions: 'What is art? What materials can art be made from? Who in our society has the power to define art?'

The furore over 'the bricks' was also of value in exposing the immense gap which existed during the 1970s between the taste of the art world minority and the taste of the majority of the British public.

12

1976: POLE-CARRYING PERFORMANCE
AROUSES DERISION

In February 1976 an example of the genre of Performance or Live art, which took place in Norfolk, produced a barrage of negative publicity, laughter and derision, and prompted a Member of Parliament to ask the Minister for the Arts why this event had been subsidised with public money.

The performance in question involved three men – Ray Richards, Dennis de Groot and Tony Emerson – dressed in hiking gear, walking around the countryside for a week with a ten-foot-long wooden pole painted yellow attached to their heads via specially made headgear resembling ice cream cones. The men, all fine arts graduates of Leeds

16. Michael Bennett, *Ddart, 'Circular Walk', Green Lane, Thetford*, 1976.
Photo: M. Bennett.

Polytechnic (who were then working as labourers), constituted the Ddart Performance Group, a name that evoked both the Dada movement and a pub's dart team. At first sight the pole appeared silly and meaningless, yet it could be interpreted as a sign of the unity of the group since it literally linked the three members together. (In future performances given in Spain, two of the group wore harnesses which enabled them to be joined by lengths of wooden dowelling.) It could also be interpreted as a visualisation of a social tie or obligation which places limits on our freedom of action as individuals.

Raymond Richards, spokesman for the group, described their 1976 work as follows to the artist and writer Giles Auty:

> The pole was worn for many reasons, one of which was to attract attention ... we walked around a huge, 150-mile circumference circle as precisely as possible using existing roads, tracks and pathways – thus creating a gigantic but transient piece of sculpture. The pole was worn at all times whilst walking and each evening we did a short performance about the circular walk in a pub en route.

The event, he continued, was 'a sincere attempt to create something new and exciting, to bring together performance and sculpture outside of an art gallery situation'. The circular 'sculpture' was thus invisible, a mental rather than a material work of art, and since it was not visual, critics were relieved of the normal requirement to see a work before they judged or condemned it. Circles are symbolic shapes with a long history of use by artists and ancient cultures, but by the 1970s they were a cliché.

Ddart's performance had close parallels with the 1960s' 'living sculptures' Gilbert & George, and the Land art of Richard Long and Hamish Fulton who both undertook journeys in the countryside and then presented documentation of their actions in the form of photographs, books and maps. In Long's case, circular sculptures made from found stones were displayed on the floors of art galleries. While these artists too have been subject to public derision, they are still highly respected by supporters of contemporary art within the art world.

Richards also claimed that as many spectators smiled and enjoyed the performance as disliked it and that local press coverage was favourable and accurate at the time of the event. The uproar in the national media occurred a few weeks later and this time the coverage involved 'a terrible distortion of the facts'.

From descriptions and photographs the performance does appear to have been a slight work of art lacking significant content, a rather vacuous attempt to take art to the people, particularly rural people, most of whom probably do not visit contemporary art galleries. But was it any worse or any more absurd than a performance of Morris dancing outside a country pub?

Giles Auty is the author of *The Art of Self-Deception* (1977), in which he attacks what he regards as the absurdities of avant-garde art. He does not really explain what he thinks was wrong with the pole-carrying event, assuming that his readers will agree that its worthlessness is self-evident; however, he does compare it unfavourably to paintings by Velásquez. Few would question the qualitative difference: making a pole and headgear and walking in a circle hardly rivals the skill and intelligence required to produce *Las Meninas*. Yet the comparison rather unfairly jumps across time, national cultures and art forms. Auty thinks it is still possible for painting to repeat the realist achievements of Velásquez, but most art historians would argue that such an artistic peak was specific to a period, place and culture and cannot be reproduced in the same medium when so much has changed.

Auty appears to have no respect for the genre of Performance art at all: the best Performance artists he claimed to have seen were the London buskers of the 1950s. However, the genre cannot be dismissed on the basis of one minor example. There have been many, much more impressive performances both in terms of form and content by artists such as Laurie Anderson, Joseph Beuys, Stuart Brisley, John Latham and Nigel Rolfe.

Perhaps the minor art event in East Anglia would have been overlooked by the national press had it not been for the fact that it was supported by public funds. Ddart received the small sum of £395 from the Arts Council, which was spent on costumes and a fee for the photographer who documented the event. Adrian Henri, the Liverpool poet, painter and author of *Environments and Happenings* (1974), was a member of the Arts Council panel which awarded the grant. He thought it was a small price to pay for three men working twenty-four hours a day to provide a week's entertainment. Henri was one of the few who praised the 'real movement sculpture' on the grounds that it was 'pure and beautiful'. David Archer, publican of the Ferry Inn, Reedham, disagreed: he described Ddart's ten minute act as 'an up and down thing without music' which left him and his 15 customers cold.

"Methinks the boy Harry doth take the mock."

17. Giles, 'Methinks the boy Harry doth take the mock' cartoon,
***Sunday Express*, 14 March 1976.**
Reproduced by courtesy of Express Newspapers.

Predictably it was the yellow pole on heads which captured the
public's and the cartoonists' imagination. Giles, of the *Sunday Express*,
drew a cartoon in which the pole-carrying trio appeared in the
background, while in the foreground a country yokel with a log on his
head and a sign on his chest saying 'Look – no grant' danced a jig
outside a pub.

Ken Weetch, the Member of Parliament for Ipswich, wrote to Hugh
Jenkins, then Minister for the Arts, asking how the allocation of public
money could be justified. Jenkins replied that it was not his responsibility 'to make aesthetic judgements'. The argument was that such
judgements were – according to the 'arm's length principle' adopted by
Parliament – delegated to the Arts Council, who delegated them to Art
Panels or Regional Associations, who in turn delegated them to officers
or commissioned exhibition curators.

Auty complained – with some justice – that with such a pass-
the-buck system, no one was prepared to take responsibility for
differentiating between good and bad art. Discrimination is particularly
difficult in the case of Performance art because commissioning and
funding usually takes place on the basis of proposals submitted in

advance of execution. In 1976 Richard Francis, an Arts Council exhibitions' officer, wrote a frank article acknowledging the problems associated with supporting what was – to the Council – a new, experimental genre, one of which was finding people with the appropriate knowledge and expertise to serve on the Performance Art Panel. Since the only people available tended to be practitioners, there was clearly a danger that the panel would become a self-serving group.

Ddart appear to have been attempting to produce a kind of contemporary, folk art, a temporary event that would live on in the folk memory. Whether or not the folk of East Anglia fondly recall the event is not known, but the artists certainly succeeded, inadvertently, in entering the folklore of British tabloid journalism and the art world.

13
1976: CAN DIRTY NAPPIES BE ART?

At the Institute of Contemporary Arts in London an exhibition by the Feminist artist Mary Kelly in 1976 was scorned by tabloid journalists because it included some stained nappy-liners.

Kelly is an American-born, Conceptual and Feminist artist, theorist and teacher now resident in the United States, who lived in Britain for over 20 years. She was born in Minneapolis in 1941 and studied at the College of St Teresa, Winona, Minnesota, where she graduated in 1963. After completing an MA in art at the Pius 12th Institute in Florence, she taught at the American University in Beirut from 1965 to 1968, and undertook further postgraduate study at St Martin's School of Art in London from 1968 to 1970. She then married the English artist Ray Barrie and they had a son in 1973 whom they named Kelly. Mary Kelly taught at Goldsmiths College in South London for a time but returned to the United States in 1987. From 1989 Kelly was director of Studio and Critical Studies at the Whitney Museum Independent Study Program in New York City. Then, in 1996, she was appointed chair of the Department of Art at the University of California, Los Angeles.

She says that being in London in the 1970s, at the start of the Women's Movement, was one of the happiest times of her life. She became involved with the Berwick Street Film Collective, which made a documentary about women's labour entitled *Night Cleaners* (1975), and she helped to organise the exhibition *Women and Work* (South London Gallery, May 1975). She also chaired meetings of the newly founded Artists' Union. During these years she was concerned with the contribution of women to the reproduction of society, their economic condition, the division of labour between the two genders, women's multiple responsibilities as workers outside and inside the home, their roles as lovers, wives and mothers. However, as a result of the publication of articles in the film journal *Screen* and Juliet Mitchell's book *Psychoanalysis and Feminism* (1974), Kelly's attention turned to the psychic dimension, the role of the unconscious and women's internalisation of patriarchal ideology.

Kelly's offending exhibition, held in the New Gallery of the ICA, Nash House (near Buckingham Palace), in October 1976, was entitled *Post-Partum Document: Documentations I–III*. At the time Ted Little was the ICA's director and Barry Barker was in charge of exhibitions. The show was an interim report about a long-term project which began with the birth of her son in 1973 and was completed six years later when he entered primary school. The final work consisted of 135 individual units organised into six sections. A summation in book form was later published in 1983.

The ICA display recorded a uniquely female experience – motherhood, raising a baby boy from his birth to the end of his second year, when he was ready to leave the home and the intimate relationship with his mother for the outside world, that is, nursery school. It was a considerable achievement on Kelly's part to combine the roles of parent and artist, and it was an intelligent, pragmatic decision to make daily maternal experiences and tasks the subject of her artistic inquiry.

Historically, the mother/child relationship has been depicted in countless paintings of Mary and the infant Jesus. In most modern families such a record takes the form of a sequence of amateur snapshots, but in Kelly's case the documentation took various forms: baby clothes; a daily diary of notes (some typed, some handwritten) concerning food and drinks consumed plus resulting nappy-liner fecal stains; her son's earliest scribbles and handprints; diagrams derived from a post-Freudian theorist; plus a text entitled *Footnotes and Bibliography*.

Hence there were physical samples of evidence, indexical traces and written discourses that were transcriptions of speech acts and also analyses of, reflections upon, those speech acts. The material was presented in

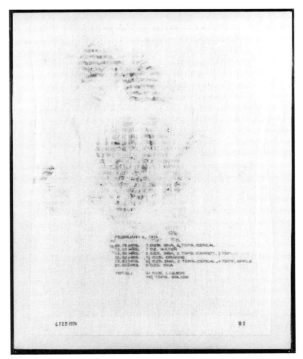

18. Mary Kelly, *Post Partum, Part I, 6 Feb 1974*, 1974.
Analysed fecal stains and feeding charts, mixed media,
28 units, 27.9 x 35.6 cm (each unit).
Toronto, Canada: Art Gallery of Ontario collection.
Photo: Carlo Catenazzi, reproduced by courtesy of the artist
and the Art Gallery of Ontario.

terms of panels and footnotes organised in three sections representing
different stages of weaning: (1) weaning from the breast; (2) (learning to
speak) weaning from dependence on the mother's completion of the
child's utterances; (3) weaning from the mother/child dyad.

What was also unusual about Kelly's work was the use of a theoretical
framework mainly derived from the French, psychoanalytic theorist
Jacques Lacan who is famous for his theory of the mirror-phase in child
development. Lacan's theories provided Kelly with a male, objective,
quasi-scientific structure within which to analyse her own subjective
experiences of motherhood and her son's acquisition of a masculine

identity. It enabled her to distance herself, to generalise from her personal biography – 'the personal is political' – to that of all mothers.

The questions Kelly addressed were: 'How does socialisation occur? How is consciousness/ideology formed? What processes are involved in the reciprocal relations between mothers and their children? When and how do children become self-conscious, gendered beings, enter into language and begin to make visual marks? And what desires and fantasies do mothers experience? What is their stake in the project called "motherhood"?'

Her exhibition was thus a remarkable combination of the concrete and the abstract, everyday detail and grand theory. Predictably, the inclusion of stained nappy-liners aroused the derision of newspaper journalists. For once the accusation, 'a load of crap' appeared to be literally true. Roger Bray, an *Evening Standard* reporter, commented: 'London's young marrieds, who may feel that they have seen enough dirty nappy-liners to last them a lifetime, may however like to know what emotions all this is supposed to stir.' In an adjoining column references were made back to the Tate's bricks affair and forward to the next ICA show *Prostitution*, thereby situating Kelly's show as one of a trio of art scandals.

Frank Robertson, writing for the conservative newspaper, the *Daily Telegraph*, reported that he had spent 40 minutes in the gallery during which time he had heard a middle-aged woman remark: 'I think it's a load of rubbish. Taxpayers should not be asked to subsidise this sort of rubbish.' Although the ICA was a private organisation which required visitors to pay a fee to become members before gaining admission, it did receive some financial support from the Arts Council.

Laura Mulvey, a film-maker/theorist writing in the Feminist magazine *Spare Rib*, defended Kelly's exhibition against its critics. In her view the show was 'a direct provocation to conventional concepts of "art". It is the form of the exhibition ... that causes so much outrage. A painting of a mother changing her baby's nappy would be easily overlooked as kitsch, but not so with dirty nappy-liners annotated and placed within a discourse that needs work to be unravelled, and refuses to place the figure of the mother on view.' (In fact, Kelly's 1983 book does feature a photo of her and her son opposite the title page.)

However, further comment in a later issue of *Spare Rib* indicated that even Feminists had problems understanding and enjoying Kelly's show. Margot Waddell and Michelene Wandor questioned the fragmented presentation of disparate objects and texts that required so much mental effort on the part of viewers: 'The exhibition ... appears to be open and accessible; in fact it is opaque, and not so much participatory as excluding and exclusive.' They went on to complain about 'weak visual metaphors' and 'esoteric intellectualisation' and then added: 'Such a heavy dependence on an inadequately presented theory can only distract attention from the "artistic" nature of the work.'

A proportion of Feminist artists and critics continue to believe that Kelly's art is too complex and cerebral for the vast majority of women to understand and that therefore it is only appreciated by a small, educated elite. Kelly's response to this criticism is to deny that there is any homogeneous mass audience for an artist to address: 'You can't make art for everyone.' She sees her audience as quite specific, that is, 'the Women's Movement, other women artists and people generally interested in the issue of patriarchy'.

Another charge levelled at Kelly's work – and Conceptual art in general – is that it lacks visual and tactile appeal. For instance, in 1979 the critic Peter Fuller dismissed *Post-Partum Document* as 'obsessive, aesthetically dead, forensic ramblings'. Some years later Edward Lucie-Smith remarked: 'Its aesthetic content, in any conventional sense of the term, is almost nil.' Her supporters, however, argue that it does have aesthetic qualities but that they are subtle ones compared to those found in a brightly coloured painting. (Long-established art forms such as painting and sculpture were deliberately rejected by some Feminist artists in the 1970s because of their historical and masculine connotations.)

Kelly herself told Terence Maloon: 'The formal qualities of typed script are very important, as well as the internal construction of the document.' As far as she was concerned, the items on display in the ICA were fetish objects which had displaced the mother's fetishisation of the child. She added: 'It's almost comical in that the value of the objects is minimal in any commercial sense, yet their affective value ... is maximum for me.' She has also stated: 'For me it's absolutely crucial that this kind of pleasure in the text, in the objects themselves, should engage the viewer, because there's no point at which it can become a deconstructed critical engagement if the viewer is not first ... drawn into the work.'

Whatever one's opinion is regarding the aesthetic qualities of *Post-Partum Document*, it was a challenging intellectual exhibit that subsequently proved to be highly influential within Feminist art circles. The sheer quantity of commentary it has generated is surely proof of its significance. Kelly's ICA show did not deserve to be trivialised by the popular press as simply a display of 'dirty nappies'. Yet again it was the unusual material presented by a radical artist which disturbed those suspicious of

all new developments in fine art. The presence of the nappy-liners provided them with an excuse not to engage with the substance of the *Post-
Partum Document* exhibit and the important social issues that it raised.

14
1976: FROM SHOCK ART TO SHOCK ROCK

In 1976 a show entitled *Prostitution* held at London's Institute of
Contemporary Arts mounted by COUM Transmissions and a performance by Throbbing Gristle incensed the press, Conservative MPs and
arts officials.

Neil Andrew Megson (b. 1950, Manchester) came from a middle-class
background and, after attending grammar school in Stockport, he
studied philosophy, sociology and social administration at Hull
University but dropped out before completing his degree. At Hull he
adopted the name Genesis P-Orridge and met Cosey Fanni Tutti
(b. 1951). In 1969 they formed COUM Transmissions, a Performance
art group. 'Sleazy' Peter Christopherson joined later.

Significantly, neither Genesis nor Cosey went to art school. They
became contemptuous of artists who pursued conventional careers via
the private gallery system. Contact with a live audience was essential
to them and, in an attempt to recapture the reality and power of tribal
rites, they emulated dervishes, shamans and witch doctors.

During the early 1970s, COUM Transmissions moved to London
where, having established a reputation as performers, they received
grants from the Arts Council for events in Britain and from the British
Council for events abroad. The public funds they received were later to
provoke angry headlines in the popular press such as 'Sex Show Man's
Amazing Free Tour', 'State Aid for Cosey's travelling Sex Troupe' and
'How Orridge and Co. got £59,000'. The large sum mentioned in the
latter headline was the Arts Council's annual funding for *all* experimental artists. For the record, the sum received by COUM from the
state during 1975–76 was around £2,000.

Some COUM events involved nudity, sexual behaviour, simulated
blood, self-inflicted suffering, wounds and burns, and were designed to
transgress social norms and to disturb audiences, but others were more
pleasing. A solo performance by Cosey at the Hayward Gallery, for
instance, consisted of a gentle, balletic display of bodily movement.

Candlelight was used to create a magical atmosphere and a large audience, which included children, found the performance hypnotic and pleasurable.

The year 1976 was momentous for Genesis. During February and March he contributed to a major show of English art held in Milan. In April he appeared at the Highbury Magistrates' Court charged with sending indecent images through the post. GP-O had mailed postcards with collaged erotic additions and this resulted in a prosecution by the GPO (the General Post Office!). Genesis was found guilty and fined £100 plus £20 costs. Then, in the autumn, the COUM show *Prostitution* held at the ICA (19–26 October) caused a public scandal. The very title was a provocation and so was a press release with a photo of Cosey posing in a manner reminiscent of the French whore Olympia painted by Manet in 1863.

'Dirt' has been defined by anthropologists as 'matter that is in the wrong place'. A short distance north of the ICA premises in the Mall was Soho with its sex shops, strip clubs and prostitutes. What COUM did was to transpose material that British society tolerated in one place to another place where it was not to be tolerated. In order to survive, Cosey had been working as a stripper and a model for porn magazines. Photographs of these activities were featured in the ICA show, presumably to make the Marxist point that most of us have to 'prostitute' ourselves to some degree by selling our mental or bodily labour powers.

Emmanuel Cooper's description of the contents of the show was as follows:

> The exhibition consists of explicit photographs of lesbian love and macabre assemblages of rusty knives, syringes, blooded hair and used sanitary towels one of which is growing mould. Less controversial are montages of press cuttings and photographic documentation of COUM performances in Milan and Paris.

The presence of used Tampax disgusted journalists, especially since it immediately followed Mary Kelly's 'dirty nappies' exhibition. Genesis claimed that the main feature of their ICA appearance was not the exhibits but the live performance or party planned for the opening night and four subsequent, spontaneous 'action performances'. In the wake of the storm of indignation that greeted the show, the latter were abruptly cancelled. Erotic photographs of Cosey were also removed from the wall and placed in a box 'available on request only'.

Nicholas Fairbairn, a Tory MP, was one of those who attended the

19. COUM Transmissions, *Prostitution*, 1976.
Flyer for exhibition at the ICA, London, 29.6 x 21 cm, with photo of Cosey
Fanni Tutti from *Curious* magazine. London: J. A. Walker collection.

crowded, evening opening at the ICA on 18 October and heard 'doom
and gloom rap' from Genesis, 'masochistic' music by Throbbing
Gristle, all wearing 'black lurex', and witnessed striptease by Shelley
who had been specially hired for the occasion (she was rather
disconcerted by the art world venue). Chelsea (or LSD), a Punk band,
was the supporting act. Fairbairn was dismayed by the presence of

'Hell's Angels [Punks more like] and men with multi-coloured hair' in the audience. As far as Fairbairn was concerned the COUM performers were the 'wreckers of Western civilisation'. He remarked: 'Now we are getting the lid off the maggot factory.'

'Sick, sadistic, obscene, filthy rubbish, pornography' were some of the opinions reported in the press the next day. In the *Daily Telegraph* the cartoonist Garland showed the muse of art being mugged outside the entrance to the ICA by the three members of COUM all dressed in black. The tabloids excelled themselves. Headlines included: 'Cosey's Sex Romp Pictures are Banned', 'Peddling Porn at the Taxpayer's Expense'. The breathtaking hypocrisy of the tabloid press was indicated by the fact that, while front pages were condemning visual art about sex, inside pages were carrying illustrated cinema advertisements for sex films showing in Soho. In other words, the press 'prostituted' itself for money just like Cosey. The double standards of the press are well illustrated by the fact that newspapers such as the *News of the World* and the *People* pander to their readers' prurient interest in sex, murder and violence but criticise artists who are also fascinated by such themes and who make use of them as iconography.

On the whole, art critics were more sympathetic to the show. Marina Vaizey's review for the *Sunday Times* was dispassionate and rational. Her report was headed 'Much Ado about Nothing at the ICA'.

COUM incorporated negative press comment into their exhibition and issued a publicity leaflet which reproduced it. Clearly, COUM hoped to use the media to demonstrate how journalists were misrepresenting the show, to turn the press against itself. (An instance of the Situationist tactic of *détournement*.) Genesis also had an opportunity to defend the exhibition in public when he was interviewed live on *Today* (Thames Television, 22 October).

As a result of all the negative press coverage, other Conservative MPs became agitated and asked questions in the House of Commons about the Arts Council's policies and methods. A Labour government was in power but was experiencing economic difficulties and hence there was a clamour for reductions in public spending, particularly money spent on such 'dubious' cultural activities. There was also concern about a national decline in standards of morality. Officers from Scotland Yard's Obscene Publications Squad were thus prompted to visit the ICA and they submitted a report to the Director of Public Prosecutions. In the event, however, neither COUM nor the ICA were charged with any offence.

Ted Little, director of the ICA, was put under pressure by the media and by his paymasters, the Arts Council (the ICA was then receiving £80,000 per annum from the Council). Little pointed out that only £200 had been paid to COUM towards the expenses of *Prostitution* and that the ICA's membership had increased sharply as a result of the COUM show. Furthermore, he felt that the ICA had a duty to act as a platform for contemporary avant-garde art whether he personally liked it or not. Roy Shaw, secretary-general of the Arts Council disagreed. Little, he considered, had a duty to be discriminating in his choice of which events he produced. Shaw visited the exhibition and found it 'boring and disgusting'. He was not in favour of banning such shows but did not think they should be funded by the taxpayer. Shaw was under pressure from the Arts Council's chairman Lord Patrick Gibson to close the exhibition but he refused on the grounds that the Council should not censor its client's exhibitions. However, he did relay the Council's disapproval to Little, and the exhibition was modified.

In terms of the history of art, *Prostitution* was not an exhibition of major importance and, aside from the live performance, there was little in the way of aesthetic pleasure. (Simon Ford has argued that the show was 'an attack on traditional artistic values, still dominated by formalist criteria'.) Nevertheless, it should be possible for contemporary art venues to present documentary exhibitions about the work of Performance artists and about such subjects as prostitution without being subjected to such a torrent of denunciation. As a moral panic and media phenomenon *Prostitution* was highly significant. Writing in 1996, Ford summed up its political ramifications as follows:

> ... it gave the Tory supporting papers an opportunity to discredit the Arts Council and the contemporary arts establishment, its liberal supporters and by association, the Labour Government, by implicating contemporary art in declining moral standards: economic crisis was equated with moral crisis.

Even members of COUM seem to have been taken aback by the fury and hysteria which, to some extent, they had set out to arouse. (During the years 1975 to 1977 the Punk rock band the Sex Pistols behaved in a similarly aggressive manner and then were unable to control the madness they unleashed.) Genesis claimed that the show had been designed as 'a comment on survival in Britain' and as a demonstration of how the media distort information, and this had been achieved. On another occasion he declared it was 'a joke ... a parody of all that is wrong with the art world'. It was a dangerous game to play and it effectively ended his participation in the realm of fine art.

While burning his boats in spectacular fashion in the art world, Genesis was switching his attention to the realm of rock music by forming the band Throbbing Gristle, which in 1981 transmuted into Psychic TV. Around the latter a youth cult was deliberately fostered entitled *The Temple ov Psychick Youth*. Despite death threats to him and his family (GP-O and his wife Paula have daughters called Caresse and Genesse), Genesis continued to employ shock tactics: dissonant sounds and videos with violent imagery – all in the service of 'sex, resistance, subversion and discipline'. His enemies accused him of being 'a vile man' who used his satanic cult in order to corrupt and brainwash teenagers, but Genesis claimed that what he was trying to do was to 'de-programme' them by providing alternative information and rituals that challenged the all-pervasive 'control' exercised by dominant social powers such as organised religion and mainstream mass media.

Psychic TV's anti-entertainment ethos generally precluded a mass appeal but in 1986 they did have a hit single and promo-video with *Godstar*, a song about Brian Jones (who died in 1969) of the Rolling Stones.

In 1992 newspapers carried reports of a video showing 'bloody ritual satanic abuse'. Scotland Yard's Obscene Publications Squad then raided Genesis's Brighton home and seized books, letters and videotapes. He was accused of making the offensive tape which included footage of the noted homosexual film-maker Derek Jarman, and which had in fact been projected during Psychic TV's multimedia concerts. Genesis has admitted to self 'body mortification' (such as the monks of old practised) in order to achieve 'altered states'. The fact is that anyone with a video recorder and a morbid imagination could easily compile a tape consisting of clips of surgical operations, scenes of rape and torture, killings in wars, and so on, from news broadcasts, documentaries and feature films transmitted on mainstream television. Such a tape might be repellent and negative but surely it would not be illegal (except perhaps on copyright grounds). It would also be realist in the sense of showing what many human beings are capable of doing to other human beings.

To escape further harassment by British authorities, Genesis moved to the United States. Genesis and his collaborators aroused extreme antagonism in many quarters because they transgressed unspoken rules not to meddle with the subconscious, the occult, sex, ritual, horror and violence. Yet it can be argued that they explored dark forces not to endorse them but to *exorcise* them and to extend human self-understanding.

15

1977: HAYWARD ANNUAL EXHIBITION
SAVAGED BY CRITICS AND A TV JOURNALIST

A selection of contemporary British art shown at the Hayward Gallery in the summer of 1977 received a bad press and was mauled on television. An Arts Council event mounted in response failed to provide illumination or reassurance.

Fyfe Robertson (1902–87), a gruff, bearded journalist and television presenter whose voice had a distinctive Scottish accent, made a series of half-hour documentaries during the 1970s entitled *Robbie*. One of these programmes (BBC1, 15 August 1977) chose to examine the state of contemporary British art as represented by a Hayward Gallery exhibition.

The Hayward Annual was instituted in 1977 with the aim of presenting, over time, 'a cumulative picture of British art as it develops'. To begin with the Annual was presented in two parts: part one took place from May to July and part two from July to September. The selectors were Michael Compton (Tate Gallery curator), Howard Hodgkin (painter) and William Turnbull (painter and sculptor). The fact that the two artist-selectors selected themselves was an indication of how cosy this exhibition was to be. The choice of artists to be included seemed to have been completely arbitrary: they were simply artists that the selectors knew, liked and could agree on. Some critics perceived the show as an 'old boys' venture by art-establishment figures who were indifferent to the work of younger artists and the needs and tastes of the general public.

In part one both abstract and figurative artists were featured. They included John Hoyland, Kenneth Martin, Anthony Caro, Bernard Cohen, Nigel Hall, Peter Phillips and Allen Jones. Critics questioned the selection on various grounds, one of which was masculine bias. Only one woman artist was included and she – Kim Lim – turned out to be Mrs Turnbull. Another complaint, made by Richard Cork, was that there was too close a connection to the dealers and private art galleries of Cork Street.

Part two of the Annual included paintings by Peter Blake, Robyn Denny, Ron Kitaj, Hodgkin, David Hockney and Bob Law, sculptures by Michael Craig-Martin, Barry Flanagan and Eduardo Paolozzi, photographs by John Hilliard, a poster series by Victor Burgin, and performances by Stuart Brisley and The Theatre of Mistakes. Blake also displayed an open letter of complaint addressed to three art critics who had had the temerity to criticise part one. An angry exchange of letters between Blake and Cork was then published in the *Guardian*. When Peter Fuller joined in on the side of the critics, an acrimonious and interminable argument ensued between him and Blake (published in the pages of *Aspects* magazine). As Lynne Cooke has observed:

> The storm of rancorous protest that erupted around this exhibition clearly revealed a hitherto dormant but deep-seated antagonism between various competing factions within the British art world, notably the orthodox painting lobby which dominated the exhibition and, increasingly, the English art scene as a whole, and a group of critics including Caroline Tisdall, Paul Overy and Richard Cork who were regarded by many of the painters as hostile since they were known supporters of art with overt social relevance.

If part one of the Annual exposed divisions within the art world, part two exposed the division between the art world and the wider culture.

Fyfe Robertson regarded himself as a tribune of the people and approached his subject with a no-nonsense, common-sense attitude. In his television programme, which focused on part two, he lambasted art critics, accusing them of 'intellectual snobbery' and of putting up 'Keep Out' notices. He admitted he knew little about art but he did not think its appreciation should require specialist knowledge. Few would expect to understand theoretical physics without intense study and a high IQ, but art – despite its many varieties and complexities – is still thought of as having a duty of public accessibility. The trouble is, many contemporary artists do not agree.

In contrast to the journalists, producers and entertainers of the media, most avant-garde artists do not see themselves as communicators using public languages or codes which can be understood immediately by an uninformed mass audience. They see themselves instead as intellectuals using private or restricted codes to address specialist, informed minorities. Viewers who are not familiar with the artists' codes are expected to make the effort to learn them. It is surely unreasonable to expect[3] that all new art should be made for absolute beginners or that it should be pitched at the lowest common denominator. Yet, if a work of art is so complex and difficult that it is only enjoyed and understood by a handful of people, then its social benefit is highly restricted and any public subsidy becomes hard to justify. However, as the history of the reception of Cézanne's work reminds us, paintings may start life with only a few admirers but then, in the course of time, they may end up being appreciated by millions. The risk of being found foolish by posterity has made many in the contemporary art world fearful of making the kind of value judgements about new art that someone like Robbie had no hesitation in making.

Robertson also attacked the live art by Brisley and The Theatre of Mistakes for its 'absurdities' and reliance on Arts Council grants. Craig-Martin's display of glasses of water on glass shelves and Flanagan's installation with ropes aroused his ire, but what really incensed him were Law's series of canvases which were all white and blank apart from lines drawn in ballpoint pens near the four edges. Law, he declared, was 'furthest down the avant-garde road to nothing and nowhere'. The painter was interviewed but his explanations and justifications of his reductive, Minimalist paintings were feeble and unconvincing.

Peter Fuller, who reviewed the show for *The Connoisseur*, shared Robbie's opinion. He wrote: 'It is difficult to understand how grown men can devote year after year of their lives to drawing single lines round the edge of blank canvases ...' He concluded: 'The sterility of artists like Bob Law and Nigel Hall can be taken as a metaphor for the sterility of British art as a whole.' Hockney also appeared and he more or less agreed with Robertson's exasperation with Law's work. In his opinion, avant-garde art was 'old-fashioned'. Paradoxically, to be radical one had to return to figuration and traditional techniques.

When Brisley was questioned by Robbie, he proved more articulate and he justified his performances by reference to a historical tradition. But surely what he should have stressed was the intrinsic merit of his work, not the fact that other artists had engaged in similar activities in the past? Sir Norman Reid, director of the Tate, was then grilled regarding his purchase of Carl Andre's 'bricks' and three women visitors to the Tate supplied puzzled comments. Giles Auty, an artist and savage critic of the avant-garde (in 1977 Auty published a sustained attack entitled *The Art of Self-Deception*), briefly discussed the problems of art education and explained how difficult it was to counter the influence of the existing arts establishment.

Robertson's overall judgement of the Hayward artists was that they were 'in retreat from art. They're degrading it to an undisciplined,

**20. Fyfe Robertson sitting on Carl Andre's *Equivalent VIII* sculpture as he
appeared in the TV programme *Robbie* (BBC1, 15 August 1977).**
Photo: courtesy of the BBC.
© Carl Andre/VAGA, New York and DACS, London 1998

despairing, free-for-all meaninglessness'. His television programme
was a populist polemic by someone whose mind was made up before he
even visited the South Bank. The half-hour programme was too short
to explore in the detail they deserved the various issues and problems
that Robertson raised in quick succession. At the same time, however,
it appeared – even to some members of the art world – that there was a
case to answer. Painters of empty canvases cannot simply refer to the
precedent of Malevich – who painted white squares on white grounds
in 1917–18 – as a justification. Malevich's intention was to clear the
decks for a new beginning. Avant-garde art is about innovation, not
repetition. Furthermore, empty canvases cannot engage directly with
the worlds of nature and society, their beauties and problems. And, in
any case, the art of painting cannot limit itself forever to such a
perpetual endgame without admitting it is an exhausted medium.

What Robbie did not discover – because his investigative journalism
was so shallow – was that, during the mid-1970s, there were significant
numbers of British artists, art students and writers who were highly
critical of Minimalism and who were seeking new directions for art
which involved pictorial critiques of mass-media imagery, Feminist
and Community arts initiatives, and engagement with socio-political
issues. The desire to reconnect art to society became evident in three
future exhibitions held in London: *Art For Whom?* (Serpentine Gallery,
1978), *Art For Society*, (Whitechapel Art Gallery, 1978) and *Lives*
(Hayward Gallery, 1979).

Attendance figures for the Hayward Annual were estimated at 10,000 for part one and 25,000 for part two. Viewing figures for the television programme probably reached several hundred thousand. When Roy Shaw, secretary-general of the Arts Council, saw that the Hayward Annual had received such a drubbing, he proposed a public discussion at the Hayward Gallery. He was concerned that much of the art appearing in shows and galleries in receipt of public funds seemed to be arid, obscure and unpopular. Those curators responsible for supporting and selecting it, he thought, should be willing to defend and explain it to taxpayers. He was told no one would come, but in fact the meeting, held on 5 September, was packed and the 600 present included many who did not belong to the London art world.

Shaw chaired the meeting and on the platform were Joanna Drew (director of exhibitions), Compton, David Hockney, Hodgkin, Hoyland and a representative of the Artists' Union. Turnbull was supposed to be there but failed to attend. Robertson arrived late and, dissatisfied with what he heard, left early. William Packer, who thought Robertson's television programme 'contemptible', reported that he strode 'peevishly from the room. The people's champion had run away.'

According to John McEwen's account, the meeting lacked structure and firm control. Statements by the selectors and artists did not provide the clarification and illumination sought by the audience. Joanna Drew performed like a blank canvas by refusing to say anything. Thus a worthy and rare attempt to bring the avant-garde faction of the art world and the public together failed. The gulf, the lack of respect and understanding between the two sides, remained unbridged. Even if the meeting had been successful, it could not have countered the impact of Robbie's programme. What Shaw should have done was to commission a film for transmission on television.

16

1979: THE ARTS COUNCIL, CENSORSHIP AND THE *LIVES* EXHIBITION

In 1979 works of art by Conrad Atkinson and Tony Rickaby – two Left-wing artists – were withdrawn by the Arts Council from an exhibition to be held in London because of their critical, political content.

Derek Boshier (b. 1937), who studied at the Royal College of Art, became well known during the early 1960s as a Pop artist. Towards the end of the 1970s he was invited to curate an exhibition funded by the Arts Council. He was given a budget of £15,000 in order to purchase work for the Arts Council's collection. Originally the show was intended for the Serpentine Gallery, Kensington Gardens, but it was later switched to the Hayward Gallery, South Bank Centre, London. It was then to tour the country. Boshier decided to focus on art that was public rather than private in order to overcome the élitism and self-referential character of so much avant-garde art, and its isolation from everyday life. He also wanted to transcend the divisions between the various media, and between high and low culture.

In his introduction to the catalogue, Boshier explained that his intention had been to mount a 'popularist (sic) exhibition' defined as 'concerning or open to all or any people'. Since everyone can relate to images of other people without the need for specialist art-historical knowledge, Boshier thought that an exhibition with figurative/humanist content was bound to be accessible, hence his title: *Lives: An Exhibition of Artists Whose Work is Based on Other People's Lives*. The show, held in March 1979, presented a disparate range of material: figurative paintings; a society portrait; a Feminist work about rape; examples of photo-journalism; videos of people at work; information on fads; Punk graphics; family photo-albums; art created as therapy in psychiatric hospitals; cartoons from national newspapers; torn-up photos collected from photo booths, and so on.

Lives was a well-meaning effort on Boshier's part but the limited extent of his freedom and independence as a selector was revealed when he was informed on 2 February 1979 that two items which he had picked were unacceptable to the General Council of the Arts Council and were being withdrawn. Texts which the artists had written for the catalogue were also being removed. (These developments revealed who the ultimate selectors were.) The two works in question were a print by Conrad Atkinson (b. 1940) entitled *Anniversary Print From the People Who Brought You Thalidomide ...* (1978) and a series of eight watercolours entitled *Fasçade* (1977–78) by Tony Rickaby (b. 1944).

Neither of the two artists was consulted before the withdrawal took place, nor was Boshier, nor were members of the Arts Council's special advisory panel for the visual arts. Some Arts Council officers were also embarrassed at having to implement a decision passed down from above. They told the artists that, as far as they were aware, this was the

first example of censorship on political grounds in the history of the
Arts Council. To add insult to injury, the General Council refused to
disclose or discuss the reasons for their action apart from saying that it
was a consequence of taking legal advice. Despite numerous protests
from leading artists, critics and politicians, the General Council
refused to reverse its decision.

Tony Rickaby studied at Portsmouth College of Art and St Martin's
School of Art in London. He produces work in a variety of media: texts,
artists books, drawings, paintings, and so on. He is a left-wing artist

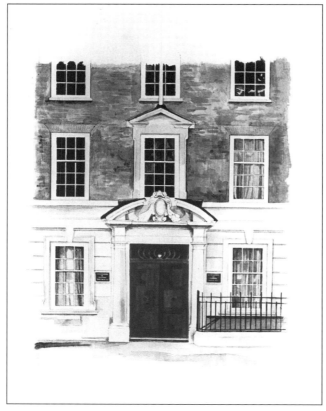

21. Tony Rickaby, *Fasçade – Conservative Party,*
***32 Smith Square, London SW1*, 1979.**
Watercolour on paper, 51 x 32 cm.
London: Arts Council collection. Photo: courtesy of the artist.

but his art is far more oblique and subtle than Socialist Realism. In the autumn of 1977 Rickaby commenced a series of 43 watercolours, drawings and etchings of the façades of selected London buildings. The series, plus an accompanying text, were displayed at the Art Net gallery in May 1978 and eight watercolours were bought by Boshier for inclusion in his planned *Lives* show.

At first sight the paintings appeared to be innocuous because their subject matter was commonplace and their medium was very traditional – watercolour is a medium in which British artists have excelled – and their technique/style was deliberately academic and unexpressive. It was their titles which gave them a political dimension: each building turned out to be the London base of a right-wing organisation (such as the Conservative Party, the Monarchist League and the National Front). Hence the overall title of the series – *Fasçade* – a synthesis of 'façade' and 'fascism'.

Rickaby considered buildings to be 'the most important and influential objects we encounter in our lives. They hold a whole range of social and cultural meanings for us, they form our environment and certain of them ... represent some of our very basic needs, fears and emotions.' He added: 'A painting or drawing is analogous to the façade of a building in that both are flat surfaces which contain, or conceal, more meanings (cultural, economic, historical, etc.) than superficially are apparent.'

So, the implication was that behind these respectable fronts a vicious future was being plotted. And indeed this proved to be the case: in 1979 a hardline Conservative government under Prime Minister Margaret Thatcher gained power. Her ten-year regime was to prove a disaster for socialism, public services, the Greater London Council and the lives of many workers and trade unionists. When Rickaby learnt of the suppression of his watercolours he offered to change their title to the less contentious *Fronts* but this proposal was rejected. He was told: 'It's too late.'

Atkinson is also a socialist by political conviction and his informational/documentary-style art has served a number of left-wing causes and struggles. It also set out to expose – to 'picture' – the power relations and injustices of capitalism. His print was a case in point. To mark an anniversary of University College London, Atkinson – who was then a tutor at the Slade School of Fine Art – was invited to prepare a print, in an edition of 55, one of which was to be presented to the Queen Mother, then Chancellor of the college. His fellow tutors laughed when they heard that the socialist artist was going to make a print for royalty but Atkinson riposted: 'It depends on what I say in my print, doesn't it?'

**22. Conrad Atkinson, *Anniversary Print: A Children's Story
(for Her Majesty)*, 1978.**
Photolithography, silkscreen and watercolour, 64.7 x 49.5 cm, from an
edition of 55. London: Arts Council collection. Photo: John Webb,
reproduced by courtesy of the artist and the Arts Council collection.

In 1978 it was also the twentieth anniversary of the introduction of the drug thalidomide by a subsidiary of the multinational corporation, Distillers. This drug had been prescribed to pregnant women to combat nausea. Unfortunately, it caused several hundred babies to be born deformed or with limbs missing. Atkinson's research showed that Distillers was being tardy and mean with compensation claims. What also incensed him was the fact that Distillers' drinks products carried the Royal Warrant, a kind of seal of state approval, on their labels.

Atkinson's print resembled a drinks advertisement: it consisted of a staged photograph of Distiller's bottled drinks with the Royal Warrant signs ringed plus a framed photo of a child with the drug's marketing name, Distaval. Behind them were two images showing a rural brewery on the left and the City of London on the right. Beneath was a text entitled: *A Children's Story* which chronicled, in a dry factual manner, the 20-year tragedy of the drug. Appeals to the Royal Family to withdraw the warrant – including petitions from Members of Parliament – had fallen on deaf ears.

When Atkinson protested to the Arts Council about the censorship of his work he received a reply from Roy Shaw, the secretary-general (later to be knighted for his services to the arts), which denied that censorship had occurred. Instead 'editorial' control had been exercised because the print might have exposed the Council to legal action. The grounds for such action were not specified. (Libel was one possibility.) The excessive caution of the Arts Council was demonstrated by the fact that Atkinson's print had been exhibited at the Serpentine Gallery months before without causing any legal action or public scandal (apart from a negative article by the journalist Bernard Levin). When this was pointed out, Shaw then maintained that it was the texts which accompanied Atkinson's and Rickaby's works which were the problem.

Writing in 1988 Shaw admitted that the Council's Art Panel headed by Lawrence Gowing, the then principal of the Slade, 'showed it had teeth' by defending, 'in private', the excluded work. However, Shaw then declared that Atkinson's print 'was of very little artistic merit anyway' and so it should not have been chosen in the first place. (Surely this judgement was the responsibility of Boshier, the selector? Shaw makes no mention of Rickaby's watercolours and their artistic merit.) Atkinson's work has repeatedly been criticised on the grounds that it is not art or that it is poor art. It certainly does not provide the sensuous aesthetic pleasures of paintings by Howard Hodgkin, for example, but it does provide cognitive content, political analysis and social relevance that Hodgkin's effete confections lack.

After months of wrestling with the Arts Council, Atkinson concluded that it was 'a state patronage bureaucracy of the utmost timidity and inflexibility ... a castrated blancmange'. He also accused it of 'servile secrecy'.

Boshier traced the origin of the censorship to the mother of Michael Regan, the Arts Council's organiser of *Lives*. Apparently, she had caught sight of the texts intended for the catalogue and been horrified by Atkinson's criticism of the Royal Family. Boshier concluded that the Council was terrified of offending these relics of feudalism. His response to the *Lives* debacle was to formulate an exhibition on the theme of censorship which was to feature a book entitled *The Arts Council Position on Censorship – A Full Explanation*. The book, of course, had its pages glued together so that it could not be opened. This work was shown in his exhibition *Drawings and Books for Artists* held at the Felicity Samuel Gallery in March 1979.

Since there was nothing about the information contained in the print that had not appeared in news reports, it seems clear that what frightened the Arts Council was the connection which Atkinson had highlighted between the thalidomide tragedy, Distillers and the Royal Family.

The last-minute switch in venue from the Serpentine to the Hayward – the first was free, the second charged a fee – was said to have been prompted by two reasons: (1) the Serpentine was Crown property located in a Royal Park; (2) Margaret Harrison's painting *Rape* might have offended mothers with children who just happened to drop into the gallery.

All these events took place while a Labour government was in power and the chairman of the Arts Council was Kenneth Robinson, a former Labour Minister of Health. It has been suggested that one motive for the Arts Council's exclusion of art criticising the right was fear of offending the next government, because it seemed likely that it would be Conservative.

While artists belonging to the Artists' Union supported Atkinson and were concerned about the general impact of censorship of the arts by a body supposedly dedicated to their support, some contributors to *Lives* evinced cowardice, selfishness and lack of solidarity. They suggested – inaccurately – that Atkinson had submitted, for publicity purposes, a provocative print knowing it would be rejected; however, the majority of the exhibitors did sign a letter of protest that was sent to the Arts Council and published in *Art Monthly*.

As a consequence of the censorship, Atkinson withdrew another of his works (about Northern Ireland) from the *Lives* exhibition, questions were put to Lord Donaldson – Minister of State, Department of Education and Science – in the House of Lords, many press reports appeared and the radical journalist John Pilger published a powerful critique in the *New Statesman*. Writing in *Art Monthly* Andrew Brighton called the Arts Council 'a pusillanimous quango'. The issues were also debated on ITV and on BBC1's arts strand, *Omnibus*. Two years later the Community arts group Interaction staged an event – the *Arts Council Show Trial* – at the Tricycle Theatre, Kilburn.

In the end some justice was achieved. Atkinson sued the Arts Council for breach of contract and loss of earnings. The case was settled out of court in 1981 when the Council paid him a small sum in compensation. Six years later Atkinson was himself a member of the Arts Council's Art Panel. Currently, he works and teaches in the United States.

Today the victims of thalidomide continue to suffer and to need financial support: in 1995 Guinness (who took over Distillers) paid a further £37.5 million into a trust fund (their annual profits were £876 million) and in 1996 the British Government paid an additional £7 million.

17

1979: *MORGAN'S WALL*:
THE DESTRUCTION OF A COMMUNITY MURAL

On 6 June 1979 at 3 a.m. contractors began to demolish a wall on which a Community mural had been painted. The company which owned the wall took this furtive action because the content of the mural was proving politically embarrassing. When Brian Barnes, one of the creators of the mural, tried to prevent the destruction he was arrested by the police.

During the 1970s, a new kind of outdoor wall painting – Community murals – appeared in deprived, decayed, inner areas of cities in Europe and the United States. What distinguished Community murals from other visual signs found in the street – billboards, graffiti, public sculptures, and so on – was a consultation process and dialogue between their makers and their immediate audience. Often, members of the local community participated in the conception, planning and execution of the murals. Process of production thus became as important as the final product. The underlying political idea was to demonstrate that, with some expert help, the people could take control and transform their environment.

In terms of content, Community murals reflected the history, aspirations, pleasures and problems of people who lived in a particular locality and who were unified by shared culture, values or issues. The market forces of capitalist economies tend to undermine such values as community, cooperation and collectivism. In retrospect, therefore, Community art can be regarded as an attempt to preserve or nurture a sense of community that was being eroded.

Community muralists were usually left-wing, professional artists/ activists with some fine art training and experience who had become disillusioned with the art gallery/museum system. Their desire to establish an alternative artistic practice, to help empower deprived sectors of society, was admirable but on the street their murals had to compete with a grassroots upsurge of graffiti which was vibrant and energetic (especially in New York), and with inventive, sophisticated advertising imagery.

Regrettably, the pictorial rhetoric of most London murals was not up to the challenge. Nor, in most instances, did the quality of the painting reach the high level previously achieved in the murals by Diego Rivera, José Clemente Orozco and David Alfaro Siquerios executed in Mexico during the 1920s and 1930s. There were, however, a few impressive and politically incisive Community murals – for instance, *Morgan's Wall* or *The Good, the Bad and the Ugly* (or *Tenants and Workers Uniting to Sweep Away the Evil of Capitalism*), Battersea Bridge Road, close to the Thames in London. It was designed by Brian Barnes/the Wandsworth Mural Workshop and painted by workshop members plus 60 volunteers – many of them local children – from August 1976 to August 1978. The previous February the mural had been officially dedicated by Sir Hugh Casson, president of the Royal Academy. Raw materials were obtained from Crown Paints and sporadic funding from several sources: the local council (then under the control of Labour), the Arts Council and a Royal Academy mural trust. The total cost of the mural was around £1,000.

The Morgan Crucible Group of companies, manufacturers of carbon and also, ironically, artist's materials, then owned a prime, ten-acre riverside site and had been seeking planning permission to develop it in terms of luxury flats, restaurants and high-rise offices. Many Wandsworth residents objected to these ideas because they would mainly benefit the wealthy and outsiders. Locals needed affordable, new, low-rise houses and industrial initiatives that would provide employment. Barnes, a Community artist employed by Wandsworth Borough Council on a low wage, had been active in the Battersea Redevelopment Action Group, a pressure group seeking a say in the future of the area, and he had earlier produced a biting series of cartoons using a cow to personify Battersea. The cow was milked for profits but she also urinated on, and kicked, her exploiters.

Set back from the road, behind a flat expanse of grass (a small public park owned by the Greater London Council), was a large, derelict factory owned by Morgan Crucible. A huge, 256-foot long, 18-foot high brick wall (4,000 square feet) shielded the factory from intruders. It was on this wall that the mural was painted. (An extension was later added on another wall running at right angles to the main mural.) There were no houses or shops near the mural. Directly opposite was a bus garage (hence the bus crews and the number 19 bus prominently featured in the mural). Viewed from the busy main road, the mural's gaudy hues – reds, blues and greens – formed a welcome contrast to the dingy, grey factory building looming above it.

The left-hand side of this epic painting celebrated the daily lives of local people and their desire for decent houses, better public transport, adventure playgrounds, swimming pools and health care. Portraits of many local people were included in order to honour their achievements as against the leaders of society who had been celebrated in the art of the past. The right-hand side depicted some of the problems of the area and attacked proposed development plans for the site. The mural, therefore, presented two visions of the present and future: the 'good', utopia or heaven, and the 'bad', dystopia or hell. At the point of division was a huge yardbrush that was sweeping the corrupt part away. Unfortunately, this optimistic scenario was shortly to be proved completely wrong. The artists badly underestimated the power of the forces ranged against them.

Part of the 'bad' half of the mural was a criticism of one of the most important figures in the history of mass entertainment: Walt Disney and his famous cartoon character, Mickey Mouse. This pictorial attack was prompted by a proposal by Trust House Forte to establish a 'Disneyland' in Battersea Park. The Disney empire earns money via character merchandising and so The Wandsworth Mural Workshop was threatened with legal action by Disney's lawyers for their unauthorised, unpaid use of the image of Mickey Mouse. In a film made by Liberation Films about the painting of the mural, a person dressed up as Mickey Mouse attempts to prevent the artists from continuing their work. Thus Barnes and his team did not succumb to pressure; instead they turned the threat from Disney into a humorous and defiant performance.

23. Brian Barnes/the Wandsworth Mural Workshop,
The Good the Bad and the Ugly or *Morgan's Wall* (detail),
(London: Battersea Bridge Road), 1976–78.
(Destroyed in June 1979.) Photo: J.A. Walker.

On the wall running at right angles to the main mural, Barnes and company painted an extension. It consisted of huge, stylised, yellow, red and orange flames. The 'bad' elements of the mural were being swept into this inferno.

The mural succeeded in attracting much public attention and press coverage. However, not all locals were pleased: one remarked that it was 'cheap and shoddy – just about ruins the estate!' To preserve the mural after the redevelopment of the site, Barnes mounted a campaign to have it declared a national monument. Its critical content proved so irritating to local Conservative politicians – the Tories had taken control of Wandsworth after an election in May 1978 – and to Morgan Crucible that they decided to knock it down. Work by the demolition firm McGhee commenced in the middle of the night to make their action a *fait accompli*. The next morning, when Barnes arrived at the site, much damage had already been done. However, he still climbed on top of the wall in an attempt to halt the bulldozers but was arrested (along with six others) and spent time in police cells. When he was released he returned to the site in order to retrieve some painted bricks. His intention was to auction them off to raise money to paint another mural. But he was arrested again for trespassing on private property.

The so-called 'Flame Wall' was protected by a round-the-clock vigil and survived a month longer. Additions were made to show who the vandals were. Burning among the flames were Ian Weston-Smith (chairman of Morgan's), Lord Harlech (director of Morgan's) and John Taylor (architect of a proposed office block). Four men were also shown running for their lives but towards a hole in the ground. They were the 'uglies' or 'gang of four', that is, the Tory councillors Michael Chartres, Chris Chope, Maurice Heaster and Dennis Mallam (leader of the Council). Mallam had his trouser leg rolled up to indicate membership of the Freemasons.

Many local people were incensed by the destruction of their mural and the damage done to the park. Pubs in the area refused to serve the demolition men. A Tory councillor recognised from his portrait was pursued by an angry crowd. Barnes was not deterred by his encounters with the law – he went on to organise the painting of several more huge murals in south London.

What the *Morgan's Wall* incident demonstrated was that the bourgeois class, which normally supports spending on art and culture and pays lip service to the artist's right to freedom of expression (after all Britain is a liberal democracy, not a dictatorship), is quite ruthless when it finds itself indicted by a political work of art. Ideology and politics in art are usually acceptable to the bourgeoisie providing they are affirmative or right wing in character – flattering portraits of the Royal Family, Conservative Party leaders or captains of industry, for example. Criticism of social conditions may also be tolerated providing they are couched in general terms. For instance, a painting criticising poor housing conditions in the rented sector might well be accepted providing it does not name individual landlords and their right-wing political supporters who profit from ownership of such property. As far as Wandsworth's Tories were concerned, the mural was not art but subversive propaganda. The fact that propaganda and art are not mutually exclusive has been demonstrated by the Catholic Church – which, in fact, devised the term 'propaganda' – for centuries.

Morgan's Wall may not have been a masterpiece of mural painting comparable to those of Renaissance Italy, but the very fact that members of the British ruling class felt compelled to destroy it was surely proof of its political effectiveness. And proof too that under their veneer of civilisation those who ordered the bulldozers in were cold-hearted philistines and vandals who cared nought for the Battersea community.

18

1980: PERFORMERS JAILED FOR WEARING 'RUDE' COSTUMES

In 1980 four people were arrested and later sent to prison for wearing strange costumes in the streets of Liverpool. The costumes were judged to be grotesque and obscene because they showed the male genitals.

Alice R. Beberman (now Chute, b. 1952) is an artist of American origin who, during the 1980s, lived in Edinburgh. She first studied art at Wesleyan University, Illinois, and then at the Faculty of Art and Design, Bristol Polytechnic. Her work has encompassed a variety of art forms and media, namely, painting, sculpture, photography and tapestry. Her most notorious creations, however, are a series of costumes for a fictional family called the Furbelows (pronounced 'fire down below'; 'fur below' also suggests pubic hair). The costumes loosely enclose the whole body and are made from soft, crocheted wool. Kitty Warnock reports that:

> It was after experimenting with life-sized rag dolls that she devised the first Furbelow as a costume. She wanted to make something that could move around and go to its audience, instead of waiting for an audience to come to it. The Furbelows engage people directly and provoke a more natural response than can a work of art in the inhibiting atmosphere of a gallery.

Beberman's costumes represent naked human bodies. When worn this makes them paradoxical because they reveal all while simultaneously totally concealing the body of the performer inside. In the case of the female figures, breasts and pubic hair are visible and in the case of the

24. Alice Beberman, *Furbelows* in Liverpool, 1980.
Photo: courtesy of A. Beberman.

male figures the genitals are prominently on view – they dangle down in an absurd manner. While some viewers found these costumes as harmless as teddy bears, others found them offensive.

On 3 June 1980 four Furbelows, played by Nick Gaskin, Mary Renouf, Hayley and Melani Fox, paraded in Church Street, Liverpool, as the 'live' part of an exhibition of photographs that Beberman was holding at the Open Eye Gallery, 90–92 Whitechapel. Apparently, the reaction of the Liverpudlians to the costumes had been mild surprise and amusement until the police arrived on the scene. A crowd then gathered and a man escorting a child complained that the costumes were 'indecent'.

At first the police arrested only the two performers wearing the male costumes – an example of sex discrimination – but the others accompanied them to the police station to offer moral support. On Monday 18 August all four appeared in Liverpool City Magistrates' Court accused of 'insulting behaviour likely to cause a breach of the peace' under Section Five of the Public Order Act. Evidence of the artistic intention or merit of the work was not provided and Beberman was not called as a witness. After the magistrate viewed a short film of the event, the defendants were found guilty, fined £25 each and bound over for a year. The defendants' solicitor thought a miscarriage of justice had occurred and unwisely advised them to appeal to the Crown Court. This course of action was also recommended to them by Artlaw in London.

Later on, the Furbelows reappeared as a jazz band on a float which was part of a street procession held during the Edinburgh Festival. Again the law intervened but this time they were let off with a caution.

At the second hearing in Liverpool, held on 4 December 1980, Judge Edward Jones described the Furbelows' costumes as 'extravagant and obscene' and the performers' behaviour as 'disgraceful and disgusting'. He claimed that the public were embarrassed by the costumes and that some individuals would have taken the law into their own hands had not the police taken action. Society, he pompously concluded, 'needed to be protected from this sort of thing'. He then sentenced them to 14 days in prison on the grounds that, since they were educated people, they 'should have known better'. The sentence was designed to 'teach them a lesson'. To friends of the defendants, however, it seemed that their real offence had been to challenge the authority of the court by appealing. One of the Fox sisters, a teenager, was led sobbing from the dock. Peter Hagerty, then director of the Open Eye Gallery, told *Time Out* magazine: 'We were absolutely flabbergasted at the verdict. Even the prosecuting counsel were shocked.' Since the defendants were first offenders, the court should at least have asked for a social worker's report before incarcerating them.

Mary Renouf, at the time of her 'crime', had just completed an MA in Victorian Literature at Liverpool University. She only agreed to wear the male costume as a favour to a friend. Stoically she endured her two weeks in Styal Open Prison, Cheshire, but afterwards she became depressed, fearful and unable to cope. On the advice of the famous ex-criminal/prisoner Jimmy Boyle, she wrote a play about her experiences as a form of therapy. It was called *Thursday* and was performed at the Gateway Exchange Theatre, Edinburgh, in 1985.

Hayley Fox found imprisonment terrifying and humiliating. Nick Gaskin, who had been working in the Open Eye Gallery, spent his fortnight in Risley Remand Centre where he had to share a small cell with a criminal who had kidnapped a policeman. It was, he said, 'the worst two weeks of my life' and after his release he suffered from nightmares.

The costume offence which resulted in trials and imprisonment was very trivial and the art in question was of minor significance. Yet, the incident does serve to demonstrate the serious and damaging consequences that can follow when the full force of the law is applied to the visual arts by police officers and judges with no sense of humour, no knowledge of the long history of erotic art, and no sympathy or understanding for even the mildest of transgressions.

19

1981: PORTRAIT OF LADY DI ATTACKED

At the National Portrait Gallery in 1981, a young man from Northern Ireland used a knife to slash a portrait of Lady Diana Spencer by Bryan Organ. The vandal was caught, tried and sentenced to six months in prison.

Organ has painted flowers, birds of prey and greyhounds but he is best known for his portraits. Born in 1935 into a humble, working-class family, he trained at Loughborough College of Art and the Royal Academy School during the 1950s, and then taught at Loughborough from 1959 to 1965. A key early influence upon his work was Graham Sutherland, especially the latter's portraits. During Organ's career he has depicted celebrities from many professions: Malcolm Muggeridge, Mary Quant, Lester Piggott, Harold Macmillan, Elton John ... and his sitters have also included several members of the Royal Family, among them Prince Charles. Furthermore, he has worked with Charles who is, of course, an amateur watercolourist in his spare time.

Prince Charles (b. 1948) first met Lady Diana Spencer (1961–97) in November 1977 when she was 16 but they did not become betrothed until February 1981. Their wedding took place in St Paul's Cathedral, London, on 29 July 1981. It was watched on television by an estimated 700 million throughout the world. This 'fairytale' event was interpreted by some on the left as providing a glamorous spectacle to distract the mass of the British from the problems of an economic recession and social unrest: 1981 was also a year in which several riots occurred in the inner boroughs of major cities. The honeymoon was a two-week, Mediterranean cruise aboard the Royal Yacht Britannia followed by a visit to Balmoral castle in Scotland. Later, Diana and Charles duly supplied two male heirs to the throne and after many tribulations – exposed in full in the news media – their marriage ended in divorce in 1996. Princess Diana was killed in a car crash in Paris in August 1997 and her televised funeral was watched by a world audience.

In June 1981 Organ used acrylic pigments to paint a 6 foot x 4 foot portrait of Lady Di, the future Princess of Wales. Organ likes acrylics because they are fast-drying and can be applied in numerous thin layers to give an effect that rivals the translucency of watercolours. The disadvan-

25. Bryan Organ, *Lady Diana Spencer*, 1981.
Acrylic on canvas, 177.8 x 127 cm.
London: National Portrait Gallery collection.
Photo: courtesy of the National Portrait Gallery.

tage of acrylics is that they lack the richness typical of oil paints. When interviewed by Graham Hughes, Organ said that he no longer painted in the presence of his subjects, that he relied instead on getting to know them and obtaining photographs, drawings and notes for reference purposes. The painting – worth £10,000 – was commissioned by the National Portrait Gallery (NPG) in London as a companion to its Prince Charles' portrait (also by Organ). Some of those who attended the unveiling ceremony on 24 July 1981 thought that the portrait – displayed behind a low rope – was very vulnerable to attack.

As Judith Williamson has explained, the royals are both like us and unlike us: they are ordinary and extraordinary. The latter quality is not because of anything they have achieved, but is due to accidents of birth and marriage. (Hence the struggle of both Charles and Diana to become socially useful over and above their value as figureheads/ national ornaments.) Regarding images of the royals, Williamson writes: 'This combination of the ordinary and the special represented *by* Royalty is manifested in the representation *of* royalty through two basic modes: the informal and the formal.' Organ's portrait clearly falls into the informal category.

Diana is shown wearing casual clothes: a white blouse, a dark bolero-style jacket and black slacks. She is placed directly in the centre of the canvas and sits facing and gazing out at the viewer with a cool, self-possessed air. Her legs are crossed and her right arm rests on them while the left arm hangs down behind. The chair she is sitting on is sideways on to the picture plane and Diana holds its rather phallic-shaped, curved back in her right hand. With her short, fair hair and unlined face she appears very young and boyish. Her feet are cut off rather awkwardly by the bottom edge of the canvas and she is framed by a light-grey door in the background which is surrounded by flowered wallpaper. The geometric vertical and horizontal lines of the door and lower wall in the background lock her in place. (Almost a prediction of the prison she was to find her marriage to Prince Charles to be.)

There appears to be more than one light source illuminating Diana from above and from the front – there are no areas of gloom and darkness but a somewhat unsightly shadow is cast by Diana's nose. The main hues of the colour scheme are black, grey, green and ochre. A green used for the chair's shiny seat covering provides the most sumptuous colour in the painting.

Anthony Everitt has observed: 'A royal portrait is much more than a likeness, although it does have to be that: its real importance is as a political statement. It transforms the flesh-and-blood sitter into an icon of state.' However, in this case the sitter and setting lack the normal trappings of royalty because of course Lady Di, at the time the picture was painted, was not yet a royal. As Everitt himself admits, the setting does not look like a palace but 'a house in Clapham', although it was, in fact, the Yellow Drawing Room at Buckingham Palace. He added that Diana was represented as 'a Royal Sloane'. Ann Barr and Peter York, authors of a humorous book about Sloane Rangers, categorised Princess Di as the 'Supersloane' of the 1980s.

Diana appears to be a demure (it was important she was a virgin before her marriage), pretty but unexceptional young woman, a person with little experience of life or hardship although she had experienced some unhappiness as a result of her shyness and the break-up of her own parents' marriage when she was a child. Biographies also suggest that at the time the portrait was being painted Diana was beginning to suffer from her eating disorder, bulimia, due to the stress of joining the Royal Family and the public exposure this entailed. John Hayes, director of the NPG, hailed the portrait as a breakthrough precisely because of its natural quality, the fact that it showed a human being as well as an imminent royal.

Organ's painting is an unoriginal contribution to one of the major genres – portraiture – of the art of painting. Given the illustrious history of this genre, the advent of Modernism, the cultural dominance of camera-based media, and the royals' loss of real political power, some theorists believe it is now virtually impossible to produce a convincing royal portrait in the medium of painting. Organ's picture is also extremely traditional and academic in its technique and naturalistic style. Compared to a van Gogh self-portrait, it is a bland confection of little aesthetic value or significance in the history of art. But then there are many portraits in the NPG which are there because of the importance of the sitters rather than the high quality of their art.

For reasons other than aesthetic ones, many artists wish to paint the royals or are commissioned to do so by charities and regiments, consequently the royals have learnt to ration themselves. After what happened to the Organ portrait, Princess Di became reluctant to pose for painters, although portraits by Susan Ryder and John Merton were sanctioned. Apparently, Princess Di was unwilling to endorse a picture by the Canadian painter André Durand which showed her touching an AIDs patient because she was embarrassed to be portrayed as a royal with saint-like healing powers. Of course, many photos and films exist which show Diana engaged in charity work.

This reminds us that the Organ portrait is simply one of millions of images of Diana which have been generated by the mass media since 1981. (Her life was made a misery by the constant, intrusive attention of journalists and paparazzi; indeed the latter were blamed for her death.) Since it is a rather dull picture it loses out in the competition with more dramatic and controversial images such as the photographs and films showing Diana wearing an off-the-shoulder, low-cut, black dress to an event in Goldsmiths' Hall in March 1981. (Princess Di functioned as a remarkable clothes horse or fashion model/leader.) Its presence in the NPG, however, ensures a high status and longevity.

Galleries of national and international significance located in the centres of capital cities act like magnets for iconoclasts and vandals. The worship of pictures encouraged by such quasi-religious environments incites certain individuals to violence. They also realise that any attacks made inside such institutions will result in national publicity. On the morning of 29 August 1981 – five days after the wedding – Paul Salmon, a 20-year-old student (actually a Dublin University drop-out who had been studying English and Sociology) and nationalist from North Belfast, attacked the portrait with a knife and cut it in three places. A diagonal, curved slash was made above Diana's head and two, vertical slashes – which left the canvas shredded – on either side of her body. Her face was thus left intact. Salmon was still holding the ripped portion of canvas when he was grabbed by security guards who had been standing only a few yards away. He was then arrested by the police and charged with criminal damage at Marylebone Magistrates' Court on 31 August.

A spokesperson for the Royal Family, who were at Balmoral at the time, reported that they were very upset to hear the news. In Southampton a shopkeeper kindly offered a painting of Lady Di in the nude, which he had executed, to the NPG as a replacement for the damaged picture. However, it was not accepted and when the painting was later displayed in the artist's shopwindow, bricks were hurled at it during the night. Meanwhile, NPG staff were removing two royal portraits in order to cover then with protective perspex and conservationists were busy repairing the damaged portrait. The repairs cost over £1,000. Peter Newman, who relined the canvas and John Bull, who restored it, did an excellent job because the slashes can hardly be seen today.

At his trial at Bow Street in November 1981 Salmon was found guilty, sentenced to six months in prison and ordered to pay £1,000 towards the cost of repairs. Quentin Campbell, the Magistrate, described Salmon as an 'immature young vandal' who was trying to 'show off'. Salmon's declared motivation, that he had 'done it for Ireland', that he had attacked 'a symbol of everything British' as a protest against 'social deprivation in Northern Ireland', was dismissed by Campbell who scornfully remarked: 'I don't think for a minute that your reasons were ideological.' Apparently, it is beyond the imagination of English judges that iconoclastic actions can be taken for reasons of principle.

Since Diana's death a huge quantity of memorial merchandise has been manufactured and a number of painters and sculptors have portrayed her. These items are mostly examples of kitsch and mediocre art. Already, media-based works by art students attempting something more critical and analytical have been subject to tabloid press disapproval and censorship by nervous art college staff.

20

1983–96: THE WAR OF LITTLE SPARTA

During the 1980s the Scottish artist Ian Hamilton Finlay and his followers became embroiled in a complex dispute with a local regional authority over rates that involved raids on his home and the Scottish Arts Council. The affair prompted much media coverage and debates about the role of art in today's society.

Artists, by definition, have exceptional talents and engage in specialist activities which set them apart from the rest of society. But they are also social beings and citizens with the same obligations to pay taxes and rates as the rest of us. For most artists no conflict arises between their two roles, but in rare instances one has occurred. The 'war' between Ian Hamilton Finlay and the Strathclyde Regional Council (SRC) which began in 1983 is a case in point.

Finlay (b. 1925) – a poet, philosopher, sculptor and gardener – is one of Scotland's most senior and original artists. Some find his work rather whimsical and lightweight but others are fanatical admirers (Dr Stephen Bann, the noted art historian and university lecturer, is one of his devotees). His oeuvre is difficult to summarise because it has involved such a wide variety of media and collaborations with architects, other artists and craftspeople – many of Finlay's works are made by others according to his ideas and instructions.

Finlay became interested in Modern art during the late 1930s and taught himself to paint. Then, for a short time, he attended Glasgow School of Art. After serving in the army during the Second World War, he turned to writing stories and plays, some of which were broadcast on the radio. During the 1960s, Finlay became noted as a Concrete poet, publishing his work via cards, booklets and a periodical. This kind of poetry emphasises the visual layout of words on the page as much as their verbal meaning. Gradually he combined Concrete poetry with carving on stone and other types of sculpture. Three-dimensional objects – some toy-like – were combined with linguistic titles, texts, puns and so on. These objects often gained meaning from their physical location; for example, a 1971 inscription carved on a stone tablet which stated 'Bring Back The Birch' had a double meaning when placed among trees of a different type.

In 1966 Finlay and his wife Sue settled at Stonypath, Dunsyre, Pentland Hills, Lanarkshire – an abandoned croft on a bleak hillside – and began to develop a garden full of symbolism that has since become famous. It has been visited by thousands of people from all over the world. The garden, which took 20 years of hard work to construct, consists of various converted farm buildings, zones of plants and of trees, hedges, pathways, two pools, a lake, a grotto ... scattered among which are sundials, columns, urns, inscriptions and other works of art. In certain respects Finlay is a radical, Modern artist but simultaneously his art connects with the culture and history of the past: the eighteenth century, English, landscape-gardening tradition, for instance. Unusually, Finlay regards gardening not as a pleasant pastime but as a *revolutionary* activity. While some think of a garden as a *retreat*, Finlay thinks of his as an *attack*. By turning nature into culture, gardening certainly demonstrates how humanity can transform the world. It therefore serves as a metaphor for the positive potential of our species.

The dominant themes and content of Finlay's art include boats, classicism, the French Revolution and modern weapons of war. Among the strangest sculptures in the garden are aircraft carriers and a submarine made from bronze and stone. Finlay's purpose is to remind us that, even in an Arcadian setting, power, violence, war and death are ever-present. In 1978, following a 'Hellenisation' of the Stonypath garden, it was renamed 'Little Sparta'.

Finlay is a combative and tenacious person who relishes battles over issues of principle with officialdom and authorities such as the Scottish Arts Council (SAC) and the SRC. Where he differs from most artists is that he uses his art, humour and wit as weapons in these battles.

One of the buildings in Finlay's garden served the function of an art gallery and because of this he was granted 50 per cent relief on his rates from 1975 to 1978. Then the SRC changed its mind and decided that the gallery was a commercial enterprise and that therefore rates were payable in full. In 1980 Finlay transformed this building into a Garden Temple in order to obtain the exemption from rates normally granted to religious buildings. The gallery, he claimed, was devoted to artistic and spiritual purposes, not commerce. Since the SRC refused to accept the change of use or even to discuss the matter, this was the beginning of a bizarre 'war' – called 'The Little Spartan War' – between the artist, his supporters and the regional body. It also involved the SAC because it was supposed to define the term 'garden temple' for the benefit of the SRC. Finlay feels that the SAC, fearful of jeopardising its public subsidies, did not give him the support he needed.

He claimed that he was perfectly willing to obey the law and to pay rates but, before agreeing to do so, he wanted the opportunity to put his case. Apparently, opportunities to appeal against the SRC's judgements were missed because of the incompetence of a lawyer. Essentially, the argument, Finlay contended, was not about money but 'about whether the spirit has any place in the world'. On 4 February 1983 the war of words became a war of deeds: the SRC sent in a Sherrif's officer called Alexander Walker to seize three Dryad sculptures to be sold in order to cover the sum of £530 the SRC claimed it was owed. (Finlay told one reporter that he was £14,000 in debt because of the garden.) This attack – witnessed by journalists and television cameras, and covered live on radio – was successfully repulsed. Finlay defended his home with mock mine-fields and imitation tanks. Walker's car was trapped by a tractor and he had to hitch a lift to phone the police. As they arrived, a simulated Panzer Mk 4 tank exploded in a ball of fire and smoke. Friends of Finlay had already removed the three Dryads and the artist hid in order to avoid arrest. Meanwhile Finlay's supporters in Europe and America bombarded Scottish officials with telegrams of protest.

To celebrate his victory Finlay struck a medal and built a bronze and brick monument on the battlefield. However, on Budget Day (15 March) the Sherrif's officer raided Little Sparta again. The rates bill was now £1,153. This time Walker managed to confiscate eleven works from the Temple which were then placed in the hands of the auctioneers Christie's in Glasgow for valuation and sale. Finlay claimed that Walker had exceeded his warrant and therefore an act of theft had occurred. He also argued that certain documentation was essential to the works and since this had been left behind, the value

FIRST BATTLE OF LITTLE SPARTA
FEBRUARY 4, 1983

THE MACHINE-GUN is a visual pun (or play!) on
Virgil's flute, with the vents in the barrel-sleeve as the
finger-stops. But – *Et in Arcadia ego* – is the flute to
begin, or the gun – or is the duet in fact to be a trio: does
the singer (if he is to continue in his pastoral) need *both*?

Bibl.: Virgil, *Eclogues*; Eyres, *Despatches From The Little Spartan War*; Hogg,
Encyclopedia of Infantry Weapons.

MEDALS OF THE LITTLE SPARTAN WAR

26. Ian Hamilton Finlay,
***Medal to Commemorate the First Battle of Little Sparta*, 1984.**
Bronze, with Michael Burton. Photo: courtesy of I.H. Finlay.

of the works was reduced. Furthermore, the artworks belonged, not
to him, but to other individuals and institutions, hence efforts were
made to recover them by legal means. One American museum did
succeed in retrieving the work it owned. The SRC was accused of
behaving in a 'Stalinist' fashion and in May Finlay called for the
intervention of United Nations troops. Meanwhile, Little Sparta
remained closed to visitors for a year. The SRC retained the
sculptures for five years before dumping them, without explanation,
at Finlay's gate.

Early in 1984 two of Finlay's neo-classical stone reliefs which had
been bought by the SAC were seized by the Saint-Just Vigilantes (a
group of Finlay supporters named after one of the leaders of the French
Revolution) from the SAC headquarters in Edinburgh – a member of
staff was manhandled in the process – and returned to Little Sparta as
spoils of war. They were then sent abroad with the names of Finlay's
enemies carved upon them.

By 1988 Finlay was facing demands for £34,000. He then discovered
that the SRC had cleaned out his business bank account by means of
an arrestment order. (This money was subsequently returned to him.)
In protest Finlay refused to participate in various Scottish art festivals
and exhibitions. The dispute rumbled on. In 1993 Finlay received yet

another rate demand for several thousands of pounds. The following year the Little Sparta Trust was founded in an attempt to protect the garden from further attacks by the SRC. One of the trustees is Nicholas Serota, director of the Tate Gallery.

Ironically, in 1996, the SRC was abolished as part of a Conservative reorganisation of local government. Finlay's Committee of Public Safety issued a triumphant postcard. But, at the time of writing, Finlay is still deemed to owe rates money to a Scottish court. He is adamant that he will not pay. Since the public role of the Temple has been denied, Finlay has decided to close Little Sparta indefinitely. Referring to the Government's policy of selling off public utilities to the private sector, the garden, he says, has been 'privatised'. He has now applied for the Temple to be recategorised as a store.

During the late 1980s another controversy beset Finlay. As a result of a false allegation by a European radio station and French art magazines that he was a Nazi sympathiser, he lost a £350,000 commission from the French government to sculpt a huge frieze to commemorate the Declaration of Human Rights in the garden of Versailles Château. The allegation probably arose because Finlay had corresponded with Albert Speer about the latter's garden in Spandau Prison. Finlay had also employed the odd Nazi emblem and a 1980s' exhibition of drawings and commentaries was entitled *The Third Reich Revisited*.

Arguably, Finlay is a political artist (with a small 'p'). The battles he has fought against modern, secular bureaucracy, have been a means of challenging the state – at both local and national levels – concerning their fundamental attitudes towards art. Many politicians and state officials pay lip service to art, but Finlay's experience is that they do not truly value it, especially when it questions the priority of money, red tape and inflexible, authoritarian systems of control. At the same time, there are those who regard Finlay as an eccentric, Don Quixote figure who wastes artistic energy by tilting at windmills. No doubt there are also Scottish ratepayers who ask themselves: 'If I have to pay rates, why shouldn't he? Are artists to be given special privileges just because of their chosen profession?' However, if they were to reflect on Finlay's achievement in building Little Sparta, they might conclude that his creativity and labour added considerable value to Scotland's culture, economy and landscape.

STRATHCLYDE REGION MADE WAR ON LITTLE SPARTA

STRATHCLYDE REGION IS NO MORE

See: *'Lyons made war on Liberty/Lyons is no more/18th day of the first month of the Year Two/of the French republic, One and Indivisible.'* – The Committee of Public Safety

27. Committee of Public Safety, Little Sparta, *Strathclyde Region ...*, 1996.
Postcard. Reproduced by courtesy of I.H. Finlay.

21
1983: THE DESTRUCTION OF *POLARIS*

In August 1983 a man poured petrol over *Polaris*, a public sculpture by David Mach made from rubber tyres. There was a conflagration which set the vandal alight. He died a few days later.

Mach (b. 1956), a prolific and energetic Scottish sculptor, was trained at Duncan of Jordanstone College of Art (1974–79) and the Royal College of Art (1979–82). After leaving art college he quickly became noted for his large-scale public projects and events. He specialises in works that are made from non-traditional, ready-made materials such as Anglepoise lamps, wire coat-hangers, shoes, telephone boxes and directories, and thousands of copies of magazines which he builds up, layer by layer, until they constitute surprising new shapes and unlikely subjects such as smoke and the sea. (A famous art-historical precedent for such visual puns are the bizarre, grotesque paintings of Giuseppe

Arcimboldo [1537–93], that is, images of librarians constructed from books, portraits of peasants made from fruit and vegetables, and so on.) Embedded in the 'sea' or 'smoke', like currants in a bun, are often other found objects such as furniture or automobiles. The piquant contrast between the materials employed and the character of the final object is amusing and intriguing to many viewers.

Sculpture made from pre-existing elements or fragments which are then organised into larger images or structures, was termed 'Bricolage', 'New Object' and 'New British Sculpture' during the early 1980s. The critic William Feaver characterised it as 'impudent, insolent, nonchalant, witty and absolutely urban in its inspiration'. Mach's work was not unique. Artists such as Tony Cragg, Jean-Luc Vilmouth and Bill Woodrow (all associated with the Lisson Gallery) worked in a comparable manner. And of course there was a history of the use of found materials in the collages of the Cubists, the ready-mades of Duchamp and the mixed-media sculptures and installations of the Surrealists.

Mach is an extrovert who is happy to work on location in full view of the public, so there is a strong element of process and performance in his artistic practice. Sometimes his works are site-specific or place-related; for example, an exhibit in Stoke-on-Trent made use of dinner plates supplied by a local pottery firm. Many of his sculptures and installations are also temporary: after a designated period of display they are dismantled. Because Mach recycles materials, he has been dubbed a 'green' sculptor but he has denied any ecological motive. His work, he informed David Lee, 'has everything to do with survival ... helping people get through their day and then the next one and ensuring that by the end of the week they're still sane'.

Although Mach is a leading experimental artist, the sculptures he makes tend to be representational and therefore comprehensible to the general public. Like Jeff Koons, he has expressed the desire to communicate with popular audiences in the same way that mass media forms of entertainment do. He told Lee: 'There is absolutely no reason why the audience shouldn't be entertained by even the most serious work.' In his opinion, too much contemporary art was not only bad but boring. Mach also expressed faith in the good sense of the general public: 'The public have all the necessary faculties to understand my work. They are not easily hoodwinked: there is a serious discrepancy between the incomprehension of crass journalism and public awareness.'

28. David Mach, *Polaris*, 1983.
Public sculpture made from 6,000 car tyres, walkway behind
Hayward Gallery, South Bank, London.
Photo: Barry Lewis, courtesy of the Hayward Gallery, South Bank Centre.

Whatever the faults of journalists, Mach's kind of art and his working methods lend themselves to media coverage, and the press and television have provided him with plenty of free publicity.

In the summer of 1983 Mach contributed to *The Sculpture Show*, an Arts Council exhibition of the work of 50 British sculptors, held at the Hayward and Serpentine Galleries in London. Mach constructed a scaled-down but still huge submarine made entirely from several thousand old rubber car tyres. Regarding his choice of material, Mach told Wendy Halstead:

> Tyres are an excellent building material and I enjoy using them. They have a strange quality, a surreal quality. They are ugly, and dirty, and brought together have a lot of friction; I feel good about using something like that.

An art-historical precedent for Mach's use of tyres was Allan Kaprow's environment *Yard* (Martha Jackson Gallery, New York, 1961) which consisted of a chaotic assembly of tyres in an enclosed space.

Mach named his vessel *Polaris* after Britain's nuclear deterrent submarine which had its base in Scotland. The older Scottish artist Ian

Hamilton Finlay may also have inspired Mach's choice of subject because Finlay had previously generated two submarine sculptures: *Nuclear Sail* (1974) and *USS Nautilus* (1979). A year earlier Mach had made a smaller submarine ploughing through a 'sea' made from magazines in an indoor space. Called *Silent Running*, it was shown at galerie T'Venster, in Rotterdam. He also created another submarine in Kingston-upon-Thames.

Polaris was located out of doors on a walkway behind the Royal Festival Hall. Apparently, Mach did not intend it as a pacifist, anti-nuclear weapons statement. More than one art critic has commented on Mach's moral ambiguity. Nuclear submarines are so politically loaded, it is difficult to see how an artist can be neutral in respect of such a subject. However, the sculpture could also be interpreted as a comment on technological obsolescence: just like car tyres, *Polaris* submarines wear out and have to be abandoned or recycled. (They have since been decommissioned.) Close to the River Thames, the submarine implied that powerful destructive weapons could be lurking under the apparently peaceful surface of the water. It was strange to find a seagoing vessel on dry land and there was irony in the fact it was made from objects with holes in the middle (the final sculpture had a honeycomb structure), objects which only function on land. As a representation of one of the most powerful weapons of war, *Polaris* could also be regarded as a parody of war memorials and monuments.

The walkways of the South Bank are used by art lovers visiting the Hayward Gallery but also by many commuters/office workers; the latter's reactions were mixed. The dirtiness of the tyres irritated some passers-by. (One would have thought that commuters would have welcomed almost anything to divert their attention from the grey, concrete, brutalist, architectural environment.) Mach claimed later than he had had 'considerable public support' while constructing the sculpture. Letters to the press citing *Polaris* moaned yet again about 'the waste of public money' even though private funds were also involved. (The show was sponsored by the Greater London Council, the Henry Moore Foundation and United Technologies.) Antagonism towards Mach was fostered by the tabloid press which falsely claimed that he was paid £50,000 for his sculpture. This figure, in fact, was *the total cost of the whole exhibition.*

On the night of 21 August a man called James Gore-Graham poured petrol over the tyres and set them alight. Unfortunately, there was an explosion and he set himself ablaze. As a result of 90 per cent burns to his body, he died a few days later at Queen Mary's Hospital, Roehampton without regaining consciousness. The art critic William Feaver commented: 'The submarine was transformed into a blazing longship, such as the Vikings used for immolation at sea.' Gore-Graham, it emerged, was a man in his thirties, a classical furniture designer from Hammersmith who had conservative tastes in art. Since Gore-Graham died before he could explain his act of vandalism, his motive remains unknown but one assumes it must have been anger at contemporary art.

The act of vandalism and the death of the perpetrator cannot be said to have harmed Mach's career. Quite the contrary. It did, after all, generate publicity. And as Glyn Banks perceptively observed: 'The destruction of *Polaris* gives back to the art world the image of the victimised artist, misunderstood by a contemptuous public (and protected of course only by administrators and critics).'

As in the case of Carl Andre's 'bricks', the materials from which *Polaris* was constructed caused offence. Certain materials – bronze, clay, marble, wood – have through time and usage come to be associated with the art of sculpture and many viewers find it difficult to accept that sculpture can be made from other materials, particularly everyday objects with which they are familiar and which are invested with all kinds of associations, functions and meanings. Of course, it is precisely because these objects have such meanings that Mach is interested in using them. His sculptures are unique phenomena constructed from mass-produced, consumer goods. As David Lee put it: 'Mach's works convey a strong sense that modern culture is being borne away on a tidal wave of unsold and useless commodities.' Confronted by Assemblage art, many unsophisticated viewers seem unable to see beyond the materials from which they are made. They seem unable to appreciate that cheap, banal materials such as magazines have been endowed with a new significance via the artist's imagination and labour, via the forms and shapes they have been compelled to take up.

The common accusation made against Modern art – 'Anyone could do it!' – is literally true in Mach's case: anyone with sufficient strength could build a submarine from old tyres but the fact is that Mach thought of doing it, while his detractors did not. Another common complaint – 'A child could do it!' – is not without relevance, because both Mach and children delight in playing with modular-type materials, such as wooden blocks, and then building unpredictable things with them. For once philistines could not ask: 'What is it made of? What is it supposed to be?' because the answers to both questions were obvious. Nor could they complain that it was too complex and difficult to understand. Perhaps its very directness and simplicity was an affront to some viewers.

The idea that sculpture could be transient rather than permanent also disturbs certain people because it challenges the traditional nostrum, 'art is eternal'. Yet we appreciate the beauty of flowers even though we know it is short-lived.

Any sculpture located in a public space is going to be seen by a wide cross-section of the populace, including many who have no interest in, knowledge of, or sympathy for, the arts. Such sculpture, therefore, is always at risk of protests and vandalism. In response to this challenge, the sculptor needs to develop a 'public language' capable of communicating with non-specialists. Many art critics believe, and Mach's track record seems to prove, that his art has a much wider popular appeal than most contemporary work displayed in private galleries.

In May 1986, as part of the Bath Festival Sixth Contemporary Art Fair, Mach recreated *Polaris* outside the Assembly Rooms. This enraged some of the locals and again there were problems with vandals: a guard dog was caged while a security guard was beaten up.

In retrospect it is clear that *Polaris* was a straightforward sculpture. Arguably, it was not a work of major intellectual significance and aesthetic value (although in Ken Hollings' opinion it was 'an extraordinary work'), but given the fact that it was planned as a short-term structure, the act of vandalism which destroyed the London version was unnecessary. Furthermore, given the plethora of media in today's society, there were many channels through which Gore-Graham could have voiced his objections without endangering his life.

22
1984: RAPE PICTURE 'TOO DISTURBING'

In Hull in 1984 a local councillor, disturbed by a picture by Sue Coe showing the rape of a woman, had it removed from the walls of the city's major public gallery. Protests, demonstrations and petitions followed demanding its reinstatement and these were eventually successful.

Kingston-upon-Hull is a pleasant port (once famous for its fishing industry) and university city situated on the north bank of the River Humber. It is somewhat remote from other English centres of population and therefore has developed a character of its own. Culturally, it is noted for its William Wilberforce Museum and the fact that the poet Philip Larkin lived there for many years. In the city centre's Queen Victoria Square is the Ferens Art Gallery, an imposing, neo-classical building which opened in 1927. It was there during September–October 1984 that the exhibition *Power Plays*, consisting of works by Sue Coe, Jacqueline Morreau and Marisa Rueda, was held.

The exhibition had been organised by Morreau and had been shown in London, Liverpool and Sunderland before its arrival in Hull and there had been no problems. Its three participants had previously shown in the *Women's Images of Men* exhibition held at the ICA, London, in 1980. According to Bryan Biggs of the Bluecoat Gallery, Liverpool, what the artists shared was a concern 'for aspects of power – political, religious, patriarchal, judicial – and the ways in which it is abused'. The critic Sarah Kent maintained that all three artists were motivated by rage about the state of human society and in response produced 'coolly rational observations of cruelty and injustice depicted with an intellectual clarity and dispassion'. Rueda (b. 1941) was an exile from Argentina. She exhibited cast *papier-mâché* figures satirising the powerful, corrupt rulers of her homeland. Morreau was a painter who studied art and medical illustration in the United States. Her paintings employed myth and symbolism to examine the conflicting demands placed on women and the patriarchical forces they have to contend with.

Sue Coe, the artist whose pictures were to be found offensive, came from a working-class family. She was born in Tamworth, Staffordshire, in 1951 but grew up in London. Her mother, who worked in a doll factory, was also an amateur painter. Coe studied at the Guildford and Chelsea Schools of Art during the late 1960s and at the Royal College of Art during the early 1970s. She then moved to New York where she discovered Feminism and produced illustrations for *The New York Times* and other newspapers, and for British magazines like *City Limits* and *New Musical Express*, and for books about such subjects as apartheid in South Africa and the life of Malcolm X. She also taught political illustration at the School of Visual Arts, Manhattan, and was a member of the American Communist Party's People's Workshop for Art, a group of artists willing to work for trade unions and other radical groups or causes.

Coe has been dubbed a 'social conscience/protest' artist because she is a passionately committed, Feminist and socialist artist whose political convictions and indignation are evident in her art. Coe has set herself three goals: (1) to depict events from real life that involve the exploitation and repression of working people; (2) to present images of hope and justice; (3) to produce more personal work relating to her own lived experience.

Coe's images challenge the distinctions between art and illustration, history-painting and cartoons. Her drawings, paintings and prints are always figurative, indeed they are often packed with people and animals occupying a shallow space or emerging from darkness. Black and red are her favourite hues. Although committed to depicting harsh realities, her pictures are not naturalistic in style – they are linear, graphic, quasi-expressionist, verging on caricature.

Exaggeration, distortion and photomontage techniques of juxta-position and superimposition, plus the addition of ransom-note style lettering, news cuttings, slogans and titles written on the surface of her images, are employed for emotional effects, to tell stories, and to penetrate to the truth hidden beneath surface appearances. Extensive research normally underpins Coe's images and they are often accom-panied by factual, contextual information in the form of texts.

Susan Gill has noted Coe's wide range of art- historical sources: 'The atmospheric quality and incisiveness of Goya; the pathos of Käthe Kollwitz; the sharp angularity of Max Beckmann; the collage technique of John Heartfield; the chilling skeletal forms of Posada and Orozco.' Donald Kuspit, a leading American critic, has praised her 'visionary esthetic' which 'eloquently conveys the suffering she is at bottom ob-sessed with'. Dissenting critics complain that her work lacks subtlety and is too close to agitprop, too aggressive, literal and violent. Coe does risk the dangers of preaching to the converted and alienating those she hopes to persuade. Thad Ziolkowski perceived 'gloomy didacticism' and claimed that Coe's 'dreary images ... mourn their own powerlessness'.

Coe's painting/collage The Rape of Rosa Velez (1976) was loaned to Power Plays by its owner Nigel Finch, a television arts producer. It depicts men wearing neo-Nazi, 'savage nomad' jackets about to rape a woman: one holds her down by the shoulders while another forces her legs apart as he prepares to penetrate her with his erect penis. This scene was based on a real crime that took place in New York. A cover-up was attempted but the perpetrators were brought to justice thanks to the efforts of a New York policeman.

29. Sue Coe, *The Rape of Rosa Velez*, 1976.
Tempera and collage on paper, 50.8 x 76.2 cm.
Copyright © 1985 Sue Coe.
Photo: courtesy of Galerie St Etienne, New York.

Hull local councillor Mrs Alice Tulley attended the preview of the exhibition in her role as chair of the Cultural Services Committee (CSC) and was upset by Coe's picture. She thought it bordered on the pornographic and might incite men to rape because it was so explicit. She decided it was too shocking to be seen by other councillors and by the public, so she ordered its removal. Her decision was later endorsed by meetings of the CSC and the full Council.

Mrs Tulley, from the evidence of a letter published in *Art Monthly*, was not a rabid philistine but a sensitive person who was genuinely troubled by 'the uncertainties of the democratic process', that is, the problem of satisfying the various interests and needs of artists, arts administrators, councillors, and voters/ratepayers. Her concern may have been a mask for a desire to suppress images which she found personally offensive, but it seems she did try to contact the chief protagonists in order to discuss the matter.

Coe reports that when she projects slides of her rape paintings to college students, women approach her afterwards to recount their own experiences. Consequently, she feels that her images perform cathartic/ therapeutic functions. She was in Madrid at the time that her picture was removed from the walls of the Ferens, but when she returned and learnt of the censorship she demanded that all her other works be taken down too. Morreau thought it was ironic that an exhibition about the abuse of power was itself subject to 'the abuse of power- censorship'. She acknowledged that Coe's picture was disturbing, but added, 'so is rape'. She then threatened the Council with legal action unless the picture was placed on view again.

Hilary Robinson and Helen Watts, two Hull residents, angered by the act of censorship, canvassed support from art students, lecturers and women's groups. They succeeded in organising a demonstration of over 100 people outside the Ferens on 5 October when another exhibition was being opened. Fortuitously, Coe arrived from London and a debate ensued with Tulley, the outcome of which was an 'open', emergency meeting of the CSC held on 10 October (the public could observe but not contribute) to reconsider the matter. The meeting took place inside the Ferens with the offending picture present. This was the first time most members of the CSC had actually seen it. A petition signed by 891 people was submitted requesting its reinstatement.

Another Coe painting which caused concern to the local press and to John Bradshaw, a senior arts administrator, was *England is a Bitch*. It depicted a riot in Brixton and included the printed text: 'British cops kill youth as royalty live it up'. Prince Charles and the Princess of Wales were featured and were alleged to be indulging in oral sex (Diana was shown on her knees with her head buried in Charles' groin). A 'father of four' com- plained to the police who scrutinised the picture, but decided to take no action. Pru Clark, a reporter for the *Hull Daily Mail*, also judged Coe's depiction of Mrs Thatcher as Lady Macbeth 'simplistic and offensive'.

This is a story with a happy resolution: a majority of councillors finally voted that *The Rape of Rosa Velez* should be placed on view again. The vote cut across party lines. Councillor Margaret Parker wanted the picture removed because she thought a gallery 'was a place where people should be able to come and relax'. Councillor Keith Russell, in contrast, wanted its reinstatement because he objected to censorship on principle and because he feared that Hull would be 'laughed at as a cultural backwater'.

All the press coverage prompted by the incident had the positive effect of doubling the attendance. However, despite their victory, the artists and their supporters felt concerned that Hull Council, alerted to the trouble

30. Jacqueline Morreau, *Protest demonstation outside the Ferens Art Gallery, Hull, October 1984*. Photo: courtesy of J. Morreau.

that contemporary art shows can cause, might seek to vet them more stringently in future. They were also worried that arts exhibition officers willing to take risks would be put under pressure not to book or mount challenging exhibitions or would feel compelled to exercise self-censorship. Remarks by Tulley indicated that their fears were justified: '... the Committee has insisted on reducing the gallery space devoted to exhibitions in order to show more of the permanent collections, especially Victorian Art'. She also stated that the CSC should, in future, be given advanced warning of any 'sensitive' shows.

In a letter to *Art Monthly* Morreau thanked Henry Lydiate of Artlaw (an organisation founded to offer legal advice to artists) for his assistance. She pointed out that all she had, by way of a contract for the exhibition, was an exchange of letters between herself and the Ferens's curators. She had not, of course, anticipated the intervention of a third party and thought a service such as Artlaw was vital because of the legal complications that can arise when acts of censorship occur and when the police become involved.

Even critics of Coe's style would have to acknowledge that the events in Hull were a tribute to the catalytic power of her art to provoke strong emotional reactions and to prompt public discussions about such important issues as the violent crime of rape, the relation of art to obscenity and pornography, democratic control in respect of professional museum staff, the pros and cons of censorship, and the political content and function of art.

23

1984: ATTACK ON 'PORNO-ART' IN LEEDS

In November 1984 a group of furious Feminists smashed plate-glass doors to gain access to the Leeds Polytechnic Art Gallery. Once inside they used hammers to destroy eight sculptures. Five women were subsequently arrested and a year later they were tried at Leeds Crown Court.

Fired Works, the Leeds Polytechnic exhibition that provoked a violent reaction was a joint staff/student display of ceramic sculptures. Certain works by students Stephen Clarke and Zena Herberts were judged by a number of Feminists to be obscene, violent 'porno-art' that degraded women. Shirley Moreno, lecturer in the Department of Adult Education, Leeds University, has described two works by Clarke as follows:

> *Fridge*, a real fridge with rotting food plus the dismembered corpse of a woman wrapped in cling film. The body parts were naturalistically rendered and the fridge and its contents were splashed with red and green paint to simulate blood and mould.

> *Reclining Nude*, a naked female figure lying on her back with her legs drawn up to expose her genitals which were slashed. Her breasts and mouth were also gouged and mutilated. Four stakes protruded from her body, two of which had shredded pornographic magazines attached to the top forming the shape of crowing cocks. Surrounding the figure were women's magazines with razor blades sticking out.

And two works by Herberts:

> *Heat*, a lifesized nude, glazed in black with braided hair, shown crawling on the floor. She was fettered from ankle to knee with a chain, and with rings through her nipples and labia attached to more chains around her body.

> *Dancer*, a black, limbless torso on a plinth again chained through her nipples and labia and in a writhing position with an expression on her face that appeared to be pain.

Moreno concluded: 'Altogether these exhibits looked like some ghastly torture chamber. The effect was really disturbing, you either had to get angry about them or just cry – they were so upsetting.' She also noted that because the gallery was on the ground floor, the sculptures were clearly visible from the street.

Some polytechnic students complained about the sculptures to the Student Union and to Geoff Teasdale, head of the Fine Art Department, but no action was taken. So, shortly after the exhibition opened, groups of Feminist students and academics gathered with the intention of protesting and picketing. The gallery was then closed against them. Male staff and students shouted at the women and threatened them with violence. The actions that ensued were spontaneous rather than planned. Stones were thrown by irate demonstrators to break the glass doors and then a few women entered the gallery and smashed the sculptures. By this time fire alarms were sounding and hundreds of people were milling about.

31. *Leeds Polytechnic Art Gallery after the attack by Feminists*, 1984.
Photo: courtesy of Yorkshire Post Newspapers Ltd, Leeds.

Following the storming of the art gallery, five women were arrested, charged with criminal damage, and kept in custody for three days. When they first appeared before a magistrate the police opposed bail. Leeds Women's Defence Group – an all-women group of solicitors and barristers – took up the case.

Dr Patrick Nuttgens, director of Leeds Polytechnic, admitted to the *Yorkshire Post* that the sculptures had been 'difficult to look at' but believed they were 'designed as a protest against male domination'. 'The whole situation', he continued, 'is, therefore, profoundly ironic. They have smashed exhibits which were themselves a protest about the treatment of women ... I deeply deplore violence to people or property.'

A three-week trial was held at Leeds Crown Court in November 1985. Two defendants were acquitted because they had not entered the gallery. The other three – Helena Coningham, aged 23, Helen Easton, aged 22, and Connie O'Donovan, aged 31 – were members of, or sympathisers with, such groups as Women Against Violence Against Women and Angry Women. Of great concern to these women was the prevalence in Britain of so much pornography featuring women and the appeal of this imagery to rapists and sadistic murderers such as Peter Sutcliffe, the so-called Yorkshire Ripper. Porno-art, according to Moreno, was even more pernicious than pornography because 'the artist operates with a privileged voice' and 'art is seen as a prestigious and respectable arena of production'. In other words, art sanitises and legitimates pornography. (Arguably, some of the work of the British painter Allen Jones and the American artist Jeff Koons can be categorised as porno-art.)

The three Feminists admitted smashing the ceramics but pleaded not guilty on the grounds that the works constituted an obscene display and they had used reasonable force to prevent a crime being committed. They had taken direct action because they had no confidence that the authorities of Leeds Polytechnic would respond to their complaints. Furthermore, they welcomed the trial as an opportunity to make their views known to the public.

Expert witnesses called by the defence were able to establish that the ceramics were indeed obscene; even tutors from the art department admitted as much. They also acknowledged that, in hindsight, there had been a serious error of judgement in allowing the public exhibition of the offending works. Clarke told the court he would not have stopped the women from destroying his work if he had witnessed the event. In fact, destruction on the part of viewers was something he had previously encouraged by exhibiting a sculpture of a baby covered with blood along with a hammer and the invitation 'Please smash this'. However, Clarke complained that his work had been misread and misunderstood, that it was intended to make men feel guilty and women feel angry. This was why he had made vivid the violence that women endure at the hands of men. Moreno countered this argument by saying: 'There was nothing in his work to show that he was critical of that violence, in fact it looked celebratory.'

Herberts also defended her work and claimed that she had made sculptures showing 'strong and dignified women'. Unfortunately, this was not how they were interpreted by others. It seems that Herberts had not understood the implications of the visual vocabulary she had employed.

The three defendants were found guilty as charged by a jury consisting of ten women and two men, but Judge Brian Bush gave them a three-year conditional discharge. He did not award Leeds Polytechnic any costs or damages. (The total cost of the damage caused was estimated to be £1,894.) By not punishing the defendants with fines or imprisonment, the court implicitly endorsed their action.

This case raised, in an acute form, the conflict which periodically occurs between, on the one hand, the artist's desire for absolute freedom of expression and comment, and, on the other, the artist's duty as a member of society to respect society's norms, values and standards, and the feelings of others. Of course, radical artists can decide to break or challenge such norms but they need to think carefully about the way they do it and to be prepared to take the consequences of their actions.

The case also illustrated the discrepancy that can arise between the artist's intended meanings and the meanings experienced by viewers. Because visual signs can be ambiguous, obscure and complex, and because the ideas, politics, religions and cultural capital of producers and receivers can be so different, communication is not simply a matter of transmitting a fixed meaning – via a medium of some kind – from one person to another.

For these reasons, it appears that the art education at Leeds Polytechnic was to some degree inadequate and that the students who made the offending ceramics had not thought enough about the problematics of visual representation/communication. Nor had they envisaged their likely public impact. When the students were questioned by defence barristers during the trial it emerged that they had not read any art-historical or Feminist critiques of images of the female nude, nor had they received any guidance from the predominantly male teaching staff concerning the treatment of such sensitive subjects.

One can understand and sympathise with the outrage felt by the Leeds Feminists, but what is somewhat disturbing about their iconoclasm is that there are probably hundreds of 'masterpieces' in the world's museums which are equally suspect, equally misogynist – pictures showing the rape of the Sabines, for instance – which, according to their principles, also merit destruction. Furthermore, there are many horrific murder scenes found in novels, true crime books, and in feature films about serial killers, as well as the tableaux of tortures and executions typical of waxworks museums and popular tourist attractions such as the London Dungeon. No doubt there is a case for all such scenes to be suppressed, but would this not simply sweep the fundamental problem of human brutality under the carpet?

The American writer Wendy Steiner would also find the iconoclasts guilty of the sin of literalism which she claims is committed by fundamentalists whatever their politics, that is, taking the sign for the reality, for instance, treating a picture of a rape as if it was an actual rape.

Those who smash art at least pay tribute to its power to influence and move people.

24

1986–87: ART, MONEY
AND THE BANK OF ENGLAND

J.S.G. Boggs, an American artist, achieved some notoriety in Britain during the 1980s as a result of being arrested and tried for copying English banknotes.

Paintings and sculptures are produced for a variety of reasons – aesthetic, religious/spiritual, intellectual, political, and so on – and their content may be other-worldly and idealistic, but within a capitalist system they are nevertheless bought and sold for money every week. Art is part of the ideological/cultural superstructure of society which relies upon a material/economic base, but since there is a market in art, it has its own micro-economy. Producing art is one way of earning money/making a living. However, the supply of artists greatly exceeds society's demand for them: a 1996 report by the National Artists Association revealed that 85 per cent of British artists earn less than £15,000 per annum and 38 per cent earn less than £5,000. It is no wonder, therefore, that money is a subject of intense interest to most artists. Indeed, some artists have even been driven to depict money (an example of wish fulfilment?) or alter banknotes: Fergus Callen, Marcel Duchamp, Otis Kaye, Larry Rivers, Andy Warhol, Michael McKenzie, Barton Benes, Baldo Diodato and J.S.G. Boggs, for example.

Because of the rule of free market, right-wing politicians in Britain and the United States, the 1980s was a very money-conscious decade.

As a consequence, both theorists and artists became preoccupied with the commodification of art. As in the field of mass entertainment, they asked themselves: 'Can culture retain use-values despite the dominance of exchange-values?' Some artists even made money and commodification the subject of their work. In New York, in 1990, The Gallery organised an exhibition with the title *Art = Money?* Earlier, in London in 1988, the British artist Rose Finn-Kelcey produced a mixed-media installation entitled *Bureau de Change* which included an image of van Gogh's *Sunflowers* literally made from coins to the value of £1,000. This work – a reaction to the fabulous sums fetched by van Gogh's paintings in auctions – commented on the virtual metamorphosis of his canvases into cash.

There are, of course, paradoxes associated with the visual representation of money: the two dollar bills silkscreened on to the surface of a Warhol canvas are worth far more than their face value.

Coins and banknotes are art to some degree, in the sense that they feature relief sculptures of heads and complex, coloured images designed by either artists or skilled artisans and engravers. Banknotes are also like prints in that they are issued in editions and each one is assigned a unique number. Coins and banknotes no longer in circulation as currency are, like art objects, collected by individuals and preserved in museums.

The special advantage of money, of course, is that it is a universal medium of exchange. It solves many of the problems associated with bartering goods. As Marx explained in *Das Kapital* (1867), money is a universal measure of value and equivalence realised in commodities, which in turn are realisations of human labour. The fact that money too can be a commodity is demonstrated by the existence of money markets.

Most people do not value money in itself but for what it can buy, consequently they only examine banknotes to check that they are genuine. Nation states ensure they have a monopoly on the production of coins and paper currency and they regard the maintenance of the integrity of their currencies as vital, hence laws against forgery, counterfeiting and unauthorised reproduction are vigorously enforced. If an artist decides to copy money, he or she is highly likely to fall foul of the law. This is what happened to Boggs.

James Stephen George Boggs (b. 1955, Woodbury, New Jersey) is an itinerant American artist who has worked in Tampa and New York, Basle in Switzerland, Hampstead in London, and other places. (As a child Boggs travelled around with a carnival. This experience taught him about illusions and tricks.) He went to school in Florida and received tuition from the artist Stephen Holm at the Hillsborough Community College; later he studied for a brief period at Columbia University in New York. In 1980 he made London his base. Four years later he was following the precedent of Jasper Johns by painting numbers. Boggs described them as 'portraits *of* numbers, wild expressionist renditions of twisted three-dimensional numerals that seemed to take on a sort of physical presence'. He had a one-man exhibition entitled *Numbers* at Artshow, London, in December 1984.

Earlier that same year Boggs had started making drawings in ink and coloured pencil (some the same size as banknotes) and paintings (some 4 x 8 ft in size) of American, Swiss and British banknotes which he then exhibited or spent. He was reluctant to sell them to art dealers for real money – partly because dealers could then re-sell them at many times their face value – but he was happy to exchange them for goods and services. If one of his notes exceeded the price of the goods and services paid for in face value, Boggs expected to receive change in the form of real coins.

Asked why he refused to sell his notes he declared: 'Because I don't want to make money out of them. I want to illustrate that works of art are valuable; people can see the value of a drawing when it says £5 or £10. This brings art directly into daily life ... I think art can be appreciated by the man in the street.' Essential to Boggs's art practice are the transactions he has with ordinary people outside the art world. This prompted Jane Jackson of *Performance Magazine* to employ the portentous expression 'transactional performance'. Boggs documented his transactions by such means as signed receipts, then if a collector wished to retrieve one of his banknote drawings, Boggs would sell him or her the receipt and leave it up to the collector to find the owner and to try to buy the drawing back.

The fact that Boggs appeared to have invented a personal currency which was supplanting the need for the official currency, aroused the interest of reporters, the police and the Inland Revenue. Clearly, if everyone followed Boggs's example and produced their own money there would be financial chaos. To forestall any problems with the Bank of England, Boggs wrote to the bank asking for permission to copy English banknotes. Permission was refused, but Boggs went ahead anyway.

In October 1986 Boggs took part in a mixed exhibition on the theme of money at the Young Unknowns Gallery, The Cut, Waterloo, organised by Peter Sylveire. On the day before the show was due to

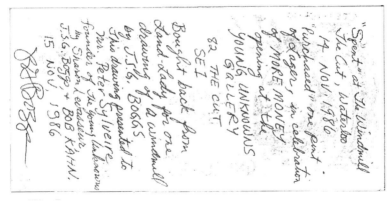

32. J.S.G. Boggs, *One Pound Note*, 1986.
Front: drawing in coloured pencils; reverse: handwritten record of
transactions, 14.9 x 7.5 cm. London: collection of Peter Sylveire.
Photo: courtesy of the artist and P. Sylveire.

open, while a BBC film crew was recording an interview with Boggs and
Sylveire, detectives from Scotland Yard arrived. After interviewing
Boggs they arrested him and confiscated eighteen works by six artists,
but Boggs was the only one eventually charged and committed for trial.
(The police also searched his Hampstead studio.)

At the Young Unknowns, the exhibition was reopened on 14
November with the title *More Money*. A 'Petition Bill', designed by

Sylveire and Jon Sellers, was distributed to a wide cross-section of people in the arts. When these were returned they were displayed in the gallery along with paintings by Jamie Reid, Larry Rivers and others. Tony Banks, a Labour MP with a particular interest in the arts, was prevailed upon to propose an amendment in the House of Commons to the current laws on the depiction of currency in order to enlarge the artist's freedom of expression. On 18 December the Young Unknowns Gallery organised an exhibition/press conference inside the Houses of Parliament.

Shortly after Boggs's arrest, his own bank – a branch of the Midland in Hampstead – mounted a display of his 'art money'. An oversized version of an English £20 note was then seized by an undercover officer. Boggs was advised by his solicitor to find precedents for artists depicting money. During his art-historical research Boggs discovered that there had been a number of nineteenth-century, American *trompe l'oeil* painters who had depicted banknotes in such a way as to fool the viewer. The best known of these artists was William Harnett (1848–92). Boggs experienced a sense of *déjà vu* when he learnt that Harnett had been arrested in 1886 – exactly one hundred years earlier – by the American Secret Service.

Boggs was tried at the Old Bailey in November 1987 on four charges of reproducing British currency contrary to Section 18 (1) of the Forgery and Counterfeiting Act of 1981. The prosecution was a private one brought by the Bank of England as a test case. It was not alleged that Boggs had forged or counterfeited money, but that he had reproduced it without permission. Thus it seems his real 'crime' was breach of copyright. (Boggs's defence was that his images were original works of art not reproductions.) The copyright of English Treasury Notes is held by the governor and company of the Bank of England, but strangely, the Bank did not invoke the law of copyright in order to sue Boggs in the civil courts. As Henry Lydiate of Artlaw has explained, it was only after the Boggs's trial that the bank added the international copyright symbol to their notes. The bank was also compelled to issue a set of guidelines for those wishing to reproduce notes in such images as advertisements and illustrations.

For those outside the legal profession the key issue in copyright cases is the degree of transformation involved. Artists and their supporters believe that if the original image on a banknote is altered to a significant extent, then the work acquires originality and uniqueness. In Boggs's case there was no intention to imitate in order to deceive. He

drew and painted by hand objects which were mechanically reproduced. Thus he made visible the human labour involved in the
production of artworks. Changes of medium, colour and scale occurred,
and the face of the Queen was made cartoon-like. Boggs created images
that were one-off rather than manufactured in large editions. Like Pop
art, all his drawings and paintings were *interpretations* of images
already in mass circulation: in the process of copying alterations and
additions were made. For example, one of his banknotes purported to
be worth three, six and ten pounds simultaneously and the chief
cashiers were named as C. 'n' D. Saatchi (the well-known, London art
collectors). So, while the final drawings and paintings still *resemble*
real banknotes, they are not exact copies. The drawings also *function*
like banknotes when people treat them as currency.

Geoffrey Robertson, Boggs's barrister, called as expert witnesses the
art dealer René Gimpel, the ex-Tate Gallery curator Michael Compton
and the Arts Council's director of visual art, Sandy Nairne. After
listening to the arguments cited above and a summing-up by the judge
which lasted three hours, and after deliberating for ten minutes, the
jury acquitted Boggs. For once 'common sense' resulted in a sensible
and just decision. The fee owed to Mark Stephens, Boggs's solicitor,
was paid with drawings of banknotes and a cheque issued by 'The Bank
of Boggs'. On his acquittal the artist vowed to live from his 'transactions' for a whole year.

One of Boggs's intentions was to make people look at banknotes
more carefully, and his work did succeed in calling attention to their
artistic/technical qualities and their iconography/history. His visual
images were intriguing and amusing rather than profound works of art
of the highest aesthetic quality. They were derivative in two respects:
they were inspired by the imagery of banknotes and by Warhol's money
pictures. But it seems clear that the visual dimension was only one
aspect of his work, that what he was in fact creating were conceptual/
social-experiments which had economic and legal ramifications. This
was surely borne out by the fact that the Bank of England thought it
necessary to prosecute him.

On a trip to Sydney, Australia, Boggs appeared in court again, but
this time the judge dismissed the case and awarded him $20,000 in
costs. Afterwards Boggs returned to the United States. (At the time of
writing he is a Professor of Art and Ethics at Carnegie-Mellon
University, Pittsburgh.) An exhibition of his work was held at the
Jeffrey Neale Gallery, New York, in the autumn of 1987. Another took

place at the Vrej Baghoomian Gallery, New York, in 1989. A third, a travelling show, was organised by the Tampa Museum of Art, Florida, in 1990. In these shows Boggs presented drawings and paintings of British and American banknotes but also documentation of his 'completed transactions' in the form of receipts, objects purchased, change received, as well as photographs and descriptive annotations. American reviewers took his work seriously and treated him as a Conceptual artist rather than as a painter.

Europeans might expect American officials to be more relaxed about Boggs's art-money than British ones, but they would be mistaken. Boggs clashed with the US Secret Service in Florida in 1990 and in Wyoming in 1991. Then, in December 1992, a dozen Secret Service agents and police raided Boggs's Pittsburgh studio and seized over a thousand items. No doubt they were concerned about Boggs's success: by then he had received approximately $250,000 worth of goods and services in exchange for his own currency and he was proposing to print, via a colour photocopier, $1,000,000 worth of new, Boggs's bills.

Boggs took legal action himself to recover his property and to stop the Secret Service from confiscating his work in future. Unfortunately, a District Court judge ruled against him. In 1994 he told *Art in America*: 'My career is destroyed, no gallery will touch my work with a barge pole.' Yet he still seems to be active across the United States.

25
1986: EROTIC OR SEXIST ART?

In March 1986 Feminists attacked and damaged a sculpture entitled *Chair* by Allen Jones while it was on display in the Tate Gallery. This action was the culmination of years of criticism by Feminists of Jones's depictions of women as sex objects.

Allen Jones, born in Southampton, Hampshire, in 1937, studied at the Royal College of Art and Hornsey College of Art from 1955 to 1960. At the end of his first year at the RCA's Painting School he was expelled 'for setting a bad example'. Although an internationally famous painter, sculptor and graphic artist, he is primarily known for his contribution to British Pop art (colourful paintings often combining abstraction and figuration, male and female figures) and for his sexual imagery and objects inspired by erotic/pornographic and sado-masochistic source material. Sexual subject matter was common in both British and American Pop art and the decade in which this kind of art flourished – the 1960s – was, of course, the age of the contraceptive pill and of sexual liberation. However, men still benefited more from the latter than women did.

Chair (1969) was one of three, related sculptures; the other two were *Table* and *Hatstand*. They were produced in an edition of six, but because of certain variations no trio was exactly the same. Examples of the sculptures were first exhibited in London at the private gallery Arthur Tooth & Sons in spring 1970, the same year that the *Sun* newspaper began to feature topless models on its page three. *Chair* consists of a life-sized figure of a woman made from painted fibreglass and resin, perspex and leather. Because of her idealised/stylised features and glossy, smooth skin, she resembles a shop-window mannequin more than a real woman. She is also close to the pin-up girls drawn by Alberto Vargas, the American erotic illustrator whom Jones admired and once visited on a trip to California.

Like a nightclub stripper she is heavily made up and has long eyelashes; she is dressed in a wig, knee-length boots with stiletto heels,

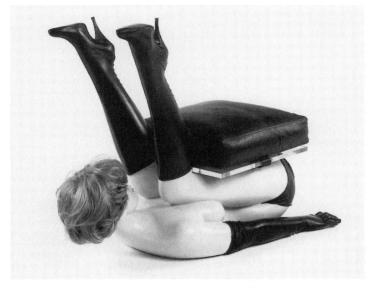

33. Allen Jones, *Chair*, 1969.
Painted fibreglass, resin, perspex, leather, a wig and other
items of clothing, 77.5 x 57.1 x 99.1 cm.
London: Tate Gallery collection. Photo: Tate Gallery Publishing Ltd.

gloves that reach the elbow and a pair of briefs or hotpants. The boots, gloves and briefs are all made of black leather, a 'second-skin' material popular with fetishists. She is depicted lying on her back with her legs raised so that her knees press against naked breasts and with her head raised from the floor. Such a pose would become very painful for a real model if held for any length of time. Her torso and thighs are bound together by a large strap which also holds in place a square, cushioned seat again made from black leather. In other words, a woman has been forced to become a chair upon which viewers – implicitly male – are invited to sit. *Table* and *Hatstand* similarly transform the bodies of women into pieces of furniture.

Precedents for such works can be found in African carvings where wooden stools sometimes included crouching female figures and in Surrealist objects which fused humans and everyday utensils. Female figures carved from marble were also employed by Greek architects as pillars to hold up the roofs of buildings.

In an illustrated book with no text published at the time of the exhibition, examples of Jones's work were reproduced alongside his source material, that is, bondage and sado-masochistic (S-M) images taken from fetish magazines. Jones continued the Pop art practice of using secondary, mass-culture imagery rather than first order reality. This has enabled him to argue that he is concerned with woman-as-sign or as 'personifications of some kind of drive' rather than real women. Paradoxically, in S-M imagery it is often men who are treated as slaves by powerful women – dominatrix – who inflict punishment upon them. There is no denying that such images, however crudely drawn, exert an erotic power. Indeed, some viewers believe that the impact of the source imagery is greater than Jones's own because it is rawer and more compulsive.

Since Jones is so dependent on other people's images, he could be accused of a lack of artistic imagination. He also relied on other people's skills to manufacture and adorn the sculptures (which in any case resemble kitsch artefacts rather than sculptures in the traditional sense): the figures were based on Jones's wife Janet and were modelled in clay by the professional sculptor Dick Beech working according to Jones's instructions, and were then cast in fibreglass by Gems Wax Models. Flesh tints were added by Lucina della Rocca and their leather costumes were made by John Sutcliffe of Atomage, a London firm specialising in sexual clothing. The wigs were supplied by Beyond the Fringe, the boots by Anello and Davide and the gloves were bought ready-made from Weiss, Shaftesbury Avenue.

Bernard Denvir, reviewing the Tooth show, asked the vexed question: 'Is it erotic art or pornography?' which has been raised repeatedly in discussions of Jones's work. Denvir judged that the sculptures were erotic art rather than pornography and concluded: 'Lusts and aberrations of all kinds lurk in even the most virtuous. Jones has monumentalised and projected some of them in a way which does credit to his standing as an artist, and enhances our own comprehension of *la condition humaine.*'

Other critics, and Jones himself, have defended his art on the grounds that its sexual iconography makes it universal and democratic, because eroticism makes it accessible to those outside the art world who normally find it difficult to respond to contemporary art; and also on the rather strange grounds that Jones is 'exploring formal problems'. Some of his supporters scornfully dismiss Feminist criticisms as instances of puritanism and political correctness. Marco Livingstone has even contended that 'Jones is fighting the same battles as the feminists' because he is exploring the way sexual identity is formed via visual stereotypes.

Historians of Pop art admit, however, that Jones's images of female passivity and submissiveness were meant to shock and succeeded in their aim. Jones himself has explained that his intention was to provoke a direct physiological, emotional response that would pre-empt cerebral and aesthetic reactions. Furthermore, 'The furniture idea was to further dislocate the expectation of the viewer by introducing a motor response [that is, the reflex habits of sitting or hanging up coats] that was common to everyday life ...' He denied that any violence towards women was intended.

Given the interest Feminists have shown since the early 1970s in the 'Images of Women' topic, it was inevitable that Jones's art would attract their attention. Their critiques have taken two forms: theoretical and practical (that is, physical assaults). At first, the complaint was that Jones's exploitation of already exploitative material was compounding a wrong. His art could not be regarded as politically neutral because it was adding to the objectification and degradation of women. But then, in a justly celebrated 1973 article published in *Spare Rib*, the film-maker/theorist Laura Mulvey ingeniously argued that Jones's work was not about women at all but about a castration complex in the male unconscious of which Jones, the so-called 'Thinking Artist', was unaware. Without doubting its veracity, Mulvey applied a male's – that is, Sigmund Freud's – theory of fetishism to the content of Jones's work considered as a totality. When men discover that women do not have penises they develop castration anxiety and the absent phallus becomes displaced on to fetish objects and materials. Even a woman's body can become a phallic substitute. Thus, according to Mulvey, 'Man and his phallus is the real subject of Allen Jones's paintings and sculpture.' It follows that women need not worry about Jones's images of them, because it is Jones's problem, not theirs.

Su Braden, an art critic, thought that both Jones and Mulvey took his work too seriously. In her view there was an obvious commercial motive: Jones used art to camouflage sexually titillating material in order to sell highly-priced, erotic objects to wealthy collectors.

Lisa Tickner, a Feminist art historian, wrote an article in *Block* magazine and also appeared on a television programme with Jones. She made the argument more complex by considering the gender of the spectator: Jones's work and statements always assumed a male viewer, therefore it was not universal in its appeal because the experience of half the world's population was ignored; and women's responses were bound to be different from those of men. Tickner denied that Feminist critics were seeking to censor him but stressed that, for Feminists, representations of women were a site of political struggle; such signs, they believed, were imbricated in social relations and were bound to have social effects.

A version of *Chair* was acquired by the Tate Gallery in 1981 from Waddington Galleries Ltd in Cork Street. While on display in the exhibition *Forty Years of Modern Art 1945–85* (February–April, 1986) paint-stripper or acid was thrown over it. The attack took place on Saturday 8 March, International Women's Day, so the culprits can be assumed to have been Feminists even though they were not appre- hended or even seen by the guards. This assumption was supported by the fact that two women telephoned the quality Sunday newspapers to report the attack. The face of the sculpture – estimated market value £50,000 – was particularly badly damaged – part of it was eaten away – and this posed major difficulties for Lyndsey Morgan, one of the Tate's conservationists.

Jones's sculpture has not been displayed in the Tate since the attack. Does this mean the Tate is now afraid to show it? Perhaps the danger of further vandalism could be overcome by displaying *Chair* with contextualising information that would put the arguments for and against it before the public. In other words, the Tate Gallery would openly acknowledge the contentious character of the sculpture.

Besides the Feminist critique of Jones's art, there have been other criticisms on the grounds of artistic deficiencies. For example, Terence Mullaly, a critic of conservative tastes writing for the conservative newspaper, the *Daily Telegraph*, delivered this devastating judgement in 1979:

> He is a clumsy painter with little to say ... The facts are simple. Allen Jones cannot draw, has no feeling for oil paint, and so trite and familiar are his vulgar images that they do not even excite interest. The only effect his work has is to irritate us by the crudity of his colour, his total lack of painterly ability, and the pretentiousness of his proclaimed aims.

It is clear from the above that Jones's art prompts mixed reactions. Critical opinion within the art world is divided as to its artistic merit and women too are divided regarding the issue of sexual iconography/pornography. Compared to such figures as Käthe Kollwitz, Hans Bellmer, Francis Bacon or Jackson Pollock, Jones is a minor artist. However, he does transform his source material to a certain extent and there is some illumination in the way he often foregrounds the role of the male voyeur in the composition of his pictures. But, on the whole, the Feminist complaints about his work are justified. The defence so frequently mounted – 'Just because I depict women as the objects of male sexual desire does not mean that I personally approve of this attitude, I simply reflect reality' – cannot be accepted because it would absolve male artists from all moral and political responsibility for contributing to social improvements.

26
1987–89: THE CASE OF THE FOETUS EARRINGS

In 1989 an artist and a gallery director were tried at the Old Bailey in London and found guilty of the offence of outraging public decency for creating and displaying earrings made from human foetuses.

Rick Gibson (b. 1951, Montreal) is a Canadian artist who came to live in London in 1983. Nine years earlier he had obtained a degree in psychology from the University of Victoria. For a while he trained for the teaching profession at Goldsmiths College but was then rejected as 'unsuitable'. It was he who had the macabre idea of making two, three-inch-long earrings from human foetuses which were twelve weeks old at their time of death, presumably by abortion. Gibson told one newspaper that he was given them by a lecturer in pathology after placing an advert for 'legally preserved human limbs and foetuses' in a gallery window. (One surprising fact revealed by this case was the public availability of, and trade in, dead body parts.) Gibson learnt of the technique of freeze-drying from the Natural History Museum which had pioneered it during the 1950s as a means of taxidermy. During the late 1970s he had been researching holography as an art form but abandoned it once he discovered the delight of freeze-drying a strawberry.

In November 1984 Gibson exhibited 'sculptures' made from human and animal body parts at the Cuts Gallery in Kensington (the show was entitled *Dead Animals*). One was a wall plaque made from a human uterus; another consisted of a dissected, pregnant cat whose foetus was impaled on a fork. The latter's bad-taste title was *Kitten à la Carte*. It would seem that Gibson pioneered the kind of sliced-open, animal art that Damien Hirst would later capitalise on so successfully.

Gibson questions current attitudes to food and the way we dispose of dead bodies. For instance, he sees no reason why human flesh should not be recycled as pet food or fertiliser. Challenging the law and testing the limits of a citizen's freedom of speech are also of interest to him. In December 1985 he tested the attitude of the British law by walking around the town centre of Reading wearing a sign saying: 'Wanted: legally preserved human limbs and human foetuses.' The local police provided him with an escort and no trouble occurred, although headlines in the local paper described him as 'sick'. However, when Gibson, accompanied by a dog, tried the same performance in Brighton, he was arrested, spent a day in police cells and was then bound over for a year to keep the peace. Naturally Gibson was bemused by the inconsistency of the British police and legal system. Canadian law, he claimed, was simpler, easier to understand and more democratic.

The earrings were part of a sculpture displayed in a perspex case which consisted of female mannequin's head, a dark wig and a face that was luridly made up. To make the foetuses into earrings Gibson pierced their skulls with hooks and attached them to the ears of the mannequin. *Human Earrings* (1985) was featured in an exhibition called *Animal*, held at the Young Unknowns Gallery, The Cut, Waterloo, London, in December 1987. Altogether 41 paintings and

34. Rick Gibson, *Human Earrings*, 1985.
Mannequin's head, make-up, wig and human foetus earrings.
Photo: courtesy of Peter Sylveire.

sculptures were on display. The show's premise was that humans had once been or were still part of the animal kingdom.

Peter Sylveire, the Young Unknowns' director, was also a painter. He had established the gallery in 1985 in order to provide a space for experimental art by young artists. One of the key principles of the gallery was that work should be presented anonymously so that it was the art that received attention rather than the name and personality of the artist, but in the event some artists did not adhere to this principle. In relation to *Animal*, Sylveire half-expected some protests from animal rights activists, particularly concerning a performance piece involving live gerbils encased in the perspex heels of shoes.

Human Earrings was insured for £1,000 and its sale price was said to be 'negotiable'. Gibson's intention, he claimed, was not to offend visitors but to intrigue them, to make them think about what materials are suitable for art and adornment, and about the ethics of using such loaded objects. One cannot help but conclude that Gibson was being disingenuous. Another of his fashion statements consisted of a transparent waistcoat inside of which were 200 live locusts.

A press release about the exhibit on gallery notepaper was issued by Gibson to various newspapers without Sylveire's knowledge, so it is clear that he wanted publicity and was prepared to ignore the gallery's policy of anonymity. Following a tip-off from the *Daily Mail*, officers from Kennington Police Station visited the gallery, examined the work and then decided to take action. Gibson's sculpture was removed within half an hour of the exhibition's public opening. But instead of using the Obscene Publications Act of 1959 to charge Gibson and Sylveire, the police employed the old common law for the offences of (1) committing 'an act of a disgusting nature outraging public decency'; and (2) causing a public nuisance (because the sculpture, they claimed, was visible from the street). This law dated back to 1663, was very vague and had never been used before in relation to art. Unlike the 1959 Act, it did not permit a defence on the grounds of artistic intentions or merit.

The case took a year to reach the Old Bailey. To coincide with it the Young Unknowns Gallery defiantly mounted an exhibition entitled *Animal II*. The trial lasted ten days but much of the time was spent on legal arguments with the jury absent. Michael Worsley QC, acting for the prosecution, argued that *Human Earrings* was not a work of sculpture at all. He accused Gibson of mutilating the foetuses and appealed to the jury to use their common sense when considering whether or not public decency had been outraged. Geoffrey Robertson QC, for the defence, claimed that the sculpture was a 'profoundly moral' comment on the double standards of a society in which tens of thousands of foetuses were destroyed every year and animals killed for their pelts to be worn as adornment. In his summation Judge Brian Smedley invited the jury to 'set the standards'.

On 9 February 1989, after deliberating for five hours, the jury found the two defendants guilty of the first offence. The judge directed the jury to find the defendants not guilty of the second offence. The jury consisted of ten women and two men – a highly unusual gender balance. There was a majority verdict of ten to two. Gibson was fined £500 and the gallery £350 with a threat of prison if the fines were not paid. Given the lightness of the sentences, it seems strange that the whole apparatus of the law should have been mobilised against two, little-known artists, especially since the case was estimated to have cost £200,000. A right of appeal was subsequently granted but when the appeal failed, permission to take the case to the European Court of Human Rights was refused.

It is important to stress that no member of the public had been offended by Gibson's sculpture while it was displayed in the Waterloo gallery. (In fact the sculpture had only been seen by around 200 members of the art world who had attended the private view.) One of the main concerns of the defence lawyers was that artists charged under common law would not know if they had committed a crime or not until a jury reached a verdict. And the jury – which might not include anyone with a knowledge of contemporary art – would decide on the basis of their common sense what was indecent and outrageous. No expert witnesses could be called to argue for toleration of artistic expression and to explain the tradition of shock in Modern art.

This case was an extreme example of disgust provoked by an unusual material selected by an artist. Clearly, Gibson had unwittingly broken a taboo of British society. At first sight, there is something distasteful about the use of the remains of humans whose lives were so brief. The tiny bodies in their crouched positions, with their wizened flesh and disproportionately large skulls with metal hooks screwed into them, were disturbing and aroused feelings of compassion and pathos.

Yet, if we consider the habits and art of tribal peoples – and many Modern artists have admired and borrowed from this source – then the use of human remains such as shrunken heads, scalps, and so on is not uncommon. Furthermore, as the defence lawyer pointed out, in public institutions such as the British Museum ancient, dried, Egyptian mummies and other corpses are on view for all to see, including children. Gibson said he preferred to reuse human remains rather than to burn or bury them. Wanting to be the first cannibal to 'come out of the closet' he also ate human tonsils in a 1988 performance in Walthamstow High Street entitled *Meet a Cannibal.*

In December 1987 the *South London Press* passed an instant judgement on Gibson by carrying the front page headline 'Stop the Freak Show'. Ironically, the report appeared next to an advert for a jewellery shop. The trial a year later prompted several articles discussing the pros and cons of using human body parts in art. One of the most thoughtful was by Rosalind Coward who observed: 'Gibson's sculpture is particularly disturbing because it touches on the emotive and unresolved status of the foetus. It stirs up anxieties about whether or not the foetus is actually a person' (rather than part of the mother's body). She then pointed out that 'equating an embalmed foetus with a dead person carries as a logical concomitant the idea that abortion is murder, which is currently neither law nor a point of shared morality'.

Yvonne Say, in a letter to *City Limits*, criticised Gibson's sculpture from a woman's perspective:

> This so-called 'art' is offensive to *women*. The 'artist' does not *mention* women ... To use a foetus in this way is to deny the feelings of many women who have had abortions, miscarriages and still-births. If he is so keen to shock, why not use a dried penis?

Television arts programmes also considered the case: BBC2's *The Late Show* mounted a debate with five speakers including Victoria Gillick (anti-abortionist and mother of ten) and Jonathan Miller (doctor, stage director and author). Opinions were so sharply divided, that the discussion quickly became acrimonious. Another television arts programme, produced by the independent production company Holmes Associates for Channel 4, dramatised the trial itself. Beverley Brown, an expert in law at Edinburgh University, wrote a lengthy analysis – delivered as a conference paper – of the case's legal implications. In her view, the court's decision was a watershed one that reversed '35 years of legal protection for serious art'.

Most of the writers who accepted that *Human Earrings* was a work of art, thought it a trivial or minor one with little or no aesthetic appeal. (But few had actually seen it.) What they and others did consider important was the threat posed to freedom of artistic expression represented by such charges and court cases. A pressure group, The Campaign for Artistic Freedom, was formed in order to combat the threat but the campaign fizzled out after the trial. Rick Gibson returned to Canada in 1989. All the publicity had a negative effect on the Young Unknowns Gallery and Sylveire closed it in 1991.

If one takes into account all the events and media coverage caused by Gibson's actions then, arguably, his sculpture was not so much a physical artefact as 'a social sculpture' (a term invented by the German artist Joseph Beuys), that is, an experiment designed to see what would happen when extreme art collided with the law, the mass media and British common sense. The latter was to be tested again in 1997–98 when another sculptor, Anthony-Noel Kelly, was charged with stealing body parts.

27

1988: NUDE PAINTING DEEMED TOO RUDE FOR
ROYAL EYES

In November 1988 an oil painting of a naked man by Rebecca Scott
on show at Goldsmiths College of Art in South London was deemed
too rude for the eyes of a member of the Royal Family and so it was
removed from an exhibition by college officials. The rest of the show
was dismantled in protest and the story made front page news.

The *Sun*, owned by the Australian-born tycoon Rupert Murdoch, is an
aggressive, mass-circulation tabloid newspaper with sales of over four
million copies. Its readership may reach a figure as high as eleven
million. This paper is not noted for its interest in, sympathy for, and
coverage of, contemporary art but on 3 November 1988 its front page
was graced by a cropped photo of the painting *Porsche Cabriolet* (1987)
by Rebecca Scott, a postgraduate art student, with the headline 'Get
him Orf: Rude painting taken down before Anne's Visit'.

The oil painting in question was a large canvas showing a naked
young man fondling his erect penis standing in front of an image of the
bonnet of an expensive, red sports car placed in a landscape setting.
(One presumes the man was standing next to a billboard with an
automobile advertisement.) The point of the juxtaposition was simple
enough: many men enjoy the power and status provided by fast,
expensive cars; such cars are common phallic symbols. As Ruki Sayid,
the journalist responsible for the story put it: 'The implication is that
the flashy sports car is a sexual turn on.' In the *Sun*'s cover photo a
sticker entitled 'censored' was placed over the man's private parts –
which had the effect of drawing the eyes to that spot – and the caption
beneath coyly declared: 'Suitably censored for a family newspaper'.

The Anne of the story – featured in a photo falsely labelled 'Anne at
the exhibition' – was Princess Anne of the British Royal Family. (The
familiar way in which the newspaper referred to her indicated a
spurious closeness or matiness.) In her capacity as Chancellor of the
University of London, Princess Anne visited Goldsmiths College – a
division of the university – on 2 November. A reception had been
planned in Goldsmiths Art Gallery, Lewisham Way. Fearful of an
appalled reaction to Scott's painting, Peter Cresswell, the then head of
the Fine Arts Department, took the decision to remove it from part one

of an exhibition entitled *The Invisible Man: The Construction of 'Male' Identity* which had opened in October. With consummate irony, Scott's naked man was thus literally made invisible.

So incensed were the staff and students of Goldsmiths by this craven act of censorship that they decided to remove all the exhibits for the day of Princess Anne's visit rather than let the show continue in a mutilated form. The show had been conceived and designed as an installation of related but contrasting images, consequently the removal of Scott's painting undermined its rationale and coherence.

35. Rebecca Scott, *Porsche Cabriolet*, 1987.
Oil on canvas, 224 x 148cm.
London: artist's collection. Photo: courtesy of R. Scott.

The exhibition's curators were Kate Love (an artist and lecturer) and Kate Smith (an artist). They decided to write to the press office of Buckingham Palace in order to inform Princess Anne of what had happened. Their exhibition was a consequence of more than a decade of Feminist debate about visual representation and sexual identity/ difference. Early analyses had focused upon images of women, especially ones depicting their naked bodies. Such images had generally been commissioned by, and produced for, the visual pleasure of heterosexual, male voyeurs. In an interview with Derek Manley, Scott noted: 'A body defined is a body controlled, and by controlling the look men have left themselves outside the picture.'

Later on Feminists turned their attention to images of men, both gay and heterosexual. Margaret Walters, in her 1978 book *The Nude Male: A New Perspective*, discussed the shyness of male artists and viewers in regard to their own bodies, especially their penises. As Love and Smith pointed out, men's penises are generally not shown in art and advertising, therefore, pictorial substitutes such as guns and cars tend to be used instead.

However, in 1980, the Institute of Contemporary Arts, London, mounted a travelling exhibition entitled *Women's Images of Men* which included several paintings and photographs of naked men with penises visible (most of which were in a flaccid state). The show at Goldsmiths of 28 works by both men and women set out to examine the visual stereotypes of men found in the mass media and the ideological construction of masculinity. Of course, the *Sun* was not seriously interested in these issues nor, one suspects, was Princess Anne.

Scott derived her iconography from glossy advertising, playing cards and postcards of Old Master paintings. She also resorted to gay, pornographic photographs because they featured naked men with erections. There was a danger, Scott acknowledged, that her use of pornography might result in pornographic pictures. Nevertheless, she felt this was a risk worth taking. She remarked: 'Pornography's like a well-kept secret. It's a secretive, reserved territory with its own power. By representing it, you break some of that power.' As a Feminist painter, her 'reading' of pornography was not purely theoretical. Furthermore, it engaged with the pleasure inherent in images of the nude body. Heterosexual women, Scott contended, should admit that they enjoy looking at images of attractive men and fantasise about having intercourse with them.

Her aim was deliberately confrontational: she wanted viewers to be surprised and shocked. Both male and female viewers, it seems, were embarrassed by the representation of an erect penis. Although perfectly natural and essential to the reproduction of the species, it is a taboo image in Britain outside the realm of hard pornography. She used a large format and the medium of oil painting to contrast with the earlier, Feminist art of the 1970s, much of which had employed photographs, performances and installations. In an interview with Mark Currah, Scott gave additional reasons for choosing painting over other art forms:

> I intended the paintings for women. I wanted to seduce them into enjoying that kind of imagery through painting ... it's still a standard art school attitude – that the paintbrush is a sublimation of the man's penis and the gestures he makes with the brush are given so much importance, so it's not surprising when women say they can't deal with paint. But I was determined to operate directly with the masculinity of painting and the act of painting.

At first Scott was angry when she read the *Sun*'s jocular account of the censorship incident but then she realised that the paper illustrated the very points she was trying to make: there was a hypocritical contrast between the censored, male nude on page one and the uncensored, female nude on page three (a regular feature, indeed a minor national institution); furthermore, in that issue of the paper there were two reports about badly behaved men who owned Porsches.

Academic freedom of expression was clearly of little concern to the officials of Goldsmiths faced by the prospect of losing face. What was particularly absurd about their act of censorship – which rebounded against them in terms of bad publicity – was the belief that somehow the British Royal Family are exempt from sexual desire, activities or knowledge. Despite this, officials and bureaucrats feel that they must protect members of the Royal Family from any reference to sex or images that might be in the least controversial. A writer in *Art Monthly* remarked: 'A story not so much of censorship as of a knee-jerk application of petit-bourgeois gentility which is apparently inseparable from royalty.' This incident was symptomatic of the nauseating grovelling associated with royal excursions. Republicans can only regret the absence of the spirit of Oliver Cromwell in modern Britain.

Scott was not deflected from her path by the Goldsmiths's affair. She continued to generate paintings of men sporting erections – witness her *American Footballers* series of the early 1990s – in order 'to question perceptions of masculinity' and 'to demystify the phallus' (Manley).

28

1992: BRITISH GULF WAR PAINTING ACCUSED OF ANTI-AMERICANISM

A war painting by John Keane prompted a furore in the tabloid press because its content seemed to be critical of the American and British involvement in the Gulf War of 1991.

Since the Imperial War Museum in South London is not primarily an art gallery, it is surprising that it possesses a substantial collection of British paintings and drawings. This is because the museum has a long history of acquiring and commissioning pictorial records of war. Thus certain artists gain financially and in terms of publicity from every major war that occurs, although, of course, they also put their lives at risk by visiting war zones.

In 1990 John Keane (b. 1954), a British figurative painter who trained at Camberwell School of Art (1972–76), was commissioned by Angela Weight of the Imperial War Museum to record the so-called Gulf War. (Art to the value of £10,000 was to be purchased for the permanent collection.) In 1991 an international force authorised by the United Nations and led by the Americans invaded Kuwait to expel the Iraqi army which had illegally attacked and occupied that country at the behest of Iraq's dictator Saddam Hussein.

Keane, a member of the Labour Party and the Campaign for Nuclear Disarmament, and a veteran of trips to Northern Ireland and Nicaragua, was a Social Realist painter of some verve; he was also reputed to be 'anti-establishment'. Mark Lawson has remarked: 'More than any other modern British artist, Keane has demonstrated a desire to get out of the studio and into the social and political frontline. What he produces is a kind of editorial art.' Regarding the subject of war, Keane told Nicholas de Jongh: 'I'm not obsessed with warfare but I am interested in how warfare affects life and how people suffer.'

During January and February 1991 Keane spent four weeks in Saudi Arabia staying in the Bahrain Sheraton Hotel along with some RAF bomber pilots. He made forays into the desert and entered Kuwait City shortly after it had been liberated. Keane employed modern recording technologies – videotape and still cameras – to 'sketch' in the field but, somewhat paradoxically, what emerged from his London studio after his return were traditional, hand-painted canvases and drawings executed in a hectic, quasi-Expressionist style. Pigment and brush-strokes were strongly foregrounded. However, in some instances a collage/mixed-media method was employed. For example, he sur-rounded one painted image with a border of still photos taken from video and glued postcards and dollar bills to the surface of other works. He also painted over newspapers so that print showed through in places. Keane is an artist who is keenly aware of the rival mass media but, rather than rejecting them, he uses them and incorporates them into his art.

When an artist is selected to become an 'official recorder', this in itself is a newsworthy event as far as the media are concerned. The British press also made certain that knowledge of Keane's war pictures was widely disseminated: one was reproduced in full colour in the *Guardian* (5 April 1991) and later, when the series was complete, other newspaper articles ensured that their appearance was accompanied by public controversy and misinformation.

A show of Keane's Gulf War paintings was held at the Imperial War Museum in April 1992. A work which included pages from the Koran was omitted for fear of offending Muslim fundamentalists. Earlier, in December 1991, a selection committee from the museum headed by Jonathan Scott had visited Keane's studio to choose a painting for purchase. They acquired *Mickey Mouse at the Front* (1991), a picture which was to prove highly contentious. Its content was prompted by Keane seeing the devastated seafront near Kuwait City. He took several colour photographs of different items which he later integrated into a single composition.

The painting depicts a melancholy vista of mud, sand, sea, distant buildings and shattered palm trees, together with a supermarket trolley loaded with turquoise-coloured grenade launchers. One of the trolley's wheels rests on the flag of Kuwait. On the right is the thick trunk of a palm tree whose top droops down to the ground (a phallic symbol of the force that has been defeated?). Neither the Iraqi aggressors nor their Kuwaiti victims are depicted, indeed no people or bodies are visible. However, the absent citizens of Kuwait are implied by the everyday relics of peacetime which now bear the traces of war.

At the very centre of the painting, between the trolley and the palm tree, is a broken but still grinning Mickey Mouse child's ride. Its bright, cheerful colours – red, blue, yellow, green and white – stand out against the light brown background of the earth. In front of the ride are piles of

36. John Keane, *Mickey Mouse at the Front*, 1991.
Oil on canvas, 172.8 x 198 cm.
London: Imperial War Museum collection. Photo: Imperial War Museum.

human excrement – the amusement arcade where Keane discovered the ride had been used as a latrine. The ride is an incongruous object, redolent of children's pleasures. The figure of Mickey naturally reminded some viewers of the strong American presence in the Gulf and the painting caused adverse comment in January 1992 because it was assumed by tabloid journalists that criticism of the United States was intended. Arguably, the Gulf conflict was a just war but it was also fought to protect and restore undemocratic Arab regimes and Western oil interests. The overwhelming firepower of the victors also made them seem brutal.

For a while the Disney Corporation considered suing Keane for breach of copyright. Newspapers such as the London *Evening Standard* and the *Daily Mail* carried headlines such as 'War is ... Mickey Mouse on a Toilet' and 'Outrage at Artist's View of Tragedy in the Gulf'. The *Daily Mail*, a right-wing paper, claimed there was anger in high places. It obtained a quote from Archie Hamilton, the Armed Forces's minister, stating that Keane's pictures 'trivialise an important event'.

On 15 January the painting was reproduced in the *Sun*, another right-wing newspaper, along with a quote from the father of a British soldier killed in the Gulf saying it was 'depraved'. An editorial headed 'Black Art', asserted that Mickey was 'sitting on a lavatory'. The writer went on to accuse Keane of sneering at the sacrifice of soldiers and of taking money as an official war artist when he was anti-war. The press also thought Keane was insulting the war dead by 'taking the Mickey out of Gulf troops'. The painter protested that no insults had been intended, that his picture was true to his experience of things seen in Kuwait City. Since he had camera-based evidence of what he had seen, the Imperial War Museum stood by its decision.

The *Evening Standard*'s and the *Sun*'s view that Keane had depicted Mickey sitting on a toilet was a factual error. The 'toilet' was, in reality, the white cover of the plinth which enclosed the machinery of the ride. This was a case of journalists reading too much into an image, of seeing what they wanted to see.

However, Keane had decided to include the symbol of American mass culture rather than some other relic, and Mickey's grin was disturbing and macabre because it was in such contrast to the surrounding desolation. Mickey's smirk reminded some viewers of the triumphalism of American generals when announcing victories on television. There was surely some justification for such associations even if Keane's intention had been to suggest 'the Mickey Mouse defences' of the Iraqis who had expected an invasion from the sea.

The various responses to Keane's painting constitute an example of reception history. It is now a commonplace of aesthetics, art history and cultural studies that images are capable of ambiguity, polysemy (many meanings) and that they can be 'read' or interpreted by different viewers in different ways. However, if there is no limit to the number of meanings that can be derived from an image, if no consensus can be reached as to its meaning, then effectively it is meaningless. The fact that we have all misread a word and then discovered our mistake shows that a legitimate distinction can be made between correct and incorrect readings. The 'toilet' example demonstrated that pictures can be misinterpreted because some viewers have not taken the trouble to examine the work closely enough to determine exactly what is there in terms of content or iconography, which is a fundamental prerequisite of art criticism. Where the media so often go wrong, is that they leap to conclusions as to the meanings and significances of new works of art before they have truly looked at them and thought about their import.

In February 1992 BBC2's arts strand *The Late Show* transmitted a discussion of the issues surrounding Keane's painting. After a filmed report of the media fuss and Keane's reactions, Sarah Dunant chaired a debate involving Linda Kitson (Falklands's War artist), Richard Cork (art critic) and Paul Fussell (war historian). Drawing upon her own experience, Kitson claimed that the tabloid press whipped up controversies in the interest of selling papers in order to gain profits. The war artist, she remarked, then becomes 'a pawn in an enormous game'. Cork pointed out that war art began as propaganda for the home side, but he saw no reason why contemporary artists should not produce anti-war pictures which are 'indignant, angry and crusading'. Given the censorship associated with reporting the Gulf War, he thought the artist's responsibility was to communicate 'a bitter truth'. He concluded: 'The intensity of the response to Keane's paintings proves that he is saying something new and something that needed to be said.'

Fussell thought that paintings of war now had to be made with irony. Despite the contradiction between the ugliness of war and the beauty conventionally associated with art, he considered war artists to be of value. Photographs did not reveal who had made them, whereas Keane's pictures had been constructed by hand, hence it was obvious that the artist was providing a subjective reaction and making a comment. (One is reminded of Emile Zola's definition of Realism as 'nature seen through a temperament'. In this case, one might say 'war as viewed through a pacifist/socialist ideology'.) A supporter of the documentary ability of film and photography might well disagree and argue that the handwork of the artist, the aesthetic dimension of art, places an unnecessary filter between viewers and the content of the image, and that the atrocities of war are more vivid and searing in camera-based media than in painting. Film footage exists of the terrible carnage that occurred along the Basra Road when a convoy of fleeing Iraqi forces loaded with loot were annihilated by Apache helicopters.

In Western democracies modern wars are normally reported immediately and in detail by television, radio and the press. Many images and much information reaches the public in spite of government censorship and the selection/editing procedures of the media themselves. Given the availability of such information, the question arises: 'What can a work of art say about war that news reports do not?' Critics loyal to art argue that it is capable of being more complex and truthful because artists have more time and more freedom to digest the information and to reflect upon its significance. Unlike news reporters and photo-journalists, artists do not have to be 'objective' and 'balanced', they can include personal feelings and make critical comments if they wish to do so.

Keane's painting *Day for Night* (1991) can be cited as an example of comment. Keane painted his images of Arabs, a burning oilfield and a red Mercedes on top of a copy of the *Financial Times* sprinkled with sand in order to indicate that the world markets – 'speculation and commodities' – were inextricably involved in the Gulf War. This was a somewhat obvious point to make but it did at least situate the events of the war in a broader context.

Artists are also capable of generating pictures and sculptures that are more imaginative, memorable, monumental and physically more permanent than news photos or film footage, and if these enter the collections of national institutions such as the Imperial War Museum, then they may have a much longer lifespan. In the view of Keane's admirers, *Mickey Mouse at the Front* is such a work.

29
1993: THE HOUSE THAT WAS
NO LONGER A HOME

In 1993 the interior of a house in the East End of London was transformed into a concrete sculpture by Rachel Whiteread. It became notorious, produced very mixed responses and generated much media comment. Despite protests, and to the dismay of many, the construction was demolished in 1994.

Whiteread was born in Ilford, Essex, in 1963. Her mother Pat was a Feminist/Socialist artist but at first Rachel wanted to become a doctor. Later she changed her mind and studied at Brighton College of Art as an undergraduate and then as a postgraduate at the Slade School of Art, London. She had her first one-person show in 1988 and within three years she had become a name to reckon with in the art world. In 1992 she spent a year in Berlin on a German scholarship. Her fame and reputation were confirmed in 1993 when she won the Turner Prize, the K Foundation Prize (even though this was for the 'worst' artist of the year) and her public sculpture *House* (1991–94) received massive publicity.

There are certain contemporary artists, and Whiteread is one (Christo is another), who have built whole careers on one idea/ technique. As the artists progress, the concept is generally applied on a larger and larger scale. The idea of using the technique of casting – an ancient and traditional fabrication method – to generate sculptures occurred to Whiteread following a workshop on the subject given by Richard Wilson in Brighton. At the Slade in 1987 she made casts from her own body. Tutors in drawing classes tell their students to pay as much attention to negative space – the space between objects – as to the objects themselves. In Whiteread's case, she focused upon the negative spaces inside such things as wardrobes, sinks and rooms by casting their interiors in plaster. *Ghost* (1988–90), for instance, was a plaster cast of the bedroom of a Victorian house on the Archway Road, North London. Paradoxically, the space was transformed from a void into a sealed block with all the room's surface details – doors, fireplaces, picture rails, and so on – imprinted on the plaster. The room's projections and hollows, of course, were reversed in the sculpture. 'Melancholy monument' was one critic's description.

An art-historical precedent for casting negative spaces was Marcel Duchamp's *Female Fig Leaf* (1951), a plaster cast of a woman's groin. Such a procedure does not involve certain traditional skills associated with the art of sculpture, that is, modelling or carving, the conceiving and organisation of a sequence of forms in space to represent figures or some kind of narrative. This is because in casting an existing object the shape and iconography are ready-made. This kind of 'sculpture' is thus highly conceptual: it depends on the artist's choice of what negative space to cast and what final material to use. As in the case of *House*, the artist may not even directly execute the work – that can be contracted out to specialist companies. In so far as the cast is a physical trace of something that previously existed, it is an indexical sign, but it is also an iconic sign because it resembles the original in certain respects. Whiteread has defended casting against the charge that it is merely copying by saying that it always *changes* the original object in some way, thereby making it strange.

In 1991 Whiteread conceived the idea of casting the interior of a whole house. One became available – 193 Grove Road, Bow – in the East End of London (an area with the highest concentration of artists in Britain). It was the last of an old terrace of three-storey dwellings that was being demolished to make way for a small park called Wennington Green. It was clear from the outset that the piece would only exist for a limited time. *House* was commissioned by the Artangel Trust – a charitable organisation founded for the purpose of fostering innovative, site-specific but temporary art projects – funded in part by Beck's Beer.

Further sponsorship money for the sculpture – which cost around £50,000 – was provided by Tarmac Structural Repairs, the London Arts Board, the Henry Moore Foundation and the Arts Council. Permission for the sculpture was given by Bow Parks Board in the absence of their chairman, Councillor Eric Flounders.

Structural plans were drawn up by Neil Thomas of Atelier One and work on the sculpture began in August 1993 and was completed in October. Fittings and wallpaper had to be removed and the

37. Rachel Whiteread, *House*, (Grove Road, London E3), October 1993 (destroyed January 1994).
Lokrete with metal armature. Photo: courtesy of the Artangel Trust.

structure strengthened with steel bolts and mesh. New foundations had to be laid to take the weight of the Lokrete that was gunnite-sprayed by Tarmac Structural Repairs inside every room after the roof, attic and porch had been removed. Once the concrete had cured, the exterior brickwork and windows were stripped off to reveal a three-dimensional impression of the house's previously hidden interiors. Some critics were reminded of bunkers, sepulchres or tombs. Like a death mask, it evoked loss, memories and mortality.

As already indicated, defamiliarisation is one of Whiteread's objectives. Certainly, her whitish concrete blend of architecture and sculpture was both familiar and strange, particularly since it stood alone in a shallow depression in the ground surrounded by air and grass. Without the rest of the terrace, the dwelling could now be seen in profile, and the smaller rear extension with its outside toilet was visible from the street. One side of *House* had strong vertical and horizontal lines. These, together with the flat roof, gave the impression of geometric abstract art or the white architecture of Modernism.

Directly opposite were houses and churches whose occupants had a grandstand view. Some of them came to resent the crowds of visitors the sculpture attracted. Unlike Flanagan's 1972 sculpture in Cambridge, *House* was too strong to be destroyed by vandals, but in its short life it did attract graffiti demanding 'Homes for All, Black + White' and asking 'Wot For?', answered by 'Why Not?' Whiteread also encountered a group of anarchist squatters equipped with drills and sledgehammers who were intending to break into the concrete shell.

In November 1993 Whiteread was awarded the Turner Prize. Simultaneously Flounders, a PR spokesman for the shipping line Cunard and a severe critic of *House*, announced its imminent demolition. The public's and the media's interest in her work escalated. Hundreds of Londoners, as well as people from other parts of Britain and from abroad, visited Grove Road daily and demands were made that the sculpture remain for ever or for a longer period. Flounders disagreed and insisted that it be removed as contractually agreed. After pressure from Members of Parliament and Artangel, an extension was granted until January 1994, when the sculpture was destroyed by a mechanical digger in two hours. No trace of *House* remains today on Wennington Green, a rather featureless public space which would have benefited from the continued presence of a sculpture which had stimulated such widespread curiosity. As Richard Cork remarked on television, *House* was 'a real landmark that enhanced the park'.

Despite petitions from local schoolchildren asking for the sculpture to be preserved, the attitude that prevailed in the Bow Neighbourhood Council was: 'Local amenities for local people, outsiders/art tourists keep out'. Flounders's view was that the sculpture was an imposition by arty-farty Hampstead types who would not tolerate such an ugly structure in their own backyard. The material from which it was made also offended him; he remarked: 'We have enough concrete in Bow already.' Some residents who admired *House* protested that, although Flounders was an elected representative, he did not, in fact, represent their views.

Given the public character and location of *House*, it was more or less inevitable that it would become embroiled in local political issues. Whiteread says she is a socialist and *House* was interpreted by some writers as a political statement. The work was described as a monument to the lives of ordinary people, the East Enders who, during the Second World War had suffered the Blitz, and in the post-1945 era had experienced poverty and housing problems. It was perceived as a tribute to 'the frailty and resilience of people's private lives'. Women critics detected a gender issue in the fact that the interior of the house – a space associated more with women than with men – was externalised.

By calling attention to the demolition of houses in the East End, the sculpture indicted the Conservative government's indifference to the need for new council housing for the homeless. Flounders and his colleagues were Liberal Democrats and there was no love lost between them and the Labour Party in the London borough of Tower Hamlets. (This may help to explain Flounders's antagonism towards *House*.) However, while such meanings could be derived from *House* with some effort, arguably the political dimension of the sculpture was overstated, a case of 'reading in' or analysing the physical and social context of the work rather than its actual content. After all, the work itself made no explicit condemnation of the Conservatives or the Liberal Democrats; it made no specific proposal as to how social change could be achieved.

Local 'psychogeographers' (a Situationist term) pointed out in a newsletter that it was the council which, by serving a possession order on Sidney Gale, the 71-year-old, ex-docker resident in 193 Grove Road for decades, had transformed his private, domestic space into public space against his will. (Gale's opinion of Whiteread's sculpture was: 'If this is art, I'm Leonardo da Vinci.') They also accused Whiteread of 'imperialism', of 'robbing those who once lived in Grove Road of their own past' and 'replacing it with a supposedly "higher set of values"'. Furthermore, they compared her *House* unfavourably to a tree house built and occupied by environmental activists who were resisting roadbuilders who cut down trees. For the activists, the company Tarmac was an enemy force, whereas for

Whiteread it was a collaborator. In short, they were highly critical of Whiteread's politics.

There is ample evidence of the intense public interest aroused by *House*. Unlike so many public sculptures, it evoked a positive emotional response. One reason for this was its simplicity and popular character, that is, everyone can relate to the experience of living in houses. In Andrew Graham-Dixon's opinion, '*House* was stubbornly unheroic and democratic: an image of how we all live, caught between solitude and sociability ...'

However, there was no consensus as to its aesthetic and social value or its meaning. Brian Masters found *House* 'chilling ... necrophilic in concept and effect ... there was not a flicker of life about it, no echo of the human presence which would normally have imbued it with charm, with character, with health; it was white, stark, ghostly and obviously dead'. Other responses ranged from the usual – 'This isn't art ... a load of rubbish ... a joke ... a monstrosity ... experimental nonsense' – to the view that it was 'beautiful ... extraordinary ... fantastical ... a modern masterpiece'. What was unusual was the fact that opinions did not fall into familiar categories: art world opinion versus those of laypeople, because some locals liked and welcomed the sculpture while others detested it; opinion in the art world was similarly split. As James Lingwood, a director of Artangel, observed, responses did 'not divide conveniently into local against national, public against private ... Such binary oppositions could neither explain nor contain the multiple shades of opinion and sentiment which *House* engendered.' Lingwood also questioned the received idea that art did or should aim to achieve a consensus because, in his opinion, no work of art could succeed in pleasing everyone.

Arguably, *House* was overrated by its art world enthusiasts – witness the excessive praise and over-elaborate discourse of interpretation found in a Phaidon Press book published in 1995. (The commissioners and sponsors of such sculptures have so much invested in them that they cannot stand back to judge the works dispassionately. Whiteread's dealer Karsten Schubert also contributed support and he cannot be considered a disinterested party. He is now her ex-dealer because in 1996 Whiteread shifted her allegiance to another gallery. Schubert was so upset he closed his gallery.) The sculpture's celebrity surely stemmed from a unique concatenation of circumstances: the Turner and K Foundation awards, the Channel 4 television coverage, the newspaper articles and cartoons, Flounders's unrepentant philistinism, plus the short life, large size, street location, emotional resonance and accessibility of the sculpture itself. For all that, it was an intriguing artefact that could usefully have been left in place for a number of years rather than a number of weeks.

Although Whiteread was distressed by the intense media pressure that fame and success brought in its wake, it did bolster her international reputation. For instance, she subsequently won a competition to design an important public memorial to the Holocaust in Judenplatz, Vienna. Plans for this monument – a concrete cast of the inside of a library – caused even more controversy in Vienna than *House* did in London because of the legacy of anti-semitism and quarrels between various interest groups and political factions within Austria. Its construction, therefore, was postponed many times. However, in 1998 it was announced that the memorial would be built.

30

1993–94: OUTSIDERS SEEK TO OUTRAGE THE ART WORLD

In 1993 the K Foundation attempted to spoil the Turner Prize celebrations by awarding £40,000 to the 'worst' artist on the shortlist. The following year they subverted the monetary values of the art world by burning £1 million as an art event. The art world remained unperturbed – it was business as usual.

Bill Drummond and Jimmy Cauty, who were born in the 1950s, are two anarchistic individuals who enjoy playing games with culture both high and low. They have lived out the Punk rock principle 'Cash from Chaos'. To begin with both men were interested in the visual arts. Drummond, a 6' 5" Glaswegian, studied at Liverpool Art College in the mid-1970s. Then, after a spell as a guitar player for Big in Japan, he switched to managing bands. Cauty, also a guitarist, taught himself illustration and designed a successful poster for the company Athena. Their collaboration began in 1987 as the Pop music duo The Jams or The Justified Ancients of Mu Mu, which had a hit with a version of the Beatles' *All You Need is Love* with material culled from news broadcasts, AIDs information and other songs. Then, in 1988, as The Timelords, they had a number one record with *Doctorin' the Tardis*, with sounds based on the *Dr Who* television series' theme tune. The fact that they seemed to change the name of their band annually was a parodic comment on the turnover of bands and names in the music business.

In 1990, as KLF (Kopyright Liberation Front), they released *Chill Out*. The very title of the group signalled their piratical, parasitical attitude to existing culture, in this case music: appropriate or sample it, and then use home technology to remix it. Naturally, Drummond and Cauty faced legal actions for breaches of copyright. Despite, or because of, their borrowed character, some of KLF's records proved very popular in clubs and in the charts.

The two men also devoted much energy to devising publicity gimmicks to help the sale of their records. They wore weird headdresses made from antler horns, sprayed graffiti, faked corn circles, added tasteless slogans to billboard advertisements and dumped dead sheep outside venues where they had been invited to receive awards. In 1991, 50 journalists were persuaded to travel to the island of Jura and to dress in Druid-like, yellow costumes. They then took part in a pagan-type ritual – *The Rites of Mu* – in which a 60-foot high Wicker Man and some money were burnt. A video was made of this ceremony which had been inspired by the sci-fi novels of Robert Anton Wilson.

In 1992 Cauty and Drummond 'withdrew' from the Pop music business by deleting all their records and by firing blanks from a machine-gun at the Brit Awards audience. Having succeeded so effortlessly in the field of mass culture, they decided to cross over into high culture, that is, the realm of fine art. Using their profits from record sales, Cauty and Drummond established the K Foundation (started 18 February 1993, but suspended for 23 years on 5 November 1995) to support struggling artists and 'the advancement of kreation'.

Needing an art world event upon which they could piggy-back to fame, they seized upon the Turner Prize. Via a series of newspaper adverts, they asked the public to vote for the 'worst' of the four shortlisted artists. The winner was to receive £40,000, that is, double the amount of the Turner Prize. That year – 1993 – the winner of both prizes was Rachel Whiteread, the sculptor whose concrete work *House* was widely acclaimed and denigrated. In the postal ballot, Whiteread was the clear winner with 3,000 votes. To publicise their Turner Prize activities the K Foundation spent over £20,000 on television commercials.

To involve the press, a posse of journalists was assembled at a rural location to witness a nightime event entitled *The Amending of Art History*. On display in a field was an oblong wooden panel upon

38. Kippa Matthews, *Rachel Whiteread being presented with K Foundation prizemoney outside the Tate Gallery*, November 1993.
Photo: courtesy of K. Matthews.

which bundles of notes amounting to £1 million had been nailed. This precious object – entitled *Nailed to the Wall* – was guarded by two nightclub bouncers. The journalists were then bribed to nail further bundles of money amounting to £40,000 to another board enclosed by a picture frame. The result was a shallow relief with a Minimalist grid. A motorcade of hired Cadillacs then travelled to London where the relief was chained to the railings of the Tate Gallery. This work, made from real banknotes, was a literal embodiment of the equation: art = money. Since this point had been made already by Warhol, Boggs, Finn-Kelcey and others, it was far from being an original one. However, Drummond later contended that the intention was not to 'use money to make a statement about art', but rather 'to use art to make a statement about money'.

Naturally, Whiteread was reluctant to accept the K Foundation's poisoned chalice but agreed to do so when the K Foundation threatened to set the money alight. Outside the Tate the emotional artist was mobbed by reporters and photographers. She took the money but immediately dispensed it to various charities.

Although the Turner Prize spoiling tactic did bring the K Foundation national publicity, they felt the need to make an even more extreme gesture, to show the art world they were braver than any other artists in their willingness to 'go all the way'. Finding that artists were slow to come forward to claim part of the £1 million they had put into the K Foundation, because they did not want the bother of selecting beneficiaries, and since a proposed exhibition of money-works such as *Nailed to the Wall* had not materialised, they decided to burn it instead. Drummond and Cauty later explained that their aim was to show that they were in control of money, not vice versa.

The NatWest Bullion Centre in Kent supplied the sum in new £50 banknotes packed into two suitcases and Cauty and Drummond flew by chartered plane to Scotland, and then by boat to the Isle of Jura where, on 23 August 1994, they proceeded to throw banknotes into a fire inside an abandoned boathouse. An hour-long film or video of this 'Destructive art' event was shot by their roady Gimpo (Alan Goodrick). Jim Reid, a journalist, acted as a witness and recorder. Even so, to this day doubt remains as to whether or not £1 million was actually incinerated. Scientific tests on the ash found in one suitcase showed that around £80,000 had indeed been burnt. Cauty and Drummond also keep the media and their fans guessing by telling lies all the time. One wonders why, if they wanted the world to see them destroying such a huge sum, the event did not take place in Hyde Park in front of dozens of sceptical witnesses rather than in a remote region of the British Isles? It might be that the idea was to make the event more 'legendary' or 'mythical' by making people wonder 'Did it really happen?'

Assuming that they did burn £1 million, what was the point/ motive? Cauty and Drummond seemed unable to provide a rational explanation except to say they were 'driven by inner demons'. Many people thought the burning was 'a load of rubbish, a waste of time'. If one of the aims of artists is to make money, then the K Foundation inverted this by disposing of money. It was obviously a gesture of contempt for the materialist values of contemporary society – no doubt they expected to shock those who value money highly – but it is much easier for millionaires to disdain and sacrifice money than for the poor to do so. Anthropologists could cite, as a precedent, the Potlatch ceremonies of some native American tribes in which chiefs proved their wealth and power by giving huge quantities of property away or by destroying it.

Whatever the reasons for the incineration, the questions 'Was it art? Was it good art?' remain. Certainly it could be categorised as a minor example of the Destructive/Performance genre but the event had been private rather than public. However, there were several, tangible by-products: Gimpo's film, the suitcase full of ash (from which a brick was eventually made), and a book, published in 1997, documenting the event. Cauty and Drummond consulted a marketing expert to discuss what to do with Gimpo's silent, unedited footage which resembled an early, hand-held, avant-garde film.

For a while they considered projecting it on the outside wall of the Tate Gallery in Liverpool. (This institution had earlier rejected a proposal to exhibit *Nailed to the Wall* and then to auction it with a reserve price of £500,000.) The film was first shown to the local people in Jura in August 1995 and subsequently to a variety of audiences in locations around Britain – art schools, prisons, theatres, a ladies' college – where it provoked a wide range of reactions and opinions: boredom, hostility, insults, support, animated argument and, in some places, scenes of chaos. One viewer claimed that the film was designed to make the audience think; another complained that is was like being 'sucked into a cerebral black hole'.

After a screening at a Music Business Conference, Cauty and Drummond acknowledged that the money-burning had been an 'indulgent' act but denied it was merely a stunt to sell records. They denied that they wanted to 'crawl back to the music business' and categorically stated that they were not making a new record. But, shortly afterwards, *The Magnificent* appeared on the 1995 *Help* album. (This record was again a rip-off: it was a reworking of the soundtrack of the popular Western *The Magnificent Seven*.)

Assuming that the K Foundation's money-burning ritual was essentially an expensive publicity gimmick, it was successful in the sense that Weekend Supplement articles about it appeared in the quality press and an hour-long, arts programme was transmitted on television, (*Omnibus*, BBC1). During the making of this programme, the suitcase full of ash was hawked around London galleries to see if it would be accepted/bought as an artwork. (Drummond claims this was entirely the doing of the programme-makers.) Several dealers expressed mild interest but declined to exhibit or sell it. Bernard Jacobson defined art tautologically by saying: 'It's art if it is made by artists.' But artists, he thought, could not be invented. (The implication being that artists are born not made. So much for the tuition supplied by art schools.)

The art world, it seems, was reluctant to recognise Cauty and Drummond as legitimate visual artists because they had no track record, no substantial corpus of work to their name. Significantly, René Gimpel, of Gimpel Fils Gallery, identified their Turner Prize prank as the only item on their art world CV. He reckoned that the suitcase, with documentation, might well be accepted by the art world as the residue of an iconoclastic gesture, but he valued it at a paltry £850 (a truly loss-making artwork).

In retrospect it would seem that few people were really shocked by an event intended to shock. Many thought, 'It's their money, so they can do what they like with it.' Others considered it 'a tedious, futile and childish gesture'. The London art world was not impressed either. After experiencing so many iconoclastic gestures in previous decades, it had become blasé, and there was the underlying judgement: 'These two arrivistes are not visual artists; they do not produce high quality works of art, only spoiling, critical gestures; they have no history of exhibiting; they may understand mass culture in the form of the music business, but the art business is more subtle and sophisticated – we are not so easily taken in or manipulated.'

When people new to the art world discover the extent to which art, as one commodity among others within capitalism, is associated with the greed and power of wealthy dealers, collectors and businesses (who sponsor it for their own ends), with promotion/selling/financial spec-ulation/investment/profiteering, they often become disillusioned and feel betrayed by art's promise of beauty and aesthetic pleasure. There was, therefore, some merit in the K Foundation's disturbance of the art establishment's self-congratulatory Turner Prize ceremony. Yet the best art has *use-value* as well as *exchange-value*. If Cauty and Drummond had devoted some time to the study of, say, the paintings of Vermeer, they would have realised that the value of such art transcends the money it would fetch in sale rooms. If their aim was really to 'use art to make a statement about money', then viewers and critics are left to reflect on the quality of the 'art' and the profundity of 'the statement'.

31

1993: THE ARTIST WHO ADORES LITTLE GIRLS

In March 1993 Graham Ovenden's erotic paintings and photographs of pre-pubescent girls aroused the attention of the police who raided his home and accused him and others of generating child pornography.

In recent years images of young children – especially those showing girls in the nude – have become highly suspect. This is because of increased knowledge and sensitivity concerning the sexual abuse and exploitation of children, and because of some appalling rapes and murders committed by paedophiles which have attracted worldwide publicity. Even parents who have photographed their own children naked have been subject to suspicion, police inquiries and media exposure. Any artist or photographer who habitually makes erotic images of small girls is now likely to be accused of being a child abuser, hence the problems that Graham Ovenden has experienced with the law.

Ovenden (b. 1943) studied at Southampton School of Art from 1960 to 1964 and then at the Royal College of Art from 1965 to 1968. He is now an internationally-known illustrator, painter and photographer specialising in landscapes and images of children. He is also an avid collector of images of children: he owns an extensive collection of photographs of girls by Charles Dodgson (1832–98, pseudonym Lewis Carroll), the author of *Alice's Adventures in Wonderland* (1865) and *Through the Looking Glass and What Alice Found There* (1871), an Oxford academic and clergyman who adored young females. Such adoration does not mean though that he was a paedophile in the sense that he physically abused the children he knew. Dodgson obtained the permission of parents to photograph their daughters dressed and undressed, and the sessions were supervised. The same applies to Ovenden's photo sessions. (The photos were often used as studies for paintings.) Ovenden is the author and editor of books about Lewis Carroll's photographs, Victorian erotic photography, and illustrations of fairies and nymphs.

Ovenden's interest in Victorian photography resulted in a bizarre practice of re-creation or fakery. For example, in a Court Case at the Old Bailey in 1980 he was accused along with the photographer Howard Grey of conspiring between 1974 and 1978 to obtain property by deception by passing off photographs taken by Grey of drawings by Ovenden which were themselves based on photographs taken by Grey of child models simulating Victorian beggar girls! The fakes were then sold to a collector on the basis that they were calotypes by the Victorian photographer Francis Hetling, who in fact never existed. Ovenden was eventually acquitted on the grounds that he had committed an elaborate hoax rather than a crime.

In 1975 Ovenden helped to found the Brotherhood of Ruralists, a loose association of artists who were friends, had decided to reside in the countryside (the West of England) in preference to the city and were dedicated to its preservation and celebration. The name chosen evoked that of such nineteenth-century groups as the Brotherhood of Ancients and the Pre-Raphaelite Brotherhood. Other members included Peter Blake and his then wife Jann Haworth, Graham and Ann Arnold, Annie Ovenden and David Inshaw; consequently it was as much a 'sisterhood' as a 'brother-hood'. The group exhibited figure and landscape paintings at the Piccadilly Gallery, the Royal Academy and the Camden Arts Centre, London. (So, cities had some use.) Critics who favoured avant-garde art regarded the Ruralists as reactionaries in flight from the realities of modern urban life, as academic artists who produced finicky paintings, some with literary subjects. One by Blake, which he started in 1976, featured Shakespeare's fairy-queen Titania, from *A Midsummer's Night's Dream*, stark naked with copious pubic hair visible.

In March 1993 two members of the Obscene Publications Squad of the Metropolitan Police and three local constables, acting on the basis of the indecent images clause in the 1978 Protection of Children Act, raided Ovenden's home in Cornwall. They confiscated boxes of material which included photos of children by Ann Arnold, Blake, David Bailey, Carroll, Inshaw and others. Ovenden was arrested and interviewed for several hours. Triumphantly, the police announced that that they had smashed a long-standing, international ring of paedophiles and pornographers involving hundreds of children. But they subsequently failed to press charges and Ovenden's property was returned.

Ovenden, in fact, has been exhibiting his paintings of children since 1970. Paul Overy, art critic for *New Society*, reviewing an exhibition of Ovenden's pictures held at the Piccadilly Gallery in that year, reacted with shock and distaste:

> The little girls are shown adopting extremely provocative poses, made more
> so by the fact that they are usually painted wearing a single undergarment –

> a too short vest revealing minutely detailed *pudenda,* knickers pulled half-down to reveal pale, flaunted buttocks ... Ovenden depicts his little girls' faces with a simpering sentimentality that contrasts horrifically with the precisely painted sexual parts ... Ovenden's paintings do not attempt to help us to understand or come to terms with such desires [that is, men's sexual desires for attractive little girls] but try to inflame them ... they are obscene ...

Overy concluded with a very serious observation: 'Ovenden's paintings seem only to lead in the direction of the terrible world of Ian Brady and Myra Hindley' (two notorious child killers of the 1960s). This was surely an unfair extrapolation because the vast majority of those who enjoy looking at sexual imagery do not go on to commit murder.

Ovenden has contended that the photographs and paintings of nude girls are not obscene in his eyes, though they may be in the eyes of others. He has pointed out that 'Nakedness is a natural phenomenon' and claimed that it is the pervert who wants to add fig leaves. If one took the view that all images showing naked children were intrinsically obscene, then no parents could enjoy photos of their offspring. It is surely possible for adults to find children beautiful, to find their bodies aesthetically pleasing, to kiss and cuddle them, without being sexually aroused by them. However, in many of Ovenden's paintings there is a clear sexual dimension. For instance, in 1973, he created a painting with the title *Lolita after the First Lovemaking,* one of a series inspired by Vladimir Nabokov's famous novel. Nabokov, apparently, neither liked nor approved of Ovenden's Lolita series.

The painter has had his defenders, for example, Dr Peter Webb, an art historian who is the main author of *The Erotic Arts* (first edition 1975) in which Ovenden's *Belinda* (1971) is reproduced. (Webb, a homosexual, was arrested in the summer of 1996 and is currently serving a five-year prison sentence after being found guilty of indecently assaulting under-age boys.) Webb wrote:

> His little girls are certainly very sexual, but they are not painted as titillations for old men; they express a romantic nostalgia for the mystery of childhood ... Basically, they express Ovenden's conviction that sexuality is an essential ingredient of childhood, a still unpopular belief and the cause of much bigoted criticism of his work.

Ovenden may well be right to say that children are sexual beings before the age of consent but his pictures are not made by children externalising their nascent sexual feelings but by an adult male who is voyeuristically gazing at or imagining a child's body. Furthermore, if they are not produced for old men, who are they produced for? Could it be for lustful men of all ages?

Webb then quotes Ovenden's personal confession:

> I think that little girls are very romantic creatures ... one paints the thing that moves one most in life ... of course I fall in love with them ... I would be an absolute hypocrite if I said my work was lacking in any sexual feeling. It's paramountly obvious that they are very sexual things to me ... I have to admit to myself that I'm involved with something that can never be consummated ... It's a very painful experience.

A distinction exists in the discourse about visual culture between Erotic art and visual pornography but the line between them is hard to draw and it is a highly contentious issue about which there is no social consensus. In the final analysis, the difference is determined – for a time at least – by juries in British courts of law because they decide whether or not an image is likely 'to deprave and corrupt' and counts, therefore, as an example of pornography. Webb's position, of course, was that Ovenden's work is Erotic art rather than pornography. Yet might it not be possible for a conflation of the two categories to occur?

One of the dreamlike paintings of Balthus (Balthazar Klossowski, Count de Rola, b. 1908), for example, shows a woman abusing a semi-naked adolescent girl (*The Guitar Lesson*, [1934]), yet he is a highly-rated and financially successful Polish-French artist. In the case of Jeff Koons' sculptures and images of himself and his then wife Ilona Staller (the ex-porn star La Cicciolina) engaged in various sexual acts do we not find a fusion of high art and low pornography? Why is it not possible for art with sexual content to arouse sexual feelings, to deprave and corrupt?

In Ovenden's case, some of his pictures do appear to cater for the scopophilia of adult males, in this case the desire to gaze upon the private parts of small girls and, presumably, to fantasise about touching and having sex with them. Like so much pornography, they may well be used for masturbation purposes. In their defence it could be argued they are a form of sublimation. Banning such images would be difficult because of the existence of innocent family snapshots and eroticised images of girls found in certain advertisements, in films like *Bugsy*

39. Lisa Yuskavage, *Faucet*, 1995.
Oil on linen, 182.9 x 152.4 cm.
Photo: courtesy of the Christopher Grimes Gallery, Santa Monica.

Malone (director Alan Parker, 1976) and in television series such as *Minipops* (Channel 4, 1983), and because of the problems of enforcement. There are other grounds for rejecting Ovenden's art: from the standpoint of Modernism it is anachronistic in style and aesthetically weak.

In the United States the photographers Sally Mann, Alice Sims and Jock Sturges have made studies of nude or sexualised children and have been accused of producing child pornography as a result. However, as the *World Art* writer Hannah Feldman reports in an analysis of what Japanese sociologists call 'The Lolita Complex' (the male desire for girlish women), a surprising new development in American art has been paintings by women artists such as Karen Kilimnik and Rita Ackermann which celebrate girls as sexually alluring creatures. Feldman also points to the popularity of the Lolita look in popular media and fashion design. In other words, Lolita has become a heroine for many American women because she exerts sexual power: 'Rather than being controlled by a man's desire, Lolita controls the men who want her.' Feldman concludes her article, however, by citing works by the artists Lisa Yuskavage and Collier Schorr which address the same subject matter but which also manage to incorporate critical elements in order to disturb the salacious male gaze for which, arguably, Ovenden's art caters.

32

1994: HIRST'S LAMB VANDALISED

In May 1994 in the Serpentine Gallery a vandal poured black ink into a glass tank 'sculpture' by Damien Hirst, thus transforming the dead, white lamb inside into a black one. The vandal was charged with criminal damage but at his trial he pleaded artistic justification.

Hirst is one of the most celebrated, notorious and sought-after British artists of the 1990s. His work sells for high prices to rich collectors but he is also known to many outside the art world. Hirst was born in Bristol into a working-class family in 1965 but grew up in Leeds where he attended the Joseph Kramer School of Art. Then, from 1985 to 1989, he studied fine art at Goldsmiths College, London, and showed his aptitude for self-promotion by organising a now famous exhibition called *Freeze* (1988) of his own and his contemporaries' work in a derelict building in London's Docklands. To ensure curators and dealers saw the show, Hirst arranged transportation for them.

Like Warhol before him, Hirst is an extremely versatile artist who is willing to try his hand at any medium: he has produced abstract paintings, sculptural-type installations involving live and dead animals, medicine cabinets full of bottled specimens and surgical instruments, a commercial for cable television, a billboard image, a trailer for an opera which involved live rats, record cover designs, a Pop music video for the band Blur (featuring live sheep and pigs), and a gloomy, narrative film entitled *Hanging Around* (1996). His art world reputation was sealed in 1995 when he was awarded the Turner Prize, worth £20,000.

Journalists adore Hirst because he makes such good copy: the amount of press and other media coverage he has generated in such a short career is astonishing. In 1994 *Omnibus*, BBC1's flagship arts television strand, devoted a whole programme to him as if he were already an old master. (As the credits rolled Hirst exposed himself to the camera.) Janet Street Porter has claimed that Hirst is 'a pop star and that's what annoys the dreary art establishment'. But how can such a successful artist be said to 'annoy' the art establishment when some who constitute that establishment have welcomed him with open arms?

Hirst's paintings are of three types:

1. randomly coloured discs arranged in vertical/horizontal rows like a decorator's paint chart. These so-called 'spot' or 'dot' paintings are

utterly vacuous – they make no claims to spirituality – and are travesties of abstract art. Their patterns have even been reproduced on dress fabrics by the fashion designer Rifat Ozbek. One critic has described them as 'trademark' paintings because they are churned out by assistants to meet the demand of collectors (in 1996 one fetched £32,000 at auction). Hirst himself admits they are 'dumb pictures about the dumbness of painting';

2. 'whirl' or 'spin' paintings produced by pouring liquid paint on to a circular support while it is revolving: a child's version of Action painting minus its Existentialist angst. The results are reminiscent of late 1960s' Psychedelic art or late 1980s' Acid House, rave-party decor. While decorative, these paintings are again vacuous in terms of their form and content;

3. monochrome canvases with dead butterflies attached.

Hirst's early installations which presented a life/death cycle had more substance even though Ecological artists had made similar works years before. For example, *A Thousand Years* (1990) was a glass enclosure inside of which was a rotting cow's head, maggots, flies and an 'insect-o-cutor' device to kill the latter. As a student in Leeds Hirst drew corpses and was fascinated by photographs in medical textbooks that were simultaneously horrific and gorgeous – he liked the contradiction. Critics think that the macabre element in Hirst's work is due to the influence of Francis Bacon, but his mother blames the Punk rock impresario Malcolm McLaren. Much of Hirst's art, his supporters claim, is about the fundamental issues of life and death, yet no profound or new insights are forthcoming, only gruesome reminders of the basic facts.

Hirst is best known for his morbid tableaux – huge steel and glass cases awash with formaldehyde containing the embalmed bodies of such animals as sheep, cows and a shark (killed to order) – but, arguably, this kind of work is neither original nor radical. For instance, much more shocking works involving animals were produced by Hermann Nitsch and Raphael Ortiz during the 1960s, and by Rick Gibson during the 1980s. Furthermore, Hirst's animal pieces can be seen as contributions to the traditional genre of animal painting/ sculpture in which British artists have excelled. A cynic might describe his tiger shark piece – *The Physical Impossibility of Death in the Mind of Someone Living*, (1991) – as a footnote to the popular movie *Jaws* (director Steven Spielberg, 1975), a thriller about shark attacks on humans. (Most of Hirst's creative effort seems to be expended on thinking up long-winded, portentous titles.) A more original use of a shark – which may indeed have inspired Hirst – was a 25-foot high, fibreglass great white shark which a cinema owner, William Heine, installed as if crashing through the roof of a small, terraced house in Oxford. This piece was made by local sculptor John Buckley and erected in August 1986 to mark the anniversary of the atomic bomb dropped on Nagasaki. It soon agitated the local council and became a tourist attraction.

40. John Buckley, *Shark*, 1986.
Fibreglass. Headington, Oxfordshire. Photo: courtesy of the artist.

Hirst's lamb piece is a three-dimensional version of Pre-Raphaelite-type depictions of pretty baa lambs. In any case, the term 'sculpture' hardly applies to his animal exhibits because sculptural skills such as carving or modelling are not involved. Hirst does not in fact *represent* dead animals, he *presents* them. This is because he wants to replace an illusion of reality with reality in order to achieve a more powerful emotional impact or visceral sensation. The novelty factor stems from the fact that preserved animals normally found in the Natural History Museum, South Kensington, have been displaced to London art galleries. They are enjoyed by the same audience: schoolboys who like the frisson of dissecting frogs and examining the innards of animals exposed in glass cases. Hirst's work is certainly direct and simple enough to be accessible to the general public. (Some critics think it is not just simple but simple-minded.) He has remarked: 'I wanted to make art that everybody could believe in – even people who hate art.'

In May 1994 Hirst curated an exhibition of works by 15 artists entitled *Some Went Mad, Some Ran Away* held at the Serpentine Gallery and several other venues. Apparently, this show broke all attendance records for the Serpentine. He included one of his own works, *Away from the Flock*, a glass tank containing the corpse of a

41. Henrietta Butler, *Damien Hirst with 'Away From the Flock'*
in the Serpentine Gallery, **1994.**
Photo: courtesy of H. Butler.

Suffolk lamb obtained from a Guildford abattoir (cost of a live lamb £30, cost of killing it £5). The critic William Feaver noted: 'Bubbles cling pathetically around the mouth and the saturated fleece has swollen like a life jacket.' Floating in formaldehyde, the lamb looked as if it was leaping in the air. The tank was placed at right angles to the gallery's windows, creating the effect that the lamb was eager to escape to the green grass outside. It was a rather cruel and pathetic sight.

A collector paid Hirst £25,000 for the lamb 'sculpture'. This prompted some predictable comments and puns from the *Sun* newspaper: 'Baa-rmy! £25,000 for one dead sheep ... [Hirst is] pulling the wool over our eyes.'

On 9 May Mark Bridger, a 35-year-old artist, gallery director and temporary teacher of English from Oxford, poured black ink into the tank and covered over Hirst's label with another stating: Mark Bridger, *Black Sheep*. Thus Bridger appropriated the Hirst piece as Hirst himself had appropriated the dead animal. An attendant ran after Bridger and obtained his name and address. At first Hirst considered accepting the alteration from white to black and not taking Bridger to court, but then he and the gallery realised that this might be construed as an open invitation to other vandals. Hirst worked all night to restore the exhibit. The cost of repairs was £1,000.

In June, *Away from the Flock* was parodied in advertisements for the Designers' and Art Directors' Association's Festival of Excellence. The adverts, designed by Nick Welch and Billy Mawhinney of S.P. Lintas, depicted a dead sheep floating in a tank of Boddington's beer. Hirst and his dealer, Jay Jopling, were upset by this breach of copyright and threatened to sue D & AD. An out-of-court settlement was reached and the adverts were withdrawn or blacked out. This legalistic response by a contemporary artist to an instance of plagiarism (or homage) was rather preposterous, given the number of times artists have borrowed imagery from the mass media without obtaining permission or paying for the privilege.

In August, Bridger appeared at Bow Street Magistrates' Court charged with criminal damage. Hirst returned from Berlin – where he had gone 'to avoid publicity' – in order to give evidence. Bridger denied his motive had been jealousy at Hirst's fame or the desire to damage the exhibit and claimed that, on the contrary, his intention had been to provide 'an addendum to his work'. He also said that he didn't think Hirst would mind because they were both on the same creative wavelength. The problem with Bridger's 'artistic' intervention was that it was as trite as the original exhibit. Bridger was found guilty but because of his poverty, was neither fined nor ordered to pay compensation; he was given a two-year conditional discharge.

Since Hirst is both praised and denigrated, it is clear that the art world is divided regarding the significance and quality of his art and, judging by letters to the press, so is the public. Sister Wendy Beckett, the nun who is also a television art pundit, condemned his work as 'pathetic, one-look, gossip shock-horror art'. Another writer dubbed him 'Britain's leading shock artist'. One might ask: 'Who has been truly shocked by Hirst's work? How can an artist who is feted by the art world, who shows no interest in politics, who has used his wealth to buy bourgeois lifestyle trappings such as a farmhouse and a Range Rover, be thought radical or subversive?' Yet he does seem to have offended some viewers: with regard to *Mother and Child, Divided* (1993), Sister Wendy commented that 'to see an animal cut in two in a glass case is a shocking thing'; some children thought it 'sick, disgusting and revolting'; animal rights activists were upset by his disrespectful treatment of dead cows and butterflies; and in 1996 New York health inspectors expressed concern that 'odours and fluids caused by the rotting process' might be a danger to Americans. But as Hirst himself has said apropos his animal pieces: 'I can't see any difference between going into the butcher's and seeing it in an art gallery.' The difference, of course, is that butchers do not claim their shops are art installations.

What offends some Britons is not so much Hirst's work as the importance he has been accorded by the art world and the mass media. Witness Deidre Thacker's letter to the *Observer*: 'We are forced to witness the tasteless, and many might say obscene, excesses of a young man who is sadly being offered to younger generations as an icon. Fine Art has been hijacked by showmen and entrepreneurs, stripped of its dignity, of its very soul, and battered into the ground.' Could this state of affairs, one wonders, have anything to do with the capitalist system in general and the competitive nature of the art trade in particular?

On a final note, during 1996 Hirst became involved in the refurbishment of Leoni's Quo Vadis, an Italian restaurant, in Dean Street, Soho. He was asked to select the furniture and to provide the decor which consisted of examples of his sculptures, namely, skinned cow heads preserved in tanks of formaldehyde. When the restaurant opened in January 1997 animal rights activists invaded it, deposited rubbish in the foyer (to indicate their opinion of Hirst's work), occupied the bar and handed out leaflets to the affluent diners until ejected by the police. A demonstration with placards then took place outside. A spokesperson for London Animal Action explained: 'We chose Quo Vadis in our campaign against the meat industry primarily because of Damien Hirst's contribution. It is disgusting.' Five of the activists were charged with affray and appeared before Marlborough Street magistrates. The protesters spent two weeks in prison on remand. When the case was heard in October two defendants were bound over to keep the peace for a year for £100 while the other three – who pleaded guilty to threatening behaviour – were each fined £200 plus £200 costs.

33

1994: PAINTING OF RAPE TOO BRUTAL FOR IMPERIAL WAR MUSEUM

In 1994 Peter Howson's painting of a rape scene in Bosnia was rejected by the Imperial War Museum even though it had been selected by one of the museum's curators. The painting was later bought by a leading British Pop music star.

Howson was born in 1958 in the South of England into a middle-class family which moved to Scotland when he was four. He was a reclusive child who found enjoyment in drawing and painting. Incidents of bullying shattered Howson's belief in the essential goodness of humanity. From 1975 to 1977 he attended Glasgow School of Art but left early and, on impulse, joined the Highland Fusiliers. He spent two unhappy years in the army where he witnessed acts of brutality.

Returning to art school he was encouraged by Alexander 'Sandy' Moffat, a tutor who stressed the importance of life drawing, content and 'the big idea'. Howson is physically large and strong – for a time he even worked as a nightclub bouncer. His figurative paintings, like those of fellow student Ken Currie, focused upon lowlife scenes, the football hooligans and religious bigots of Glasgow. Many of his pictures featured male figures – boxers, dossers, soldiers – with muscular necks and torsos luridly illuminated with strong modelling and chiaroscuro. In other words, macho subjects were matched by a macho style. Yet, as Robert Heller has observed, 'the muscle-bound gestures and the pained eyes tell a different story'. Howson's hard men were often shown in profile facing the edge of the canvas – they seemed to have nowhere to go. Some, beneath their belligerence, were impotent.

Howson has been influenced by and has drawn inspiration from such artists as Beckmann, Breughel, Courbet, Daumier, Dix, Géricault, Goya, Grosz and Hogarth. His style combines Romanticism, Realism and Expressionism. Although rooted in observation of reality, Howson tends to work from memory and imagination; he also invents and there is a strong element of exaggeration or caricature in his art. As his confidence grew, Howson produced, during the period 1986–92, narrative pictures and allegorical triptychs which were ambitious in size and subject matter. Apocalyptic compositions packed with figures addressed such themes as patriotism and the blind leading the blind. His recurring subject was humanity – or rather inhumanity – as theatrical visual sermons were preached about the bestiality, stupidity and violence of the human species. Clearly, such an artist was well suited to recording the subject of war.

Compared to avant-garde artists like Jackson Pollock and John Latham, Howson's style is retrograde. But because his paintings, drawings, pastels and prints are figurative, illustrative, and skilfully executed, they have proved popular with dealers, collectors and the public – they have even been purchased by such mass culture stars as Bob Geldof, Madonna and Sylvester Stallone. During the 1980s, Howson was acclaimed as one of a new School of Glasgow painters called 'New Image Painters' or 'The Glasgow Pups'.

Following the collapse of communist regimes in the USSR and Eastern Europe in the early 1990s, Yugoslavia fragmented into its ancient constituent parts – Bosnia, Croatia, Serbia, and so on – and a ferocious civil war along ethnic lines began. Over the next few years ghastly atrocities committed by soldiers against civilians and prisoners were reported in the news media. In 1993 Howson was commissioned to visit Bosnia as an official recorder, a trip sponsored by *The Times* newspaper. When he returned, the War Museum intended to select six works for its permanent collection up to a maximum value of £20,000.

Howson made two visits to Bosnia in that year, the first in June, the second in December. During his first, 16-day trip he spent most of his time with British troops at Vitez, a Croatian-held pocket surrounded by Muslims where he experienced shelling and sniping. The conditions he encountered were far worse than he had expected and the time he spent there was frightening and traumatic. He made some sketches but he found it difficult to work, especially after he developed dysentery. He later told David Lee: 'The first visit almost stopped me painting ... There wasn't any point because there's no way you can show the gravity and tragedy of what's going on there.'

On his second visit Howson was accompanied by Ian MacColl, an artist who took a video camera with him, and Robert Crampton, a journalist. Again the base used was Vitez. On his return to Britain Howson produced over 200 paintings and drawings in a variety of styles – some were precisely detailed and finished while others were crudely executed in a neo-Expressionist manner. Certain pictures stemmed from direct observation while others were imagined but based on stories he had been told. Howson informed Crampton that he wanted to 'cut out all the reportage' and added, 'My job is to do the things you don't see', by which he meant atrocities not documented by press photographers.

Howson's Bosnian experience had important consequences for the direction of his painting and also for his personal life: material values became much less important; his marriage disintegrated and he moved from Glasgow to London.

In September 1994 Howson's war pictures were exhibited at the Imperial War Museum and the Angela Flowers Gallery in East London. Outside the museum's display was the warning: 'This exhibition contains images of violence.' According to Sir Roy Strong, visitors left the exhibition 'feeling annihilated'. Their silence was 'a measure of the power of art to evoke reaction even in eyes dulled by the images of the camera on the television screen'. One of the visitors was Haris Silajdzic, the prime minister of Bosnia. He told Noel Malcolm that the war in Bosnia was no arbitrary, irrational outbreak of killing, but rather 'a planned, carefully thought-out project, to create a Greater Serbia at the expense of both Bosnia and Croatia, carried out in the first place by the former Yugoslav army'. Silajdzic thought that art could convey the pathos of victims in a way that no other medium could. But in Malcolm's opinion, 'in Howson's vision of Bosnia the dominant figures are the agents of violence, and the faces of victims are not just traumatised, but brutalised as well, till they come almost to resemble their tormentors'.

A painting entitled *Croatian and Muslim* (1994) was to prove the most controversial picture on display. It depicts a naked woman face down with her head in the bowl of a toilet. One man holds her legs apart while he rapes her from behind. Another man, standing near her

42. Peter Howson, *Croatian and Muslim*, 1994.
Oil on canvas, 213 x 152.5 cm. London: private collection.
Photo: courtesy of the Angela Flowers Gallery, London.

head, forces her body down with one hand and with the other he half
obscures a picture on a wall showing a family group portrait. In the
background there is a small figure – a child? – watching.

The painting's colour scheme is dominated by a clash between red
and green: Indian red for the men's faces and arms and a lurid, acidic
green for their clothes. By representing the rapists as squat, extremely
muscular figures, Howson successfully conveys the impression of
brute, masculine force against which most women would be helpless.
Only part of the woman's face can be seen, but a bulging eye
communicates a sense of the suffering and violation she is experiencing. Howson's title indicates the ethnic and religious hatreds – Croats
against Muslims in this instance – that fuelled the atrocities. The
presence of the group portrait on the wall indicates that abuses of
human rights took place in the homes of victims and it also signals the
breakdown of families and family values brought about by civil war.

Angela Weight, a curator at the War Museum, selected this painting (price £18,000) for the museum's art collection because she thought it best represented the horror of the war and showed that violence in war is often perpetrated by men on women. Her choice was supported by the art critic Marina Vaizey. However, the three other members of the Artistic Record Committee – all men: Sir Kenneth Robinson (former Chair of the Arts Council), Jonathan Scott (a banker) and one other, overruled the two women and selected instead a much more innocuous painting entitled *Cleansed*. It depicts a group of six figures, men and women, squatting on the ground with soldiers and houses behind them. According to Richard Brooks, the painting 'could be a picture of peasants in a French or Spanish country village'.

When questioned, Robinson denied that the rape picture had been rejected in favour of *Cleansed* and claimed it was simply a matter of selecting the finest work. Alan Borg, director of the museum, gave a different reason: Howson's atrocity pictures had been passed over because the artist 'had not witnessed them personally'. (One wonders if the museum would have refused Picasso's *Guernica* on the grounds that he had not personally witnessed the bombing raid.) As if an artist could, or would be allowed to, sit and sketch while a woman was being gang raped or a man was being castrated. Clearly, Howson's rape scene was a work of the artist's imagination, but one that was based on many reports from Muslim women who had been violated.

Weight, however, thought the rape picture was rejected because its truth was too brutal and upsetting, especially for men. Strangely, a museum about war was not prepared to show its harsh reality. The Imperial War Museum attracts many children and teenagers who enjoy the displays of guns and uniforms. There is a danger that male heroes will be celebrated and that war itself will be glamorised and sanitised.

Howson benefited from the publicity about the museum's timidity in the sense that it prompted David Bowie, the multi-millionaire Pop music star, to purchase the rape painting. Bowie has a strong interest in the visual arts: he paints and has exhibited his work in a Cork Street gallery; he also serves on the editorial board of the magazine *Modern Painters* for which he sometimes writes reviews. He has homes in England, Switzerland and the United States, consequently he has many walls on which to hang his extensive art collection. He told reporters he didn't *like* Howson's painting but considered it 'powerful, important, evocative and devastating'. He said he wanted to keep it in Britain and was willing to lend it to the Imperial War Museum.

The private collector's gain was the public sector's loss. A conventional but powerful picture of male violence in war could have been added to the art collection of the Imperial War Museum, but the opportunity was lost due to the conservatism and lack of vision of the male judges on the selection panel. In 1995 the trustees of the Tate Gallery proved to be braver when they purchased, for £18,000, Howson's *Plum Grove*, another scene of atrocity in Bosnia.

Howson claims not to be 'a social reformer' nor to be interested in party politics. At the same time he despises fascism, violence and apathy in the face of human suffering and he seeks to address important historical issues. He wants his art to communicate, to have an emotional impact, and this he has certainly achieved. He also hopes that his pictures will be therapeutic but it is difficult to see how this is possible because there are so few signs of redemption or optimism in them.

Given the fact that war atrocities have been documented so fully and searingly by such major artists as Goya and Grosz, and by the films and photographs of the First and Second World Wars, Vietnam, and so on, one doubts the value and efficacy of yet more records of humanity's capacity for brutality. Furthermore, besides the carnage which takes place in battle zones, wars are the products of decisions taken in government and business offices. They depend upon civilians who support politicians voting for war and workers who manufacture weapons in factories. Surely, what is needed from artists now are some deeper analyses of the causes of wars and some alternative solutions to war as a means of settling disputes rather than yet more images of violence which add little to our existing knowledge and understanding.

34

1994: CHILD MURDER –
A SUITABLE SUBJECT FOR ART?

In May 1994 a distressed woman with a Liverpool accent phoned the Whitechapel Art Gallery in London warning of impending danger. Later on, a car with four angry men inside parked on the yellow lines outside the gallery. They entered and demanded to see the 'atrocity' pictures by Jamie Wagg. Apparently, press reports and rumours had led them to expect oil paintings showing the dismembered corpse of the murdered child James Bulger. When a guard took them to see the works, the men were taken aback – there were no 'atrocity' pictures, only prints based on images they had seen in the mass media many times before. Baffled, the men retreated without taking any aggressive action.

Jamie Wagg was born in 1958 into a large working-class family living on a council estate in Norfolk. During the 1970s he studied fine art at Leeds Polytechnic under Geoff Teasdale and Jeff Nuttall but his thinking was also influenced by socialist and feminist lecturers from Leeds University, such as Terry Atkinson and Griselda Pollock. Wagg now lives in North London and earns a living as a studio manager at the Byam Shaw School of Art. For many years he has employed mass media imagery as a starting point for his art.

Like the majority of the British people, Wagg was gripped by the horror of the murder of the toddler James Bulger by two ten-year-old boys (February 1993, Bootle, Merseyside). Recalling his own rough, childhood games, he concluded that he could easily have been such a victim or such a criminal. The questions: 'Why has this case caused so much consternation? What does it tell us about the condition of British society?' also intrigued him and he decided to make works based on media images associated with the tragedy.

Two works taken from a larger series were eventually displayed in a mixed exhibition, sponsored by British Telecom, at the Whitechapel Art Gallery in May 1994. They were photographic images which had been treated in various ways to produce large, computer-generated, electrostatic, ink-jet, laminated prints. One was based on a photo taken from television of the child being abducted by his murderers in a shopping mall. The other was based on a newspaper photo of two policemen on a railway line at Walton some distance from the murder scene. The latter print was so highly abstracted that it resembled an Impressionist painting. Word-image montages are important to Wagg. He gave the prints the overall title *History-Paintings, Cartoons for Tapestry* to indicate his desire to make art in the history-painting tradition of Géricault and Manet, that is, art that responds to events of contemporary history rather than events of the distant past. Given the hysterical reaction of the press to Wagg's prints, it seems it is not acceptable in Britain for artists to make art about contemporary events. Wagg would like his prints to be made into tapestries which would then be displayed in the Royal Gallery, Palace of Westminster, a building at the heart of the British state, and with this aim in mind, he has produced a montage/coloured postcard (1995) showing the tapestries in place.

43. Martin Argles, *Installation shot of Whitechapel Art Gallery Open Exhibition with two prints (on the right) by Jamie Wagg on display*, 1994. Photo: courtesy of M. Argles and the *Guardian*, London.

Many artists who use mass media imagery are aware of the issue of copyright. Wagg contacted the Press Association and was informed that the shopping mall, surveillance video – which did not save Bulger's life but which did help detectives trace the killers – was not copyrighted and therefore anyone could use it. He then took still photos from television transmissions of the video footage. Later on, Wagg learnt that a vicious, false rumour was circulating in Liverpool that he had purchased all the copyrights to the Bulger case images in order to profit from their reproduction.

The artistic use of pre-existing images also raises the question of added value. Has the artist merely reproduced the image or has he or she transformed the original in order to contribute something new? In Wagg's case the photograph was subjected to a number of processes of reproduction, via computers, during which various alterations were made. For example, the shopping mall scene was simplified to make it even more graphic and iconic (the word 'Mothercare' was eliminated) and the lighter areas around the figures of the children were tinged with orange and yellow. In itself the mall picture was mundane, innocuous.

Its power to fascinate was surely due to our knowledge of what happened afterwards, to the fact that its blurred character encouraged projection, and the fact that three figures seen from the rear walking towards the top edge of the picture were suffused by light. The latter endows the image with a transcendental quality typical of religious or spiritual paintings in which figures face a heavenly prospect. Implicitly, therefore, it was already an image of death and Wagg's transformations enhanced this signification.

Wagg realises that context is an important determinant of an image's meaning. Consequently, by exhibiting reworked mass media images in an art gallery he addressed an audience which was, in the main, different from the audience to which the tabloids appeal. The display context also invited a different, slower kind of 'reading' facilitating a more thoughtful, critical appraisal. In the mass media, images appear and disappear with such rapidity that there is little opportunity for reflection.

For three weeks the prints were displayed in the Whitechapel, during which time several thousand visitors saw them. They evoked little comment. Wagg received one, polite letter of reproach and Richard Cork, the art critic of *The Times*, remarked that the orange-yellow of the shopping mall print was 'garish'. Then Jeremy Armstrong, a *Daily Mirror* reporter, suddenly evinced intense interest in the prints and their monetary value. His motive was not a love of art but the fact that Bulger's parents were visiting London to present a 282,000-signature petition to the Home Office asking that the boy killers be imprisoned for life. This provided the hook he needed for his story and to add controversy he phoned Bulger's grandmother in Liverpool telling her that a 'Southern' artist was exploiting the murder for fame and cash. Naturally enough, the relative provided the disgusted quote – 'It is sick' – required. This is an indication of the methods journalists use to set people up as hate figures and to construct the narrative they want. In virtually every story, the audience's emotional response – moral outrage – is pre-programmed by the tabloids.

Forewarned by the Whitechapel, Wagg phoned Armstrong to explain his motives and to ask the journalist to spike the story. Armstrong accused Wagg of seeking notoriety. Wagg denied this was the case but he forecast that if the story appeared, then he would indeed become notorious. (Armstrong, however, was unwilling to acknowledge that it was he who was creating the furore, not Wagg.) And so it proved: early next morning Wagg was awakened by phone calls inviting him to appear on radio and television programmes to defend himself. Reluctant to add fuel to the fire, he declined. The story and its 'disgusted', 'offensive' slant was picked up by other national and provincial papers. The magnifying power and global reach of the media was demonstrated by the fact that the story appeared in newspapers as far afield as Africa and California.

Wagg regretted any distress he might have caused the Bulger family and he tried to communicate with them directly but they refused to accept any letter until after 'the prints were removed and destroyed'. Due to the misrepresentation of the tabloid press, he then began to receive hate mail/ phone calls and death threats: one caller threatened to burn him alive by pouring petrol through his front door in the middle of the night. Wagg was as much frightened for his neighbours as for himself. The Whitechapel Gallery was also forced to close for a while.

The hypocrisy and double standards of the mass media are well known but they continue to astonish. How can journalists complain about an artist's use of an image when that very same image has been used for gain by the very same journalists? (Books about the Bulger case feature the shopping mall scene on their covers and television programmes about the murder screen footage of the mall and the crime scene. Yet no one has complained about this.) Why, one wonders, was the artistic use of the image so offensive to them? Was it due to the fact that they think art is frivolous, other-worldly and trivial, and so when it tackles the same subjects that they deal with they feel professionally undermined? The very fact that Wagg hoped viewers would pause and contemplate the image, stop and think about why it had been so potent and why the murder itself had aroused the reaction it did when children are being abused and murdered (usually by their parents) every day in Britain, questioned the 'natural order' of the tabloids.

Armstrong's charge of greed against Wagg was grossly unfair because in fact the prints were not for sale. They had only been assigned a monetary value for insurance purposes. (The insurance turned out to be necessary because the shopping mall print was damaged by a visitor to the Whitechapel, probably by scratching the surface with a key.) Even if Wagg had sold them for the insurance value of £2,235, he would not have made a profit because they cost him more than that to make. In any case, artists have as much right as any citizen to earn money from their labour. Why on earth is it legitimate for journalists to sell stories and photographs about murders for money but not artists? Barbara Ellen, of the *Observer*, is another journalist who has written about the Bulger case and who has criticised Wagg more than once. She has condemned his work as 'exploitative art'.

For a short period Wagg 'enjoyed' the attentions of the media but, unlike the example of Damien Hirst, the spotlight of publicity did not further Wagg's artistic career. Some critics believe the Tate Gallery should acquire the two prints so that its collection will include more works that relate to the social history of Britain and the mass media in the twentieth century.

The Jamie Wagg affair illuminates the British tabloid press's treatment of artists who have the temerity to make works of art about events which the press consider their special preserve. The tabloids' interest in contemporary art is sporadic rather than consistent and is governed, not by serious interest and enquiry, but by such 'news' values as entertainment, money, moral outrage, sensationalism, sex, shock and violence. Furthermore, as we have seen, tabloid journalists do not simply report events, they actively create or manipulate them to suit their own agendas – which are fuelled by the need to sell millions of copies to generate income for themselves and profits for the news-papers' proprietors. Often, negative effects – such as death threats – are experienced by those targeted by tabloid journalists, but the latter appear indifferent to the consequences of their 'factions'.

35

1996: PERVERSITY AND PLEASURE –
THE ART OF DINOS AND JAKE CHAPMAN

Two artist brothers – Dinos and Jake Chapman – working in collaboration, produced during the 1990s a series of sculptures designed to shock and offend. Their work was characterised by eroticism and violence; consequently it generated much media coverage and divided critical opinion. In some instances it attracted the interest of the police and in others it proved too strong for the art dealers who had agreed to display it. Sexualised sculptures of children led to accusations of paedophilia.

Dinos Chapman was born in London in 1962 and studied at Ravens-bourne College of Art while Jake Chapman was born in Cheltenham in 1966 and studied at North East London Polytechnic. As postgraduates they both attended the Royal College of Art but were dissatisfied with the tuition provided because they felt it was geared towards failure rather than success. Understanding the art world and 'the game of art' in order to reap the rewards of fame and money became a priority for the brothers.

Whatever complaints can be made about the content of D and J's art, their sculptures were characterised by meticulous craftsmanship and finish. The brothers worked for a time as technical assistants to the British artists Gilbert & George, so their collaboration – which commenced in 1991 – followed a well-established precedent. Yet, while D and J made art objects, their prime concern was not with the objects as such but with the discourse, media and emotional reactions they generated.

In April 1993 D and J exhibited in London a series of three-dimensional, miniature figurines using remodelled and painted toy soldiers. These small sculptures were based on Goya's *Disasters of War* prints and therefore showed gruesome scenes of mutilation and atrocity. Some viewers wondered why two British artists of the late twentieth century were bothering to recycle Goya's imagery. It could be argued that all young artists are influenced by the masters of the past but such wholesale borrowing seemed more than 'influence'. Alternatively, it could be argued that the practice of appropriation (based on the view that originality in art is now virtually impossible) is an inevitable consequence of the Post-Modern condition. Of course, there was no exact copying or plagiarism because various changes and transformations had been introduced in terms of medium/materials, scale and colour. D and J settled their accounts with the history of art disrespectfully by reworking Goya's prints as parodies, by transforming them into ornamental kitsch. At the same time, these sculptures disturbed the pleasures of war games hobbyists by insisting upon the horrors of war.

A year later, in September–October 1994, D and J exhibited in a Cork Street gallery in London a life-sized sculpture constructed from mannequins based on Goya's etching *Great Deeds Against the Dead*. This print shows a tree to which are bound the naked bodies of three members of the Spanish resistance decapitated and castrated by French soldiers during the Peninsula war. To those ignorant of the war and Goya's work, the sculpture might well appear to be the product of a sick mind, a mind like that of a serial killer who enjoys scenes of torture and mutilation. London police were certainly disturbed by the sculpture which could be seen from the street. They entered the galllery and questioned the director. However, after being shown the Goya source print, they decided to take no action. Apparently, horrific contemporary art is acceptable to authority if it has a famous, art-historical antecedent.

D and J described their sculpture as 'a dead work of art, a morally ambivalent focus for consumption'. They told Mark Sanders: 'The spectacle of culture provokes the voyeur to observe what he or she knows is prohibited, he or she transgresses that law and so the oscillation between moral observance and the bad conscience in perverse looking becomes the point of pleasure.' Since desire and guilt are both involved, and attraction and repulsion are both aimed for, it is no wonder their work produces mixed feelings and divided responses.

Having paid their dues to tradition and addressed the subject of violence, D and J turned their attention to sexual desires and fantasies. They made a series of sculptures from naked, shop-window mannequins of men, women and children whose sexual parts – penises, vaginas and anuses – had multiplied and migrated to faces and to other parts of the body. Such displacements occur in dreams and in certain Surrealist paintings. Furthermore, in the case of the child-sculptures various deformities and mutations were introduced; for example, figures had two heads or were joined together at the trunk like Siamese twins. (Some viewers may have been reminded of the dangers of genetic engineering which today's scientists increasingly engage in but D and J appear to take a perverse delight in the variety of forms cell division and mutation yield.) A piquant touch was the fact that the female children wore wigs and Fila trainers. Jake told one audience that 'men in raincoats' were strongly attracted to these sculptures.

The series culminated in a weird and memorable work consisting of 20 child figures fused together into a ring entitled *Zygotic Acceleration, Biogenetic De-sublimated Libidinal Model (enlarged x 1000)* (1995). (According to one newspaper report, this sculpture was bought by Charles Saatchi for £32,000.) While some mannequins retained the pert, innocent faces of childhood, others sported the Chapmans' notorious 'fuckfaces' (penis-noses and anus-mouths). In one instance, two girls with such faces engage in sexual intercourse; their bodies are also joined at the stomach although a vertical line divides them. D and J have remarked that when such lines occur they signal the sculpture's segmentation and thereby fuel male fears of castration.

In 1995 D and J commissioned a pornographic film, *Bring Me the Head of ...*, from producer David Dawson of KD Digital. In the film two female performers pleasure one another using a decapitated, mannequin's head which had an erect penis instead of a nose. The dildo-head was said to represent that of an Italian art dealer who had been so shocked by the sculpture *Mummy and Daddy Chapman* (1994) that he had

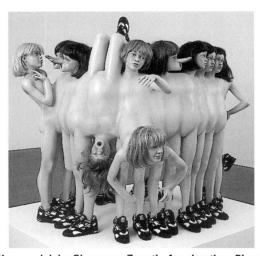

44. Dinos and Jake Chapman, *Zygotic Acceleration, Biogenetic, De-sublimated Libidinal Model (enlarged x 1000)*, 1995.
Fibreglass, resin, paint, wigs and trainers, 150 x 180 x 140 cm.
London: Saatchi collection.
Photo: Gareth Winters, courtesy of Victoria Miro Gallery, London.

refused to show it. This film appears to have been an attempt to outdo the porn-art of Jeff Koons and Ilona Staller by being pure porn. The artists' stated aim was to obtain a standard porn movie 'of no artistic value at all'; the only star was to be the sculpture. They were quite happy to see this film distributed by the sex industry rather than the art business. Its screening in art world situations was surely intended to cause embarrassment: to see if art world people really were as blasé as they pretended. A later, unforeseen consequence of D and J's venture into film-making was a bitter dispute with the producer regarding the copyright/ownership of the film. It seems that, in spite of all their cleverness, the Chapmans were naive regarding such contractual arrangements.

During 1996, D and J mounted a large-scale installation of their child-sculptures at the ICA, London. The ground floor gallery was transformed into a synthetic Garden of Eden by means of plastic green shrubs and grass. Scattered about, half-hidden by the greenery, were the sexualised figures. Given the number of deformities present this was a garden in which human evolution had gone haywire. Another installation, *Cyber-Iconic Man*, resembled a scene from a low-budget horror movie: suspended by his feet from the ceiling was a silver-coloured, male figure undergoing torture. His wounds leaked 'blood' but, via the agency of a pumping system, it was returned to his body so that death was prolonged. (This particular sculpture struck some viewers as comical rather than terrifying.) The ICA show was entitled *Chapmanworld;* it proved to be the perfect antidote to *Disneyworld.* Another version of the ICA's garden environment, entitled *Tragic Anatomies,* together with key examples of D and J's sculptures appeared in the *Sensation* show held at the Royal Academy in 1997 where they were seen by over 200,000 people.

D and J are highly sophisticated artists in the sense that they are well read in terms of psychoanalytic theories of the mind, sadism-masochism, visual pleasure, the commodity nature of art, and so on. They play with the fact that we gain sexual pleasure from looking (voyeurism, scopophilia) and that we often long to see things like sexual acts, which are forbidden by parents, prohibited by society at large or by our own fears. Bodily deformity also excites public interest – witness the appeal of fun-fair freak shows and distorting mirrors – hence the attraction of D and J's grotesque mannequins.

Their artworks are accompanied by a verbal and written discourse (talks, interviews, statements) informed by the ideas of such thinkers as Bataille, Freud and the Marquis de Sade. But just as they scramble body parts, so they scramble ideas. A rational, coherent philosophy is thus not forthcoming; instead there is an anarchic, promiscuous, intellectual cocktail. They welcome the fact that van Gogh mutilated himself because sacrifice and pain underpinned his artistic achievement. D and J also believe that all artists have to prostitute themselves, so they willingly accept commercialism, the art market and the need to produce a range of merchandise, such as T-shirts, to be sold alongside their sculptures. It would be pointless, therefore, to accuse them of 'selling out'.

Although the media and the art world know that D and J deliberately intend to seduce, disgust and manipulate them, this has not stopped the brothers from becoming highly fashionable. Their private view opening at the ICA in 1996 was packed out. Adverse critical comments such as 'second-rate art', 'ugly' and even 'fascistic' has not discouraged the press, dealers, collectors and exhibition curators from pursuing them either. Arguably, the Chapmans have developed a knowing, cynical mode of art practice which relies upon the complicity of the audience in much the same way that so-called 'exploitation' movies do. Art experts of the future may well dismiss their work as 1990s's fashionable trash; however, it is not without craft, wit and entertainment value.

36

1996: PUNISHING A GRAFFITI ARTIST

At a Sheffield Crown Court in March 1996 Simon Sunderland, aged 23, was sentenced to five years in prison for causing criminal damage by means of graffiti. A campaign was then mounted to overturn or reduce this swingeing judgement.

Probably no manifestation of contemporary visual expression provokes such opposite reactions as graffiti. For the young people – mostly male – who produce it, it is a visible sign of their existence as individuals and as a subculture, and a pleasurable and creative activity which enlivens drab, urban environments. By contrast, for the majority of city dwellers and local government officials it is a prime instance of vandalism, a form of visual pollution that contributes to urban squalor and a climate of fear.

However, there is a group of people consisting of sociologists, art students, people belonging to the arts and media worlds, and writers and publishers of books and articles on the subject, who value graffiti as a raw, grassroots type of culture and who admire its inventiveness and aesthetic qualities. Graffiti raise in an acute form the questions: 'Are they art? If so, are they any good?'

Graffiti have a very long history. For centuries they were crude line drawings, caricatures or statements scratched into the surface of walls ('graffio' is Italian for 'scratch'), but today they are almost invariably painted or written marks executed with cans of spray paint or with felt-tipped pens and magic markers. Unlike so many fine artists, graffiti writers have welcomed the new technological means of mark-making and colouring. These enable them to work at high speed with the result that there is a directness and energy in graffiti that makes much oil painting seem laboured and constipated. Another key difference is that graffiti artists are self- and peer-group motivated: initially at least, they do not produce work for the benefit of dealers, collectors or patrons; their work is not made for sale, consequently it avoids commodification. While on the one hand, their art is visually available to every pedestrian, on the other, its private-code aspect means that it is also exclusive.

There are certain types of graffiti which are unwholesome, of which virtually every public lavatory has examples. The location reveals certain recurrent characteristics: anonymity, insulting, vulgar and obscene imagery and writings; the expression of normally forbidden or repressed thoughts and opinions. Again, while some graffitied statements have a positive social content, others are expressions of racial hatred.

Graffiti have constituted a kind of subversive folk culture since the days of ancient Egypt but only in the twentieth century, as a result of Modernism's cult of 'the primitive' and 'outsider' artists, have they been taken seriously as a form of popular culture, influenced professional artists and attained the status of art in their own right. Painters whose work is indebted to graffiti include Jean Dubuffet, David Hockney, Antonio Tàpies and Cy Twombly.

A striking outbreak of graffiti occurred in New York during the 1970s when subway trains were 'bombed', that is, smothered with polychromatic 'name writings' and 'tags' (invented names, stylised signatures). Later on, much more ambitious designs were devised which involved elaborate interlocking letters, figures and imagery quoted from fine art and mass media sources. (This type of work was labelled 'Subway, Spraycan and Frontier Art'.) While the transit authorities viewed the graffiti as crime/vandalism and tried to eliminate them, others regarded them as an authentic example of grassroots culture manifesting, in many instances, considerable creativity and skill.

On investigation it emerged that they were the work of various groups of 'deprived' teenagers. Each 'crew' had its own techniques, rules, vocabulary, stylistic mannerisms (for example 'wild style'), and even martyrs (by electrocution in the tunnels and yards of the subway system). Later on, social assimilation and recuperation took place: graffiti writers were encouraged to paint public or community murals on approved walls, and to execute private murals in hotels, shops and nightclubs. They also contributed to the black, hip hop, breakdancing, rapping and scratch music scene of New York by providing backdrops for record covers and rock music videos.

In addition, a number of New York art galleries – Razor, P.S.1., Shafrazi, Fashion Moda – opened with the purpose of exhibiting and selling graffiti executed on canvas or wooden supports. This development gave rise to the expression 'Post-Graffiti Art'. As a result of the art world vogue for graffiti during the 1980s, a number of writers 'crossed over' from the subway to the gallery context and became successful professional artists; for example, Lenny McGurr, Fred Braithwaite and Lee Quinones. Also, art school-trained individuals such as Keith Haring (1958–90) made subway drawings in chalk and developed a primitivistic style strongly influenced by graffiti. Jean-Michel Basquiat (1960–88), an artist from a middle-class background, sprayed his tag 'Samo' in the street and his subsequent paintings were indebted to graffiti.

As a result of books, exhibitions, films and television programmes about New York's subway writers, the habit spread to many cities throughout the world. In London sophisticated examples appeared in the Notting Hill area. Other British examples were generated by Feminists making critical attacks upon sexist advertising. In 1990 London-based groups of so-called 'graff-ites' toured Europe giving performances in the manner of rock bands. At home they also staged events mixing music, dance and spraycan painting, a style called 'West London Pressure'.

Not all graffiti were what they seemed: record companies employed people to spray slogans and the names of bands as a form of publicity. So, the graphic spontaneity, vulgarity and subversion of graffiti became part of the repertoire of the manipulative devices used by advertising agencies.

In evaluating graffiti there is a need to discriminate between progressive and reactionary slogans, and between the rather mindless plethora of overlapping tags – motivated, it would seem, by narcissistic boasting and a horror of empty space – and the more colourful, complex pictorial designs which reveal technical skill, imaginative and aesthetic abilities. Graffiti artists capable of the latter are the most likely to to make the transition to fine art, from the illegal to the legal. However, should they cross over there is a real danger that the positive characteristics of the street writing will dissipate and the close relation to a grassroots community or subculture will be lost as the work becomes part of official culture and the trade in art objects.

Simon Sunderland hails from Worsbrough Bridge, Barnsley. For a decade he sprayed his personal tag 'Fisto' on buildings and other structures in Sheffield to such effect that in 1994 it earned the title 'Britain's graffiti capital'. His last bout of graffiti was reported to have caused £7,000 worth of damage. (Spraycan paint is difficult and expensive to remove from walls.) Shoplifting is also associated with graffiti and Sunderland had previous convictions for stealing cans of paint.

Sunderland justified his own and other writers' actions by criticising the existing society and implicitly demanding a right to freedom of

45. David Muscroft, *Simon Sunderland*, 1996.
Photo: courtesy of D. Muscroft and Trevor Smith Photography,
Brampton, Chesterfield.

46. David Muscroft, *Sunderland's graffiti tag 'Fisto'*, 1996.
Photo: courtesy of D. Muscroft and Trevor Smith Photography,
Brampton, Chesterfield.

expression: 'In a society based on image, greed, selfishness – we are the few who have broken the chains by exposing our art by any means necessary.' Certainly there is an inequality of wealth and power in British society: the rich own and control the primary means of communication; articulate and educated people can usually find legitimate ways of making their views public; powerful companies can afford to commission advertising and purchase hoarding space in order to subject the population to a constant barrage of seductive images, messages and pleas to buy consumer goods and services that some critics of capitalism would regard as a type of rhetorical persuasion and visual pollution that a better organised, more ecologically-conscious society could do without.

Graffiti, therefore, troubles people partly because it poses the questions: 'Who are the public? What is public space? Who has the right to make statements in public spaces?' By assuming the right to make such statements, graffiti artists call attention to the fact that there are commercial interests which normally command public spaces and whose right to do so has come to be regarded as 'natural'.

Following Sunderland's five-year sentence, the *Guardian* newspaper carried an editorial in which it argued that the sentence was too harsh in comparison with the case of a man in Los Angeles who had murdered a graffiti artist and who had been given three years' probation. The editorial also pointed to the irony that at the same time the American, graffiti-style painter Basquiat was being celebrated via a retrospective exhibition held at London's Serpentine Gallery. The *Guardian* proposed that graffiti artists should be assigned walls by local councils so that they could practise their art legally.

Letters from the North of England were also published both for and against Sunderland. His critics argued that aggressive and intimidating graffiti caused psychological insecurity, that he had vandalised public property and merited a long sentence because he was a persistent offender. His defenders claimed that his work was 'colourful and creative and did not threaten anyone except those architects and councillors who believe that everything on our estates should be dull, drab and uniform'. His mother, Angela Noble, supported her son and claimed that he only sprayed derelict buildings on out of the way sites; that none of his work was abusive or contained offensive language; that he had been studying art for three years and was hoping to gain entrance to art college. She announced a national campaign to overturn or reduce the prison term imposed upon her son. The sentence does seem to have been ridiculously severe. Why could not the judge have given Sunderland probation and a community service order to clean off graffiti? Surely, that would have satisfied local anger and saved taxpayer's money?

This story has a happy ending. In October 1996 the Court of Appeal in London drastically reduced Sunderland's prison sentence and he was then set free. (Including a period on remand, Sunderland spent about a year inside. While in prison he continued to draw and paint.) The positive result was due to the hard work of the defence counsel Adrian Fulford QC and Sunderland's family and campaigners; the latter included the television comedian Mark Thomas (who had staged benefits in order to raise funds) and organisers from BECTU, the trade union for the entertainments industry. A man called Mark Ticktum offered Sunderland a contract on the grounds that he had the potential to become as successful an artist as Basquiat. Barnsley College also offered him a place on an art course. Thus Sunderland was given opportunities to make a career in art as an insider rather than as an outsider.

37

1997: A 'SICK, DISGUSTING, EVIL, HIDEOUS' PORTRAIT OF MYRA HINDLEY

Outside the Royal Academy in September 1997 relatives of child murder victims demonstrated and pleaded with people queuing for the *Sensation* show not to enter because it featured a huge portrait of the murderess Myra Hindley by Marcus Harvey. Shortly afterwards two men vandalised the painting. Yards of newsprint were devoted to the story and to the ethics of making and exhibiting such a work.

In the mid-1960s Myra Hindley (b. 1942) was the notorious lover and accomplice of Ian Brady, the serial torturer and killer of children. They were known as the 'Moors Murderers' because they buried their victims' bodies on Saddleworth Moor in Yorkshire. The remains of one, twelve-year-old victim have never been found. Hindley is currently in prison serving a life sentence. Although she has some supporters, she is so reviled by the majority of the British public that it is unlikely she will ever be released. She attracts more hatred than Brady because she betrayed the love that a woman is conventionally supposed to have towards children and because she has campaigned to be released on the grounds that she is now a changed person.

Despite the fact that the murders took place over 30 years ago, Hindley is still an extremely sensitive subject for any artist to address. Harvey (b. Leeds 1963) must have realised that a large-scale image of Hindley would provoke 'a sensation' in advance of, and during, the aptly named *Sensation* exhibition held at the Royal Academy in the autumn of 1997, hence the charges of cynical exploitation that were levelled against him. The painting, entitled *Myra*, dated in fact from 1995. Its existence was well-flagged by the Academy and the press in advance of the show's opening.

47. Marcus Harvey, *Myra*, 1995.
Acrylic on canvas, 396 x 320 cm. London: Saatchi collection.
Photo shows installation in Royal Academy galleries in September 1997.
Photo: Alastair Grant/Associated Press.

Since the Royal Academy is a private institution, it needs a succession of high profile shows in order to cover its running costs and to pay off previous deficits (in 1996 its loss amounted to £715,000). The *Sensation* exhibition, sponsored by the auction house Christie's and the listings magazine *Time Out*, was organised by Norman Rosenthal and displayed works by yBas (young British artists) from Charles Saatchi's huge, private collection. It attracted 285,737 visitors and extensive media/public interest. Some artist-members of the RA were so disgusted by the exhibition's contents that they resigned.

Given the various, strongly negative responses to Harvey's painting – protests outside Burlington House by relatives of Hindley's victims and MAMA (Mothers Against Murder and Aggression), vandalism of the painting itself, moral and aesthetic condemnations in the tabloid and quality press and in art magazines – it is clear that Harvey's work was a pictorial sign of considerable power and resonance. (Even Hindley herself wrote to the *Guardian* complaining about the painting before the show opened. She also claimed to be seeking 'legal advice'.) In all the condemnation, little attention was paid to the sign itself. Arguably, the ideas of the American philosopher and semiotician Charles Sanders Peirce (1839–1914), in particular his three kinds of sign – index, icon and symbol – can clarify the way in which Harvey's painting worked.

An indexical sign is one in which there is a direct, physical relationship between mark and meaning (the imprint of a foot in sand, for example); an iconic sign is one in which there is a resemblance between marks and a referent (a drawing of a dog, for example); a symbolic sign is one in which there is an arbitrary or conventional relationship between a sign and its meaning (the White House, meaning not the building itself but the President of the United States, for example). These three kinds of sign can be distinguished from one another and considered in isolation but they can also occur in combination, in a superimposed manner.

Semioticians argue that photographs are indexical signs because rays of light act upon the sensitised film inside the camera and physically alter it. But most photographs are also iconic in the sense that they resemble the external appearance of objects, people and places. Harvey's source for his painting – a photograph of Hindley's head and shoulders taken by the police in the 1960s which has been reproduced in the mass media countless times – was thus an

48. Police photograph of Myra Hindley, 1966.
Popperfoto.

indexical/iconic sign. Looking at Harvey's painting at least one art critic was reminded of the 1970s' painting trend called Photo-Realism, in particular Chuck Close's huge, facial portraits. By appropriating/copying and enlarging/enhancing the police mug shot Harvey relayed an already striking image. Hindley's manic, staring eyes were particularly memorable.

In a work of art virtually every characteristic is a signifying element. The size of the painting, for instance – 11 x 9 foot – was compared by one writer to that of an advertising billboard. By making the image so big Harvey endowed it with a monumental quality associated with public memorials. But a contradiction arose because it is heroes, heroines and political leaders who are normally accorded such treatment, not criminals, therefore Harvey was accused of glorifying and glamorising Hindley. In my view this charge was unfair. One could interpret the large size as a metaphor for the monstrous proportions that Hindley had assumed in the consciousness of the British. Andy Warhol was an earlier artist who made use of images of criminals in his work. One recalls his contribution – *Thirteen Most Wanted Men* – to the New York State Pavilion for the World's Fair of 1965, a series of huge portraits of American criminals based on wanted men posters which were deemed so offensive by the authorities that they were obliterated.

In Harvey's white, grey and black acrylic painting the units of mark from which the iconic image was constructed were not brushmarks of pigment but a child's open palm prints. (To be absolutely precise the prints were made with a plaster cast of a child's hand not the hand itself.) When the painting was viewed from a distance Hindley's face dominated, but close up the handprints were foregrounded. Handprints are clear examples of indexical signs. They span the history of art: they appear in prehistoric cave paintings and in so-called 'abstract' paintings by Jackson Pollock. They too can be considered iconic in that they resemble the shapes of hands. Thus one set of small, indexical/iconic signs was used as the building blocks of a second, larger and different iconic sign. This is a rhetorical device well known in the history of art and illustration. Perhaps the most famous examples in European painting are Giuseppe Arcimboldo's portraits of librarians made from books, or peasants' heads made from fruits and vegetables.

The handprints can also be considered to be examples of the literary figure synecdoche – a type of sign in which a part stands for the whole (as in a sea captain's command 'All *hands* on deck!'). In this instance the parts were poignant because the small hands stood for the whole of the victims' bodies and thus implied dismemberment. What was crucial, of course, was the meaning which viewers ascribed to the children's handprints. 'Innocence absorbed in all that pain', was Harvey's preferred meaning. Since Hindley's face was literally constructed from the handprints of the group from which her victims were selected, Harvey's painting surely reiterated the idea that Hindley is inexorably marked by her crime: she can never erase the traces of her and Brady's victims – their hands reach out from their graves in reproach and accusation. Of course, the association works both ways: the murdered children are inexorably linked to Hindley and Brady, and doubtless this is a constant cause of unhappiness for the living relatives of the victims.

Considered as a totality, as a supersign, Harvey's painting could also be viewed as symbolic in the sense that Hindley's face is widely perceived as a sign for evil in general.

If my analysis is correct the painting is a layered work of art which combines all three of Peirce's famous trio of signs. This in itself does not make Harvey's painting a superb work of art but it does indicate the complexity of its workings.

Those critical of Harvey's painting argued that he should have exercised self-censorship and not tackled the subject of Hindley. While it is true that any reference to Hindley and Brady is going to distress the families of their victims, this is not a sufficient reason to preclude an artist's use of images which are widely disseminated via the mass media. Only if their use was universally banned would one expect artists to obey such a rule. Otherwise a double standard would operate: the mass media would be permitted to reproduce and profit from Hindley's image but, for some unexplained reason, living artists would not. If the artists of the past had been forbidden to comment on contemporary events then Géricault's *The Raft of the Medusa* and Picasso's *Guernica* would not have been painted.

What matters in such instances is not the fact that an artist has used an image from the mass media but what value he or she has added in the process of transformation. In the case of Harvey, critical and public opinion was divided, but arguably he did add value even if that value was not very profound.

The hypocrisy of the British mass media knew no bounds: widespread condemnation of Harvey was invariably accompanied by photographs of his painting. If Harvey was wrong to *produce* it, then it was surely wrong for the press to *reproduce* it. As a result, of course, the image of Hindley which Harvey took from the mass media was returned to its source.

When the painting was exhibited at the Royal Academy in September, security was strengthened in anticipation of vandalism but this failed to prevent two members of the public – Peter Fisher 'a-father-of-two' and Jacques Rolé 'a Frenchman' (both described by the press as 'artists') – from defacing it by throwing coloured ink and eggs over it. Many were delighted by this turn of events: one tabloid, the *Mirror* – featured the damaged painting in full colour on its front page accompanied by the caption: 'Exhibited by the Royal Academy in the so-called name of art, defaced by the people in the name of common decency.' The vandals were arrested and charged but not, in the end, prosecuted. The painting was removed for restoration and when it returned it was shielded by a sheet of perspex and flanked by guards.

In the spirit of the above semiotic analysis, we can say that the marks made by the vandals were indexical signs that communicated (a) the public's hatred of Hindley, and (b) the public's disapproval of Harvey's painting. When Marcel Duchamp discovered in 1926 that the glass from which his *The Bride Stripped Bare by Her Bachelors, Even* (1915–23) was made had been shattered while being transported, he decided to accept the damage rather than to attempt a repair. This, in my view, is what Harvey and its owner Charles Saatchi should have done. The painting would then have incorporated another layer of sign which would have added to and completed its social meaning. Harvey would thus have been seen to accept the public's disapproval of his use of Hindley's image.

A much longer account would be required to explore all the press comments provoked by *Myra*, but one particularly crass response was by journalist Julie Burchill, the professional controversialist and darling of the Right, famous for her aggression and perverse opinions. Entitled 'Art and Immorality, exploitative images of children should be censored', it appeared in *The Modern Review* and was reprinted (almost verbatim) in the *Guardian*. In her usual reckless manner, Burchill combined a dozen, different news stories in order to make spurious connections. She linked Harvey's painting and works by other artists depicting children to pornography and the sufferings of real children while in 'care' at the hands of abusers then being revealed in court cases. The artists were accused of 'celebrating paedophilia', but, as Jake and Dinos Chapman have pointed out, their sculptures adapted from shop-window dummies were examples of mannequin abuse, not child abuse.

In Harvey's case, Burchill attacked some remarks he had made about Hindley – he claimed that he found her sexually alluring – rather than analysing his painting and its meaning. *Myra* was dismissed as an 'obscenity'. Burchill's moral posturing seemed motivated by a hunger for headlines rather than by genuine compassion for children. Furthermore, her tirade revealed a loathing for the visual arts '... the brainless babble of a Visual Person (who are by definition stupid: painting, that's what children do because they can't write)'. To which one is tempted to reply: 'Verbal abuse, that's what writers resort to when they discover they can't draw or paint.'

38

1998: AN ANGEL DESCENDS ON THE NORTH
AND DIVIDES THE COMMUNITY

Antony Gormley's huge public sculpture, the *Angel of the North*, was erected on 15 February 1998 and will be seen by millions of passing motorists and train passengers. During its planning stage the sculpture aroused much antagonism and comment from local people because of its imagery, location and size. After its erection, local opinion continued to be divided.

Gormley is a leading British sculptor whose work was acclaimed by the London art world and who received international exposure during the 1980s. His reputation was further enhanced in 1994 when he won the Turner Prize. He was born in 1950 into a cultivated, Hampstead, Catholic family of Irish and German extraction. During the late 1960s he studied archaeology, anthropology and art history at Cambridge University. He then spent three years in India where he explored Buddhism and meditation. On his return to London, he attended the Central School of Art and Goldsmiths College where he made sculptures from cloth soaked in plaster and sawn-up doors. He then took a post-graduate course at the Slade School of Art from 1977 to 1979.

It was at the Slade that Gormley began to use a material – lead – which was to become central to his practice. Gormley is now best known for representations of the human body, either as empty shapes impressed in concrete or eaten out of a 'mattress' made from bread, or as free-standing, constructed figures. To make the latter, plaster moulds were made, with the help of assistants, from his own body – Gormley is slim and 6' 4" tall – and then strengthened with fibreglass. Roofing lead was beaten over the moulds to produce a metal skin. The various body parts were soldered together in such a way that the seams remained clearly visible as horizontal and vertical lines. Because the lead shells were indirect impressions of his body and they were also smoothed and rounded, Gormley's figures were not accurate self-portraits, but rather generalised statements of man's condition in the world. Bald, hairless and grey, they have reminded viewers of Hollywood Oscar statuettes, suits of armour and Egyptian mummies. Those figures that were stiff and vertical with arms close to their bodies recalled the hieratic Ancient Greek statue known as Kouros.

So-called 'Body art' was fashionable during the 1970s – it marked a reaction to Conceptualism – and since then numerous exhibitions, books and conferences have been devoted to the subject. Arguably, by prioritising the male human figure, Gormley sought to reverse the abstract, optical and conceptual trajectories of recent art by returning to the Renaissance, humanistic ideal: 'Man is the Measure of all Things.' However, Gormley himself regards his body cases as a new beginning based on the primary experience of embodiment:

> My body contains all possibilities. What I am working towards is a total identification of all existence with my point of contact with the material world: my body ... I turn to the body in an attempt to find a language that will transcend the limitations of race, creed and language, but which will still be about the rootedness of identity.

Much of his early work was concerned with the dialectic between the space inside the body and the space outside it. Gormley explored various poses and displayed his figures in related clusters on the beach or in galleries. In some instances, figures were integrated into the physical structure of rooms. For example, in *Learning to Think* (1991) figures with no heads were placed high in the air as if their heads were embedded in the ceiling. This particular installation was mounted in the Old City Jail, Charleston, South Carolina. Like many of Gormley's sculptures, it had a double meaning: ascension and lynching.

Some of his figures became permanent public sculptures: in London-derry, Northern Ireland, for instance, three sculptures made from cast iron consisting of two figures standing back to back with their arms outstretched were placed on the city's walls in 1987. Their faces were blank apart from eye-holes; one critic was reminded of the balaclavas worn by terrorists. The cruciform pose signified the importance of the Christian religion to both Catholics and Protestants but their mutual incomprehension was indicated by the fact they faced in opposite directions.

Apparently, Gormley succeeded where others have failed: he united both communities – in the sense that both disapproved of the figures, which they felt had been imposed on them by an Englishman, an outsider, and which lacked any relation to their history and to the site. Vandalism soon occurred: paint was thrown on them and they were 'necklaced' with burning tyres. Gormley was not surprised by the fierce reaction and remarked that his sculptures were intended to 'act as a poultice and draw to itself feelings and thoughts about the situation in Northern Ireland'.

Gormley's megalomaniac desire to produce huge, monumental public sculptures was first manifested in 1988 when he designed *The Brick Man* which won third prize in a sculpture competition. His plan was to build a 120-foot high structure in the shape of a man made entirely from 120,000 bricks on a site near Leeds railway station. This proposed giant would have cost £650,000. It excited much discussion and argument, but in the end was never built because the majority of the council and the public were against it (as revealed by a poll conducted by a local newspaper). Sceptics predicted that it would be 'a hideous eyesore'.

However, Gormley had better luck in 1994 when he was asked to design a huge, winged figure to stand on a hill near the A1(M) motorway, the A167 road and the East Coast main line railway south of Gateshead. The sculpture, erected in 1998, is made from steel and so it should be vandal proof. There is a central, hollow figure from either side of which sprout two huge, rigid wings. Both figure and wings have vertical and horizontal bracing ridges at intervals standing proud from their surfaces. They recall the structure of a metal ship's hull turned inside out. In other words, the internal skeleton typical of most large sculptures has been externalised.

The Gateshead monument was developed from an earlier series of sculptures entitled *A Case for an Angel* (1989–90). The word 'case' in the title signifies a bodycase or container plus an argument for an angel. Clearly, angels evoke religion, the spiritual and flight. Gormley does not think of them as real phenomena but as emblems of 'inspiration and imagination', as beings 'that might be at home in the air, but brought down to earth'. Angels deliver messages from heaven to earth, hence they are mediators between two realms: the spiritual and the material. As far as atheists are concerned, angels are products of the human imagination indicative of human desires to fly and transcend the physical world.

Paradoxically, Gormley's angels would find it difficult to fly because they are so heavy and their wings are solid and lack feathers. (He describes his angels as 'fatally handicapped'; they 'cannot pass through any door' and are 'desperately burdened', consequently their meaning is ambiguous. Furthermore, they are obstacles which block

49. Antony Gormley, *Angel of the North*, 1998.
Photo: Keith Paisley, courtesy of Gateshead Metropolitan Borough Council.

the sight and the passage of the viewer.) Being rigid, the angel's wings resemble those of aircraft rather than those of birds. They are, as Gormley puts it, 'a marriage of anatomy and aeronautics/ technology'.

The *Angel of the North* weighs 200 tonnes and is 20 metres high; the width of its wings is about 51 metres, almost as much as the wingspan of a jumbo jet. Since the sculpture is made from special, weather-resistant steel containing copper, the surface has oxidised to form a rich, red-brown patina. To secure the sculpture against winds that can reach 100 mph, it stands on concrete piles set deep in the earth. The statue was prefabricated in sections and then erected on site, bolted and welded together by Hartlepool Steel Fabrications, the company which won the manufacturing contract. It is designed to last for at least a century.

As usual in such cases, when plans for the sculpture were announced the local community was divided in its reaction. A petition
against the statue was signed by 4,000 local people and 83 per cent of
those asked during a telephone poll opposed it on the grounds that it
would be an eyesore and a traffic hazard. Some considered the statue
blasphemous and renamed it 'Hell's Angel'. According to Paul Wason,
Gormley's design resembled the trademark of a German car manufac-
turer in business between the two world wars and also the emblem of
the National Socialist Flying Corps. The implication was that the
statue's design was derivative and had commercial/fascist overtones. A
headline in the local paper ran: 'Nazi ... but Nice?'

**50. 'Nazi ... but Nice?', front cover of the *Gateshead Post*, 2 February
1995.** Reproduced by courtesy of *the Gateshead Post*.

A 'Gateshead Stop the Statue' campaign, led by Ron Beadle, was
instituted. In Beadle's opinion the design was 'a monument to
arrogance'. Local councillors in opposition – all Liberal Democrats –
headed by Kathy King, a long-term critic of public sculptures, voted

against giving the statue planning permission but they were defeated by the ruling Labour majority.

Some of the reasons why the Labour councillors favoured the sculpture were that its manufacture would provide work for a local shipyard or engineering works and for other local contractors; it would serve as an emblem or logo of the region; it would not cost the local council taxpayers anything because the money required – around £800,000 in total (including landscaping and road improvements) – would be met by National Lottery funds for the arts and various other public and private sources. There was no point in citizens suggesting: 'The money should be spent on needy causes such as hospitals ...', because it was earmarked specifically for art. Furthermore, research showed that arts tourism is a source of income for a region. As one councillor observed: 'Instead of asking how much will it cost, perhaps people should be asking how much money will it make?'

Gormley's *Angel* is Britain's tallest sculpture and will be seen by as many as 30 million people each year, that is, the train passengers and the motorists travelling north and south on the busy motorways. Since the audience for the work encompasses the latter, it seems reasonable that its design should not be limited by what the people who live in the immediate locality feel and think – although they, of course, see it on a daily basis. (Some local scrap merchants threatened to dismantle it.) The sculpture, therefore, is not really site- or local people-specific. No doubt Gormley's supporters would argue that its appeal is universal. Gormley himself claims it is a 'collective work' related to the region because the image was selected by local councillors and the manufacture of the sculpture depended upon local labour and skills.

Gormley was sanguine about the controversy his planned sculpture aroused. He has come to expect it and no longer minds if his work provokes strong feelings. Appearing in an episode of *Art Marathon*, a 1995 television series, he told some of his critics that they 'lacked imagination', and asked them: 'Would you rather have nothing on the site?' The new, he argued, nearly always prompted anxiety and resistance, but his statue was 'an expression of change, an aspiration'. His questioners were laypeople from Northern Ireland who already held the Derry sculptures against him. After the conversation – which ended in mutual incomprehension and exasperation – they described him as an arrogant artist who was indifferent to the views of local residents.

Negative criticism was also expressed in the London art world. David Lee, editor of *Art Review*, claimed that Gormley was 'one of the state's favourite and most pampered artists'. The *Angel* reminded Lee of the Socialist Realist monuments of the old USSR 'informed by the same enslavement to size, bombast and low symbolism'. (Gormley denies that his art is 'symbolic'.) Lee judged it to be 'Logo art' rather than authentic sculpture: harsh words about a work that was still being produced.

When the statue was finally erected on site in February 1998 there was a flurry of publicity and comment which again revealed polarised opinions. Those against: 'hideous rusting monstrosity ... ugly and offensive ... an intruder ... no movement or energy ... why?' Those for: 'daring, awesome, formidable ... lovely physique ... rusty majesty ... a mix of finesse and brutality ... a silent witness ... a memorial to the miners killed in the pits ... a symbol of regeneration'. William Feaver, a London critic, declared: 'The *Angel* commands attention and respect.'

From some viewpoints the statue forms a stark silhouette against the sky and it appears to be located in a rural setting, but from others in built-up zones it looms rather strangely above the rooftops of houses or stands between tower blocks. As one moves around the statue its appearance, of course, changes. From the side its wings disappear and the profile of a naked man becomes dominant.

Perhaps a final judgement should be deferred until the statue has been in place for some time. In all likelihood it will gradually become more popular because landmarks are welcome on long car and train journeys. The sculpture is visible and recognisable at a great distance, and from afar it resembles the Christian cross. Travellers may well interpret its outstretched wings as a gesture of embrace. Many motorists will pause to pay it a visit (150,000 visitors a year are expected) and its imagery is readily comprehensible.

Lord Gowrie, chairman of the Arts Council, predicted that Tyne-siders would learn to love the *Angel*. It is certainly the case that a large statue can eventually become a famous, popular icon without being a work of art of the highest aesthetic merit. Auguste Bartholdi's academic, mediocre *Statue of Liberty* (1886) in New York Harbour, is a prime example.

Whatever its artistic value, Gormley's statue serves as positive propaganda for the North East by exemplifying the engineering/manufacturing skills still available in the region. It is also a visible sign of the determination of Gateshead's Labour politicians to use culture to assist regeneration. There is no doubt that the *Angel* has already put Gateshead 'on the map'.

39

1998: SCULPTOR FOUND GUILTY
OF STEALING BODY PARTS

In 1997 police from the organised crime unit arrested Anthony-Noel Kelly on the grounds that he had stolen human remains in order to make sculptures. A junior lab technician from the Royal College of Surgeons was also charged with stealing body parts and supplying them to Kelly. Cartoonists had a field day and the news media showed intense interest in Kelly, partly because he had royal and aristocratic connections. The following year he was tried in court and found guilty.

Two silver-coated, relief sculptures which realistically depicted the back and front of the head and shoulders of an elderly man with part of his brain cut away were displayed at the Jibby Beane stand, Contemporary Arts Fair, Business Design Centre, in London, in January 1997. Kelly (b. 1956) made them by moulding rubber, glass fibre and plaster over the embalmed torsos of the dead. Catherine Pepinster, a journalist who visited Kelly's Clapham studio (always described in press accounts as 'ice-cold'), reported that, 'After embalming, which always takes place before dissection, the body becomes flatter, more solid, and less supple, and marks from the table on which one body had been placed are noticeable on the cast.' Kelly told her that his aim was to challenge notions that health and life are the prerequisites of beauty. The addition of gold and sliver gilding was intended to immortalise the dead.

The sculptures, one of which carried a price tag of £4,500, attracted a stream of curious visitors, including Judge Stephen Tumin, but no buyers. Adrian Searle, art critic of the *Guardian*, characterised them as 'vaguely sadomasochistic, sub-expressionistic' and judged them to be 'tacky decor of an imitative and immature kind'. Lucy Sicks, the fair's organiser, was worried that the exhibit might be considered 'overtly insensitive'. During a press conference, Kelly admitted that he had used corpses as models for his work but he refused to disclose where he had obtained them and how they had been disposed of after use.

Since Kelly consulted a solicitor before attending the press conference, he must have realised that his sculptures and working methods were likely to cause revulsion and prompt the interest of the authorities. And since he also remarked that he was afraid someone might recognise the face of the man depicted in his sculptures it was clear that he had not obtained the consent of the man's relatives.

51. Charles Ommanney, *Anthony-Noel Kelly with his cast body parts sculptures*, 1997.
Photo: courtesy of C. Ommanney and Rex Features, London.

Dr Laurence Martin, HM Inspector of Anatomy, the official responsible for the way bodies are used in medical research, read the press reports and then asked every hospital and research institute to check their records pertaining to body parts. When discrepancies were discovered at the Royal College of Surgeons, Lincoln's Inn Fields, Martin contacted the police. An investigation began and in April Kelly was arrested and taken to Vauxhall police station for questioning. When the police searched his refrigerated studio, his girlfriend's flat, and dug in the grounds of the Kelly family seat – Romden Castle, near Ashford, Kent – they discovered remains from many bodies. Hardened policemen described their findings as 'unbelievable' and 'sickening'. The *Daily Mail* carried a front page story headlined 'Bodysnatch Police Dig up Castle' plus a colour photo of Kelly standing next to one of the offending sculptures. Examples of the latter were seized by the police as evidence.

Four months later, at Horseferry Magistrates' court, Niel Lindsay, a 24-year-old former employee of the Royal College of Surgeons, was jointly charged with Kelly with stealing anatomical specimens of unknown value from the college between June 1991 and November 1994. Kelly faced the additional charge of dishonestly receiving human remains knowing that they had been stolen.

The case made the front pages of the tabloids. Since social class is so titillating to the British, journalists were as interested in Kelly's aristocratic origins and his links to the Royal Family as in the issue of art and dead bodies. Bernard Kelly, the artist's father, is a merchant banker while his mother, Lady Mirabel, is the sister of the Duke of Norfolk, one of Britain's leading Roman Catholic peers. His family were reported to be supporters of Kelly's art and to be standing by him in his hour of need. At the time of his arrest he was employed part time as a tutor and technician at the Prince of Wales's Institute of Architecture. Some press reports referred to Kelly as 'Prince Charles's favourite sculptor'.

Kelly originally trained as a painter but then switched to sculpture which he studied for two years. He later worked as a butcher and in an abattoir. Apparently he has been fascinated by death, anatomy and medicine since his youth. When his grandmother died he made a death mask of her face and casts of her hands. He also cast parts of dead horses, sketched surgical operations at North Hampshire Hospital, Basingstoke, and made drawings for doctors undertaking cancer research. (If Kelly had been content to remain a 'medical artist', he could have had a successful career.) He has explained his motives as follows: 'I find beauty in death ... these are rotting bodies. You look at them and remind yourself, this is how we all end up.' Although many people found Kelly's obsession with death morbid and his sculptures macabre, his supporters declared that he was a serious artist, not one given to stunts designed to attract headlines.

As books and exhibitions with titles like 'Images of Man and Death' and 'The Art of Death' testify, death and corpses are subjects which have been addressed by countless artists, especially those making funerary monuments for tombs and graveyards. They also fascinate humankind in general but simultaneously they are subjects the majority of us are frightened of and wish to avoid, hence the mixed emotions evoked by Kelly's sculptures. He should be given credit, however, for encouraging us to confront our inevitable mortality. Executed with finesse, this type of art could be educational and therapeutic, because, as Andrew Clifford has observed: 'There is no sense in which [British] society "prepares" its members for death.' In contrast, Mexicans celebrate a 'Day of the Dead' every year. Yet in Kelly's work a general social meaning may be precluded by the fact that his dead bodies were not whole and belonged to a specific category: corpses mutilated by modern medicine.

Attitudes to displaying corpses in public vary from culture to culture and from era to era. In the past contact with corpses was far more common than today. In Britain most corpses are buried or cremated and yet in other societies corpses are embalmed, preserved and even placed on long-term public display – think of Lenin in the Kremlin, Moscow. The exception is the famous, British corpse of the philosopher Jeremy Bentham in a wooden cabinet in University College, London. Of course, in Kelly's case the sculptures were reproductions of corpses, not actual corpses, but they did invoke a frisson of dread of the kind associated with viewing real corpses.

One issue raised by the Kelly case was the legitimacy of casting as an artistic technique. Casting is an ancient reproductive method and a historic method of manufacturing editions of sculptures. It is also an ancient method of producing three-dimensional records of the appearances of the dead. Yet in the nineteenth century it was considered suspect as a means of achieving first-order art: Rodin's *Age of Bronze* (1875–76), a lifelike, standing male nude, was criticised for this very reason. (Rodin was angry because he had not cast the figure from a live model.) However, in the twentieth century casting from live bodies gradually became acceptable, especially after the 1970s' vogue for Verist sculpture (for example, the work of the Americans John de Andrea and Duane Hanson). Furthermore, in the decades since 1960, many artists have contributed to the avant-garde genre known as 'Body art'. A morbid tendency has also been detected within contemporary British art (the work of Hirst and Marc Quinn, for instance). In the context of recent art, therefore, Kelly's subject-matter and working methods were not exceptional. (It is also worth remembering that casts of body parts are made by medical practitioners and preserved in medical museums.) However, there are many artists and critics who continue to believe that the goal of art is not the exact imitation of external appearances.

Another issue raised by the Kelly case, of course, was the law regarding the fate of dead bodies and who has the right to dissect them. The British government passed an Anatomy Act in 1984 which allows bodies and body parts to be preserved for three years and used for medical purposes by people and premises licensed by the Department of Health. (Any other use is a crime.) After that period the remains are supposed to be given a proper burial. Also, a body can only be used if the person has given permission in their will. Among those offended by Kelly's sculptures were funeral directors and medical people; the former were concerned about the respect due to the dead, while the latter feared that the supply of bodies would reduce if the public felt that hospital staff could not be trusted to look after them.

Few people object to medical students dissecting corpses and yet there is a long history of respected artists doing the same thing in order to learn about the structure of the human body. (Leonardo and Michelangelo did so, and George Stubbs – the British animal painter – cut up horses. When Géricault made figure studies for his 1817 painting *Raft of the Medusa* he used the severed heads and limbs of criminals.) It would seem that there is now one law for the medical profession and another for artists. Otherwise, why would Kelly have felt it necessary to 'smuggle' body parts into his studio via an intermediary and to dispose of them secretly? Jonathan Meades, writing in a Sunday broadsheet, defended Kelly's actions and pointed to the division between art and science that has developed over recent centuries. Today, 'science is held in awe and art is not ... a body may be willed to scientists but not to artists'.

One presumes there are art lovers who would be willing to donate their bodies to artists in the same way that some individuals are willing to leave their bodies to surgeons. This is the strategy Kelly should have pursued in order to challenge the existing law and to avoid any offence to the relatives of those he cast and then buried in secret.

There seems no doubt that Kelly broke the law and this is why the press employed the pejorative term 'bodysnatching' and, in the case of the *Daily Mail*, went so far as to recall the 1828 case of Burke and Hare (who murdered drunks in order to supply corpses to Edinburgh anatomists for money). This was surely an unfair comparison because Kelly did not plunder any graves or kill anyone.

In March 1998 Kelly and Lindsay were tried at Southwark Crown Court charged with stealing body parts. In their defence the two men accused the Royal College of Surgeons of keeping body parts longer than the legal limit and disposing of them illegally. After viewing the sculptures and listening to the evidence, a jury of ten women and two men found the defendants guilty. Judge Geoffrey Rivlin told Kelly that his offence was 'revolting', that it was 'deliberate, criminal and disgraceful conduct', and sentenced him to nine months in prison. After an appeal, the sentence was reduced to three months. Rivlin added that the quality of his art was not a matter for the court. Lindsay, thought to have been influenced by Kelly, was given a six-month suspended sentence. Kelly's sculpture moulds were forfeited and given to the Royal College of Surgeons.

Given the focus of the news media on corpses and legal matters, it was not surprising that the issue of the artistic quality of Kelly's sculptures was hardly raised. In fact, the realistic casts sprayed with gold and silver paint had a cheap, kitsch look which prevented them from attaining the status of major art. A creative transformation of the materials used was absent and the body fragments hung on the wall by chains lacked formal integrity. One can excuse an artist almost anything if the results are aesthetically satisfactory, but Kelly's sculptures failed in this regard.

Brian Masters, a writer who has made studies of serial killers, suspected that Kelly has a perverted personality, that he suffers from necrophilia or love of the dead. Masters thought that comparisons with Renaissance artists were inappropriate because their anatomical investigations had resulted in art that was positive and life-affirming, whereas Kelly's 'necrophilic art' was 'negative, static and stagnant'.

Notes

Introduction

1. Peter Bürger, *Theory of the Avant-Garde* (2nd edn, 1980) (Minneapolis: University of Minnesota Press/Manchester: Manchester University Press, 1984), p. 18, p. 80.
2. Campaign for Artistic Freedom, *Human Earrings* by Rick Gibson (London: CAF/Young Unknowns Gallery, 1989), press release.
3. Pierre Bourdieu, *Distinction: A Social Critique of the Judgement of Taste* (London and New York: Routledge & Kegan Paul, 1984), p. 496.
4. Re. American examples see Steven C. Dubin, *Arresting Images: Impolitic Art and Uncivil Actions* (London and New York: Routledge, Chapman and Hall Inc, 1992) and Wendy Steiner, *The Scandal of Pleasure: Art in an Age of Fundamentalism* (Chicago and London: University of Chicago Press, 1995).
5. Bürger, *Theory of the Avant-Garde*, p. 81.
6. M. Woolf, 'Raiders of the Lost Art Come Clean', *Observer* (26 May 1996), p. 5.
7. D. Lee, 'In Profile: Craig-Martin', *Art Review*, Vol. XLVII (December 1995/January 1996), pp. 6–10.
8. Bryan Appleyard, in his book *The Pleasures of Peace: Art and Imagination in Post-War Britain* (London and Boston MA: Faber & Faber, 1989) pp. 55–7, quotes from a letter to *The Times* (20 December 1945) written by the novelist Evelyn Waugh dismissing Picasso and he also cites a columnist in *Apollo* magazine (Vol. XLIII, [January 1946], p. 2) who wrote, 'For me this stuff means precisely nothing', and who complained about the lack of standards and solid craftsmanship in contemporary art. Many art students and young British artists did, however, respond to the exhibition positively.
9. The term is Anne Massey's. See 'Welfare State Culture', *The Independent Group: Modernism and Mass Culture in Britain, 1945–59* (Manchester and New York: Manchester University Press, 1995), pp. 4–18.
10. For a detailed history of this development see John A. Walker, *Arts TV: A History of Arts Television in Britain* (London, Paris, Rome: Arts Council and John Libbey, 1993).
11. R. Cork, 'Dropping a Brick', *Evening Standard* (30 December 1976), reprinted in *The Social Role of Art: Essays in Criticism for a Newspaper Public* (London: Gordon Fraser, 1979), pp. 86–8.
12. Ibid.
13. Lee, 'In Profile: Craig-Martin', pp. 6–10.
14. For a detailed examination of this interaction see John A. Walker, *Art in the Age of Mass Media* (London: Pluto Press, rev. edn, 1994).

15. For an anthology of Sewell's criticism see *The Reviews that Caused the Rumpus and Other Pieces* (London: Bloomsbury, 1994). In 1994 a letter signed by supporters of contemporary art was sent to the press protesting about Sewell's 'destructive' art criticism. He was accused of 'virulent homophobia and misogyny'; deep hostility towards and ignorance of contemporary art; a 'tedious menu of formulaic insults and predictable scurrility – the easiest and cheapest form of demagogy'; a 'dire mix of sexual and class hypocrisy, intellectual posturing and artistic prejudice'.

16. R. Hoggart, *The Way We Live Now* (London: Chatto & Windus, 1995), p. 188.

17. Lynn Barber, 'The *Observer* Interview: In a Private World of Interiors', *Observer Review* (1 September 1996), pp. 7–8.

18. M. Lawson, 'Shock tactics', *Guardian* (18 September 1997), p. 8.

19. Of course, it is not only modern works of art that are attacked: valuable masterpieces of the past are also targets for knife and gun assaults by individuals, some of whom turn out to be mentally ill. For a discussion of the motives of those who vandalise pictures see Peter Fuller, 'The Psychology of the Ripper', *New Society* (31 July 1987), pp. 14–15.

20. S. Kent, 'Mistakes', *Time Out* (8–14 October, 1976), p. 7.

21. A. Graham-Dixon, *A History of British Art* (London: BBC Books, 1996), tie-in book of a BBC television series, p. 34. For a detailed survey of iconoclasm during the past two centuries see Dario Gamboni, *The Destruction of Art: Iconoclasm and Vandalism since the French Revolution* (London: Reaktion Books, 1997).

22. Graham-Dixon, *A History of British Art*, p. 202.

23. J. Lingwood, 'The Limits of Consensus', *Random Access 2: Ambient Fears*, eds Pavel Büchler and Nikos Papastergiadis (London: Rivers Oram Press, 1996), pp. 61–72.

24. M. Peckham, *Man's Rage for Chaos: Biology, Behavior and the Arts* (Philadelphia and New York: Chilton Books, 1965), p. 314.

25. 'Art for Artists' Sake' (Editorial), *Spectator* (4 March 1989), p. 5. This statement echoes the opinion of the British painter Keith Vaughan. See his remarks quoted on p. 226 of Malcolm Yorke's *Keith Vaughan: His Life and Work* (London: Constable, 1990).

26. R. Kimball, 'Uncensored and Unashamed', *Index on Censorship*, Vol. 25, No. 3 (1996), pp. 128–33.

27. One of the few intellectuals to express sympathy for the tastes and pleasures of working-class people is the French sociologist Pierre Bourdieu. In his mammoth tome, *Distinction: A Social Critique of the Judgement of Taste* (London and New York: Routledge & Kegan Paul, 1984), he comments on their enjoyment of narrative plays:

> The desire to enter into the game, identifying with the characters' joys and sufferings, worrying about their fate, espousing their hopes and ideals, living their life, is based on a form of *investment*, a sort of deliberate 'naivety', ingenuousness, good-natured credulity ('We're here to enjoy ourselves'), which tends to accept formal experiments and specifically artistic effects only to the extent that they can be forgotten and do not get in the way of the substance of the work. (p. 33)

Bourdieu argues that high culture is characterised by aesthetic distance and an icy formalism:

> ... conspicuous formality, both in art and life, i.e., a sort of censorship of the expressive content ... a distancing, inherent in the calculated coldness of all formal exploration, a refusal to communicate concealed at the heart of the communication itself ... (p. 34)

He contrasts this uptight, bourgeois approach to culture with the working class's more spontaneous revelry, plain speaking and hearty laughter. (One suspects Bourdieu idealises the working class. His book was written before the rampages of British football hooligans and lager louts. Of course, many young men are not strictly 'working class' any more because they can't find any work.) His theoretical conclusion connects cultural differences to the maintenance of class differences:

> The denial of lower, coarse, vulgar, venal, servile – in a word, natural – enjoyment, which constitutes the sacred sphere of culture, implies an affirmation of the superiority of those who can be satisfied with the sublimated, refined, disinterested, gratuitous, distinguished pleasures forever closed to the profane. That is why art and cultural consumption are predisposed ... to fulfil a social function of legitimating social differences. (p. 7)

If Bourdieu's analysis is correct, then delivering high culture to the masses – as the Arts Council tries to do – is a problematic and contradictory enterprise. This surely explains why so many ordinary people resist and reject the modern and contemporary art their social 'superiors' seek to foist upon them.

1   1949: Munnings and Modern Art

Sir Alfred Munnings, *An Artist's Life, The Second Burst, The Finish* (London: Museum Press, 1950–52). Douglas Cooper, *The Work of Graham Sutherland* (London: Lund Humphries, 1961). Ian Jack, 'In Colour: the Only Record of Sutherland's Churchill', *Sunday Times Magazine* (12 February 1978), pp. 12–15. Mary Soames, *Clementine Churchill* (London: Cassell, 1979). Roger Berthoud, *Graham Sutherland: A Biography* (London: Faber & Faber, 1982). T. Wilcox, *Munnings v. The Moderns* (Manchester: Manchester City Art Gallery, 1987), Munnings's speech is reproduced in this catalogue. Jean Goodman, *What a Go! The Life of Alfred Munnings* (London: Collins, 1988). Mary Soames, *Winston Churchill: His Life as a Painter* (London: Collins, 1990). Peter Fuller, 'Alfred Munnings', *Peter Fuller's Modern Painters: Reflections on British Art*, ed. J. MacDonald (London: Methuen, 1993), pp. 92–7.

2   1951: Gear and Abstraction

(Numerous reports and letters), *Daily Telegraph* (April-May 1951, March 1952). Arts Council of Great Britain, *60 Paintings for '51* (London: Arts Council, 1951). 'The Man They Hang Upside Down', *Picture Post*, Vol. 55, No. 3 (19

April 1952), pp. 6–7. W. Januszczak, 'All the Fun of '51', *Guardian* (4 July 1978), p. 8. A. Massey, 'William Gear', *Art Monthly*, No. 58 (July/August 1982), pp. 14–15. *William Gear* (Kirkcaldy, Fife: Kirkcaldy Art Museum, 1985. C. Hall, 'William Gear, Redfern Gallery', *Arts Review*, Vol. XLII, No. 20 (5 October 1990), pp. 529-32. Isobel Johnstone and Hilary Lane, *Festival of Fifty One* (London: South Bank Centre, 1990). Sarah Wilson, 'Cosmopolitan Patternings: the Paintings of William Gear', *William Gear: 75th Birthday Exhibition* (London: Redfern Gallery, 1990), pp. 5–12. L. Jackson, *The New Look: Design in the Fifties* (London: Thames & Hudson, 1991). A. Massey, *The Independent Group: Modernism and Mass Culture in Britain 1945–59* (Manchester & New York: Manchester University Press, 1995), pp. 14–17. Michael Tooby, 'Sombre and Dark Hues' (Obituary), *Guardian* (3 March 1997), p. 11. Peter Shield, David Gear and James Coxon, *William Gear and COBRA* (Aberdeen: Aberdeen Art Gallery, 1997), 8 pp.

3   1953: The Cold War Monument That Was Never Built

R. Calvocoressi, 'XI: Public Sculpture in the 1950s', *British Sculpture in the Twentieth Century*, eds S. Nairne and N. Serota (London: Whitechapel Art Gallery, 1981), pp. 134–53. A. Bowness, J. Davies and R. Calvocoressi, *Reg Butler* (London: Tate Gallery, 1983). R. Burstow, 'Butler's Competition Project for a Monument to *The Unknown Political Prisoner*: Abstraction and Cold War Politics', *Art History*, Vol. 12, No. 4 (December 1989), pp. 472–91. R. Burstow, 'The Limits of Modernist Art as a "Weapon of the Cold War"': Reassessing the Unknown Patron of the Monument to the Unknown Political Prisoner', *Oxford Art Journal*, Vol. 20, No. 1 (1997), pp. 68–80.

4   1958: The Strange Case of William Green

W. Green, 'Errol Flynn: an Operation', *ARK*, No. 24 (1959), pp. 36–40. Michael Chalk, *William Green* (London: New Vision Gallery, 1958). D. Mellor, *The Sixties Art Scene in London* (London: Barbican Art Centre/Phaidon Press, 1993). R. MacDonald, 'The Rebel Rides Again', *Observer Magazine* (7 February 1993), pp. 26–30. Tim Kirby (Film about Green), *The Late Show*, BBC2 (24 February 1993). David Mellor, Jane England and Denis Bowen, *William Green: The Susan Hayward Exhibition* (London: England & Co, 1993). M. Garlake, 'Lost and Found in Sidcup', *Art Monthly*, No. 115 (April 1993), pp. 11–13. A. Seago, *Burning the Box of Beautiful Things: The Development of a Postmodern Sensibility* (Oxford: Oxford University Press, 1995), pp. 125–8. Steven Gartside, 'Disturbing the Surface: William Green and Filmic Fascination in the 1950s', *Art & Design Profile No. 49: Art & Film* (1996), pp. 8–15.

5   1966: Art and Destruction

G. Metzger, 'Machine, Auto-Creative and Auto-Destructive Art', *ARK*, No. 32 (Summer 1962), pp. 7–8. G. Metzger, *Auto-Destructive Art* (London: Destruc-tion/Creation, 1965). (Issues on violence and destruction in art) *Art & Artists* Vol. 1, No. 5 (August 1966) and *Art & Artists*, Vol. 1, No. 7 (October 1966). 'Art

That is Ripe for Destruction', *Guardian* (9 September 1966). J. Landesman, 'September is the Cruellest Month', *International Times* (14–27 October, 1966). 'Excerpts from Selected Papers Presented at the 1966 Destruction in Art Symposium', *Studio International*, Vol. 172, No. 884 (December 1966), pp. 282–3. B. Farrel, 'The Other Culture', *Life Magazine* (17 February 1967). *Happening & Fluxus: Materialien Zusammengestellt von H. Sohn* (Cologne: Koelnischer Kunstverein, 1970). Kristine Stiles, 'Synopsis of the Destruction in Art Symposium (DIAS) and its Theoretical Significance', *The Act*, Vol. 1, No. 2 (1987), pp. 22–30. D. Schwarz and V. Loers (eds), *From Action Painting to Actionism: Vienna 1960–65* (Kassel: Museum Fridericianum/Klagenfurt: Ritter Verlag, 1988). Kristine Stiles, *Rafael Montañez Ortiz: Years of the Warrior, Years of the Psyche 1960–88* (New York: El Museo del Barrio, 1988). John A. Walker, *John Latham – The Incidental Person – His Art and Ideas* (London: Middlesex University Press, 1995). G. Metzger and Others, *Gustav Metzger: 'Damaged Nature, Auto-Destructive Art'* (London: coracle/workfortheeyetodo, 1996). Kate Connolly and Adrian Searle, 'The Devil in a Grey Beard' (H. Nitsch), *Guardian* (15 November 1997), p. 6.

6.   1967: Swingeing London

Jonathan Aitken, *The Young Meteors* (London: Secker & Warburg, 1967), pp. 192–3. 'Private View' (Proceedings of court case against Fraser), *Art & Artists*, Vol. 1, No. 10 (January 1967), pp. 68–9. David Bailey and Peter Evans, *Goodbye Baby & Amen: A Saraband for the Sixties* (London: Condé Nast Publications, 1969), pp. 48–9. Reyner Banham, 'Representations in Protest', *New Society* (8 May 1969), pp. 717–18 (reprinted in *Arts in Society: A 'New Society' Collection*, ed. Paul Barker [Glasgow: Fontana/Collins, 1977], pp. 61–6). *Richard Hamilton* (London: Tate Gallery, 1970). *Richard Hamilton* (New York: Guggenheim Museum, 1973). R.S. Field, *Richard Hamilton: Image and Process 1952–82* (Stuttgart & London: edition hansjörg mayer/Tate Gallery, 1983). Constance W. Glenn, *Jim Dine: Drawings* (New York: Abrams, 1985), p. 196. J. McEwen, 'Robert Fraser 1937–86' (Obituary), *Art in America*, Vol. 74, No. 7 (July 1986), pp. 25–7. *Richard Hamilton* (London: Tate Gallery, 1992). C. Anderson, *Jagger Unauthorised* (London: Simon & Schuster, 1993). M. Faithfull and David Dalton, *Faithfull* (London: Michael Joseph, 1994). Barry Miles, *Paul McCartney: Many Years From Now* (London: Secker & Warburg, 1997).

7   1971: The Catfish Controversy

M. Tuchman and J. Livingston, *11 Los Angeles Artists* (London: Arts Council of Great Britain/Hayward Gallery, 1971). Peter Hopkirk, 'Catfish to be Killed at Art Exhibition', *The Times* (29 September 1971), p. 4. 'Milligan in Art Show Protest', *Evening News* (30 September 1971). 'Arts Council Stops US Artist from Killing Fish', *The Times* (1 October 1971), p. 3. Leslie Watkins, 'Arts Council Stops Killing Catfish', *Daily Mail* (1 October 1971). Su Braden, 'Exhibitions: A Selected Guide. Letter to Spike Milligan', *Time Out* (15–21 October 1971), p. 61. Bernard Denvir, 'London Letter', *Art International*, Vol.

15, No. 9 (20 November 1971), pp. 67–70. Colin Moorcroft, 'Portable Fish Farm', *Architectural Design*, Vol. XLI (November 1971), pp. 721–2. J. Benthall, 'Newton Harrison: Big Fish in Small Pool', *Studio International*, Vol. 182, No. 939 (December 1971), p. 230. R.C. Kenedy, 'London Letter ...', *Art International*, Vol. 15, No. 10 (20 December 1971), p. 83–7. J. Benthall, *Science and Technology in Art Today* (London: Thames & Hudson, 1972), pp. 130–4. John Russell, 'London: Catfish Row', *Art News*, Vol. 70, No. 10 (February 1972), p. 36. Michael Aupling, *Common Ground: Five Artists in the Florida Landscape* (Sarasota, Florida: The John and Mable Ringling Museum of Art, 1982). A. Sinclair, *Arts and Cultures: The History of the 50 Years of the Arts Council of Great Britain* (London: Sinclair-Stevenson, 1995), pp. 160–1. Plus letters and phone conversations between Harrison, Norbert Lynton and the author in 1996.

8.   1972: Modern Sculpture Vandalised to Destruction

Philip Oakes, 'No Old Rope', *Sunday Times* (17 October 1971), p. 38. 'Peter Stuyvesant Foundation City Sculpture Project ...', *Studio International*, Vol. 184, No. 964 (July/August 1972), pp. 16–32. 'Barry Flanagan', *The Tate Gallery 1972-4: Biennial Report and Illustrated Catalogue of Acquisitions* (London: Tate Gallery Publications, 1975), pp. 133–5. Tim Hilton and Michael Compton, *Barry Flanagan: Sculpture* (London: British Council, 1982).

9.   1973: Womanpower Exhibition Provokes Strong Reactions

Liz Moore and others, *Exhibition of Womanpower: Women's Art* (London: The Artists, 1973), 6 pp. 'Porn Probe at Library Art Show', *Evening News* (19 April 1973). Clive Borrell, 'Police See "Women's Lib" Art Show', *The Times* (19 April 1973). Peter Cole, 'Porn Squad Eyes Women's Lib Art', *Guardian* (19 April 1973). Caroline Tisdall, 'Women Artists', *Guardian* (19 April 1973). N. Gosling, 'Art', *Observer Review* (22 April 1973). Greta Cerasale, 'Women's Art Aims to Shock Public into Awareness', *Kilburn Times* (27 April, 1973). M. Sjöö, *Some Thoughts About Our Exhibition of Womanpower ...*' (Bristol: Sjöö, May 1973), 2 pp. Su Braden, 'Visual Arts: Don't Waste that Anger Sisters', *Time Out* (11–17 May 1973), pp. 23–4. Mama Collective, *Mama! Women Artists Together* (Birmingham: Mama Collective/Arts Lab Press, 1977). Margaret Harrison, 'Notes on Feminist Art in Britain 1970–77', *Studio International*, Vol. 193, No. 897 (March 1977), pp. 214–20. Moira Vincentelli, 'Monica Sjöö' (interview), *Visibly Female: Feminism and Art: An Anthology*, ed. Hilary Robinson (London: Camden Press, 1987), pp. 80–90. 'Monica Sjöö', *Voicing Today's Visions: Writings by Contemporary Women Artists*, ed. Mara R. Witzling (London: The Women's Press, 1994), pp. 154–73.

10. 1974: The Oak Tree That Looked Like a Glass of Water

Caryn Faure Walker, 'Michael Craig-Martin at the Rowan Gallery', *Studio International*, Vol. 187, No. 967 (June 1974), p. 12 (Review Section). Anne Seymour, *Michael Craig-Martin: Selected Works 1966–75* (Leigh, Lancashire: Turnpike Gallery, 1976). Lynne Cooke and others, *Michael Craig-Martin: A*

Retrospective 1968–89 (London: Whitechapel Art Gallery, 1989). J. Roberts, 'Michael Craig-Martin', *Contemporary Artists*, ed. C. Naylor (Chicago and London: St James Press, 3rd edn, 1989), pp. 217–18. David Lee, 'In Profile: Craig-Martin', *Art Review*, Vol. XLVII (December 1995/January 1996), pp. 6–10. Sarah Craddock and others, *New Contemporaries '96* (Liverpool: Tate Gallery/London: Camden Arts Centre, 1996). Kam Patel, 'Brit Art's foundation figure', *The Times Higher* (6 February 1998), pp. 18–19. Letters and phone conversations with Leeds United.

11. 1976: Bricks and Brickbats

G. Battcock (ed.), *Minimal Art: A Critical Anthology* (London: Studio Vista, 1968). *The Tate Gallery 1972–74: Biennial Report and Illustrated Catalogue of Acquisitions* (London: Tate Gallery Publications, 1975), pp. 73–4. B. Levin, 'Art May Come and Art May Go But a Brick ...', *The Times* (18 February 1976). M. McNay, 'Somehow ...', *Guardian* (25 February 1976). C. Andre, 'The Bricks Abstract', *Art Monthly*, No. 1 (October 1976), p. 25. R. Morphet, 'Carl Andre's Bricks', *Burlington Magazine*, Vol. CXVIII, No. 884 (November 1976), pp. 762–7. P. Fuller (interviewer), 'Carl Andre on his Sculpture', *Art Monthly*, No. 16 (April 1978), pp. 5–11. 'A Pile of ... The Bricks Abstract: A Compilation by Carl Andre', *Art Monthly*, No. 164 (March 1993), pp. 16–17. Andrew Nairne, 'Building a Wall', *Frieze*, No. 27 (March/April 1996), pp. 35–7.

12. 1976: Pole-Carrying Performance Arouses Derision

Richard Evans, 'Publican and Poet a Pole Apart ...', *East Anglian Daily Times* (12 March 1976). R. Francis, 'Performance and Arts Council Patronage', *Studio International*, Vol. 192, No. 982 (July/August 1976), pp. 31–2. G. Auty, *The Art of Self-Deception: An Intelligible Guide* (Wharley End, Bedford: Libertarian Books, 1977), pp. viii, 161. Robin Morley, 'Holidays in Harness', *Performance Magazine*, No. 27 (December/January, 1983–84), pp. 32–6.

13. 1976: Can Dirty Nappies be Art?

M. Kelly, *Footnotes and Bibliography, Post-Partum Document* (London: ICA, 1976). Roger Bray, 'On Show at ICA ... dirty nappies!', *Evening Standard* (14 October 1976). F. Robertson, 'Soiled Nappies "Are Art"', *Daily Telegraph* (15 October 1976); Jane Kelly, 'Mary Kelly', *Studio International*, Vol. 193, No. 985 (January/February 1977), pp. 55–6. Jane Kelly, 'Mary Kelly', *Studio International*, Vol. 193, No. 987 (March 1977), pp. 186–8. Terence Maloon, 'Mary Kelly (Interview), *Artscribe*, No. 13 (August 1978), pp. 16–19. P. Fuller, *Beyond the Crisis in Art* (London: Writers & Readers, 1980), p. 165. M. Kelly, *Post-Partum Document* (London: Routledge & Kegan Paul, 1983). Hilary Robinson (ed.), *Visibly Female: Feminism and Art: An Anthology* (London: Camden Press, 1987) (reprints *Spare Rib* articles from three issues 1976–77), pp. 100–5. Mara R. Witzling (ed.), *Voicing Toady's Visions: Writings by Contemporary Women Artists* (London: The Women's Press, 1994), pp. 198–219. E. Lucie-Smith, *ArToday* (London: Phaidon Press, 1995). M. Kelly, *Imaging Desire* (Cambridge, MA and London: MIT Press, 1996). Margaret Iverson and others, *Mary Kelly* (London: Phaidon Press, 1997).

14. 1976: From Shock Art to Shock Rock

Colin Naylor, 'Couming Along' (interview with GP-O), *Art & Artists*, Vol. 10, No. 9 (December 1975), pp. 22–5. '"Dirty" Porridge', *Time Out*, No. 318 (16–22 April 1976), pp. 8–9. 'Prostitution', *ICA Magazine* (October 1976). Michael McCarthy, 'Bust-up at Gallery of Porn', *Daily Mirror* (18 October 1976), p. 15. Neil Blincow, 'Cosey's Sex Romp Pictures Are Banned', *Evening Standard* (19 October 1976), p. 6. 'MP's Fury at Porn Palace', *Daily Mirror* (19 October 1976), pp. 1–2. Thompson Prentice, 'Adults Only Art Show Angers an MP', *Daily Mail* (19 October 1976). Brian Park, 'Sex Show Man's Amazing Free Tour', *Evening News* (20 October 1976), p. 1. Michael O'Flaherty, 'State Aid for Cosey's Travelling Sex Troupe', *Daily Express* (21 October 1976), p. 3. Nicolas de Jongh, 'British Council Attacked for "Porn Subsidy"', *Guardian* (21 October 1976), p. 6. Garland, 'Muggings Increasing' (Cartoon), *Daily Telegraph* (21 October 1976). Keith Dovkants, 'Sex Show Report for DPP', *Evening Standard* (22 October 1976), p. 1 and p. 48 (plus editorial, p. 19). Caroline Tisdall, 'Genesis and Cosey', *Guardian* (22 October 1976), reprinted in *Caroline Tisdall, Grist to the Mill: Selected Writings 1970–1995* (London: Red Lion House, 1995), pp. 328–30. 'Yard Acts over that P. Orridge Sex Show', plus editorial, *Evening News* (22 October 1976), p. 2. Nicola Tyrer, 'You've Just Spent £37m Looking for a Genius', *Evening News* (22 October 1976), p. 14. Anthony Holden, 'No More P. Orridge at the ICA', *Sunday Times* (24 October 1976), p. 3. M. Vaizey, 'Much Ado about Nothing at the ICA', *Sunday Times* (24 October 1976), p. 37. Emmanuel Cooper, 'The Politics of Art', *Morning Star* (25 October 1976). Tony Parsons, '"But Darling, Mutilation is So Passé ..."', *New Musical Express* (30 October 1976), p. 47. Sheldon Williams, 'Genesis P-Orridge', *Contemporary Artists*, eds C. Naylor and G. P-Orridge (London: St James' Press, 1977), pp. 770–2. Sarah Kent, 'Visual Arts: Prostitution Didn't Pay', *Time Out* (24 December 1976 – 6 January 1977), p. 17. 'Tutti Frutti', *Guardian* (20 August 1983), p. 11. J. A. Walker, *Cross-Overs: Art into Pop, Pop into Art* (London and New York: Comedia/Methuen, 1987), pp. 129–34. Sir Roy Shaw, 'Art for Whom? The Arts Council's Mixed Performance', *Modern Painters*, Vol. 1, No. 1 (Spring 1988), pp. 64–7. Simon Dwyer, 'From Atavism to Zyclon B', *Rapid Eye* No. 1 (1989), pp. 65–94. Eileen Fairweather, 'Video Offers First Evidence of Ritual Abuse', *Observer* (16 February 1992), p. 4. David Rose, 'Scotland Yard Seizes Videos and Books after TV Film of "Ritual Satanic Abuse"', *Observer* (23 February 1992), p. 11. Simon Ford, 'Doing P-Orridge', *Art Monthly*, No. 197 (June 1996), pp. 9–12.

15 1977: Hayward Annual Exhibition Savaged by Critics and a TV Journalist

1977 Hayward Annual: Current British Art (London: Hayward Gallery/Arts Council of Great Britain, 1977). R. Cork, 'The Hayward Annual and the Power of the Dealer', *Evening Standard* (26 May 1977), reprinted in *The Social Role of Art: Essays in Criticism for a Newspaper Public* (London: Gordon Fraser, 1979), pp. 47–50. P. Fuller, '1977 Hayward Annual', *The Connoisseur*, Vol. 195, No. 786 (August 1977), pp. 310–11. J. McEwen, 'Page Two' and Anon. 'What Critics Say', *Art Monthly*, No. 10 (September 1977), pp. 2–3, 20–1. J. McEwen, 'Page Two', *Art Monthly*, No. 11 (October 1977), pp. 2–3. 'Robbie Programme (Art) ...' *Art Monthly*, No. 11 (October 1977), pp. 4–9. W. Packer, 'Robbie, etc.', *Art Monthly*, No. 11 (October 1977), p. 10. 'Peter Blake Meets Peter Fuller: Two Versions of a Conversation', *Aspects*, No. 6 (Spring 1979), pp. 1–3 and 15. Sir Roy Shaw, 'Art for Whom? The Arts Council's Mixed Performance', *Modern Painters*, Vol. 1, No. 1 (Spring 1988), pp. 64–7. L. Cooke, 'The Prevarication of Meaning', *Michael Craig-Martin: A Retrospective 1968–89* (London: Whitechapel Art Gallery, 1989), p. 27. Patricia Burgess (ed.), 'James Fyfe Robertson', *The Annual Obituary* (Chicago and London: St James Press, 1990), pp. 102–4.

16. 1979: The Arts Council, Censorship and the *Lives* Exhibition

D. Boshier, *Lives* ... (London: Arts Council of Great Britain, 1979). J. Pilger, 'Not in Front of the Children', *New Statesman* (March 1979), reprinted in Nairne, pp. 70–1. 'Censored? Or: How to Put Your Foot in It', *Art Monthly*, No. 24 (1979), p. 1. A. Brighton, '*Lives* and the Pusillanimous Quango', *Art Monthly*, No. 25 (1979), pp. 14–15, plus letters pp. 20–1. C. Atkinson, '*Lives* lives' (letter), *Art Monthly*, No. 27 (1979), pp. 27–9. John Latham, 'Censoring a Concept' (letter), *Art Monthly*, No. 29 (1979), p. 23. T. Rickaby, '*Fasçades*', *Block*, No. 1 (1979), pp. 48–9. Jennifer Oille, 'Three Weeks in the Life of *Lives*', *Vanguard* (May 1979), pp. 16–19. S. Nairne and others (eds), *Conrad Atkinson: Picturing the System* (London: Pluto Press/ICA, 1981). T. Rickaby, 'The Powers that Be', *Block*, No. 6 (1982), pp. 32–3. Sir Roy Shaw, 'Art for Whom? The Arts Council's Mixed Performance', *Modern Painters*, Vol. 1, No. 1 (Spring 1988), pp. 64–7. 'Thalidomide Victims Win Extra £7m from Government', *Guardian* (6 June 1996), p. 3.

17. 1979: Morgan's Wall: The Destruction of a Community Mural

Morgan's Wall (London: Arts Council/Liberation Films, 1978), 16mm film, colour, 53 mins. Richard Cork, 'A Hod Full of Bricks, A Fistful of Dollars', *Guardian* (11 June 1979), p. 7. 'Page Two: A Bad Taste in the Mouth', *Art Monthly*, No. 28 (July/August 1978), p. 2.

18. 1980: Performers Jailed for Wearing 'Rude' Costumes

A.R. Beberman, '"3 Women" Alice Beberman', *Open Eye* (May 1980), p. 4. Jack Ashton, 'Jail Shocker for the Four Woolly Nudes', *Liverpool Daily Post & Echo* (5 December 1980). Ron McKay, 'Furbelows Jailed: Threat to Civilisation

Averted', *Time Out* (12–18 December 1980), p. 9. (Court case report), *Open Eye*, No. 13 (January/February 1981), p. 2. 'Knitpicking in Liverpool', *Art News*, Vol. 80, No. 1 (January 1981), p. 27. Edna Ellis, 'Our Nights in Jail: the Most Terrifying of Our Lives', *Liverpool Daily Post & Echo* (6 March 1981); K. Warnock, 'Tapestries by Alice Beberman', *Crafts*, No. 50 (May/June 1981), p. 50. Marina Cantacuzino, 'How a Short Stretch can Devastate the Man in the Street', *Guardian* (20 August 1985), p. 8. Plus letter from Alice Beberman/Chute March 1998.

19. 1981: Portrait of Lady Di Attacked

G. Hughes, 'Bryan Organ' (interview), *Arts Review*, Vol. 33, No. 14 (17 July 1981), p. 305. 'Bryan Organ' (portraits reproduced), *Arts Review*, Vol. 33, No. 15 (31 July 1981), pp. 344–5. Staff Reporter, 'Princess Portrait Slashed', *Observer* (30 August 1981), p. 1. Dennis Barker, 'Royal Portraits Are Removed After Knife Attack', *Guardian* (31 August 1981), p. 16. 'Student Jailed for Slashing Di Portrait', *Belfast Telegraph* (16 September 1981). Christopher Warman, 'Repaired Portrait of Princess on Show', *The Times* (27 November 1981), p. 4. A. Barr and P. York, 'Supersloane', *The Official Sloane Ranger Handbook: The First Guide to What Really Matters in Life* (London: Ebury Press, 1982), pp. 20–1. Ken Hollings, 'Art Year Zero', *Performance Magazine*, No. 27 (December/January 1983–84), pp. 9–15. Diana Simmonds, *Princess Di: The National Dish* (London and Sydney: Pluto Press, 1984). J. Williamson, 'Royalty and Representation', *Consuming Passions: The Dynamics of Popular Culture* (London and New York: Marion Boyars, 1986), pp. 75–89. C. Paglia, 'Diana, Myth and Media', *Guardian (Review)* (30 July 1992), p. 23. A. Everitt, 'The Palette of Majesty', *Guardian* (29 August 1994), pp. 6–7.

20. 1983–86: The War of Little Sparta

Stephen Bann and others, *Ian Hamilton Finlay* (London: Serpentine Gallery/Arts Council of Great Britain, 1977). Peter Hill, 'Page Two: Hamilton Finlay v. Hamilton Rates', *Art Monthly*, No. 64 (March 1983), pp. 2–3. Peter Hill, 'Page Two: Sherrif's Officer turns into Bumbailiff', *Art Monthly*, No. 65 (April 1983), p. 2. Peter Hill, 'Page Two: UN Troops May Parachute Into Little Sparta', *Art Monthly*, No. 67 (June 1983), p. 2, plus letters pp. 23–5. Leslie Geddes Brown, 'Digging in at Little Sparta', *Sunday Times* (7 August 1983), p. 34. Graham Rose, 'The Garden of Unrest', *Sunday Times Magazine* (13 October 1985) pp. 52–6. Alec Finlay, 'Correspondence', *Art Monthly*, No. 145 (April 1991), pp. 27–8. Yves Abrioux, *Ian Hamilton Finlay: A Visual Primer* (Edinburgh: Reaktion Books, 1985, 2nd edn 1992). Plus letters to author 1996.

21. 1983: The Destruction of *Polaris*

K. Hollings, 'Burnt Wreckage: A Consumer's Guide to Sculpture', *Performance Magazine*, No. 26 (1983), pp. 29–31. G. Banks, 'Polemics: Any Old Irony', *Art Monthly*, No. 72 (December 1983/January 1984), p. 32. W. Feaver, 'New British Sculpture', *Art News*, Vol. 83, No. 1 (January 1984), pp. 71–5. Mel Gooding,

David Mach: Fuel for the Fire (London: Riverside Studios, 1986). Tom Baker, 'Fuel for the Fire', *The Face*, No. 83 (March 1987), pp. 82–7. W. Halstead, 'Jute, Jam, Journalism, Rubber Tyres and Video Screens', *Alba*, No. 3 (Spring 1987), pp. 19–21. D. Lee, 'In Profile: David Mach', *Art Review*, Vol. XLVI (May 1994), pp. 6–10. *David Mach: Likeness Guaranteed* (London: Academy Editions/ Newlyn Art Gallery, 1995).

22. 1984: Rape Picture 'Too Disturbing'

Sarah Kent (introduction), *Power Plays* (London: Morreau & Rueda, 1983), 18 pp. Sue Coe and Holly Metz, *How to Commit Suicide in South Africa* (New York: RAW Publications, 1984). Reports in the *Hull Daily Mail* (2, 3, 4, 5, 6, 9, 10, 11, 30 October 1984) and in the *Yorkshire Post* (5, 6, 9, 11 October 1984). H. Robinson, 'Shock Horror in Hull: Local Council Censors Art' (letter), *Art Monthly*, No. 81 (November 1984), p. 21. A. Tulley, J. Morreau (letters), *Art Monthly*, No. 83 (February 1985), pp. 24–5. Sue Coe, J. Morreau (ed.), *Paintings and Drawings by Sue Coe* (Metuchen NJ and London: Scarecrow Press, 1985). Mandy Coe and others, *Police State* (Richmond, Virginia: Virginia Commonwealth University/Anderson Gallery, 1987). Susan Gill, 'Sue Coe's Inferno', *Art News*, Vol. 86, No. 8 (October 1987), pp. 110–15. D. Kuspit, 'Sue Coe', *Artforum*, Vol. 29, No. 10 (Summer 1991), pp. 110–11. Frank Gettings, *Sue Coe* (Washington DC: Hirshhorn Museum/Smithsonian Institution, 1994). Thad Ziolkowski, 'Sue Coe', *Artforum*, Vol. 33, No. 3 (November 1994), p. 87. Steven Heller, 'Sue Coe, Eyewitness', *Eye*, Vol. 6. No. 21 (Summer 1996), pp. 32–41.

23. 1984: Attack on 'Porno-Art' in Leeds

'Art Demo Hits "Own Goal"', *Yorkshire Post* (7 November 1984). Michael Parkin, 'Sculptor Defends Women "Vandals"', *Guardian* (26 November, 1985), p. 4. S. Moreno, 'Art in Conflict with the Law – Makers or Breakers, Whose Responsibility?', *And: Journal of Art & Art Education*, No. 8 (1986), pp. 20–2. W. Steiner, *The Scandal of Pleasure: Art in an Age of Fundamentalism* (Chicago and London: University of Chicago Press, 1995).

24. 1986–87: Art, Money and the Bank of England

Jean Lipman, 'Money for Money's Sake', *Art in America*, Vol. 58, No. 1 (January–February 1970), pp. 76-83. Jürgen Harten and Horst Kurnitzky, *Museum des Geldes* (Düsseldorf: Städtische Kunsthalle, 1978). Phillip Ward-Green, 'J.S.G. Boggs, Art Show, Fulham', *Arts Review*, Vol. 36, No. 23 (7 December 1984), pp. 614–15. Robin Dutt, 'J.S.G. Boggs' (interview), *Art Line*, Vol. 2, No. 6 (January/February 1985), pp. 24–5. Mazher Mahmood, 'Police Seize Paintings of Pound Notes', *Sunday Times* (2 November, 1986), p. 2; Jane Jackson, 'The Currency of Art', *Performance Magazine*, Nos 44/45 (November 1986/February 1987), pp. 23-5. Andrew Marr, 'MPs' Cash Support for Accused Artist', *Independent* (19 December 1986), p. 4. David Tulissio, 'Correspondence: Counterfeit Art', *Art Monthly*, No. 102 (December 1986/January 1987), pp. 29–30.

J.S.G. Boggs, 'Art under Arrest', *Art and Antiques* (October 1987), pp. 99–104 and 126, 128. 'Artist defies Banknote Ban', *Hampstead and Highgate Express* (6 November 1987). 'Artist takes his Money and walks from Court', *Guardian* (27 November 1987), p. 4. Henry Lydiate, 'Artlaw: Art & Money', *Art Monthly*, No. 141 (November 1990), pp. 38–9. David Lanchner, 'The Art of Making Money', *Art News*, Vol. 86, No. 9 (November 1987), pp. 14–16. Carlo McCormick, 'J.S.G. Boggs', *Artforum*, Vol. 26, No. 3 (November 1987), p. 137. Thomas Frick, 'J.S.G. Boggs at Jeffrey Neale', *Art in America*, Vol. 76, No. 1 (January 1988), pp. 138–9. Lawrence Weschler, *Shapinsky's Karma, Boggs's Bills, and Other True-Life Stories* (San Franciso: North Point Press, 1988), pp. 178–260. Sally Heller, 'Miguel Angel Rios, J.S.G. Boggs', *Art News*, Vol. 89, No. 6 (Summer, 1990), p. 177. Mark Jones (ed.), *Fake? The Art of Deception* (London: British Museum Publications, 1990). R. Andrew Maass and others, *J.S.G. Boggs, Smart Money (Hard Currency)* (Tampa, Florida: Tampa Museum of Art, 1990). 'Pittsburgh: Is Making Money a Crime?', *Art News*, Vol. 92, No. 3 (March 1993), p. 36. 'Currency Cops Prevail in Boggs Art Suit', *Art in America*, Vol. 82, No. 2 (February, 1994), p. 25. Jonathan Williams (ed.), *Money: A History* (London: British Museum Press, 1997).

25. 1986: Erotic or Sexist Art?

B. Denvir, 'London Letter', *Art International*, Vol. 14, No. 3 (20 March 1970), p. 63. *Allen Jones: Figures* (Berlin: Galerie Mikro/Milan: Edizioni O, 1969). *Allen Jones Projects* (London: Mathew Miller Dunbar, 1971). *Allen Jones: New Paintings and Sculptures* (London: Marlborough Fine Art, 1972), 28 pp. L. Mulvey, 'You Don't Know What is Happening Do You Mr Jones?', *Spare Rib*, No. 8 (February 1973), pp. 13–16 and p. 30 (also includes an article by Su Braden). Peter Webb and others, *The Erotic Arts* (London: Secker & Warburg, 1975). A. Vargas and Reid Austin, *Vargas* (New York: Harmony Books/London: Plexus, 1978). H.A. Peters and others (eds), M. Livingstone (text), *Allen Jones 1957–78: A Retrospective of Paintings* (Liverpool: Walker Art Gallery/Baden-Baden: Staatliche Kunsthalle/Arts Council of Great Britain, 1979). T. Mullaly, 'Exhibition, Serpentine Gallery: Allen Jones', *Daily Telegraph* (21 May 1979). L. Tickner, 'Allen Jones in Retrospect: A Serpentine Review', *Block*, No. 1 (1979), pp. 39–45. 'Allen Jones', *South Bank Show*, London Weekend Television (27 May 1979). Krystina Kitsis, 'Para Adultos: An Interview with Allen Jones', *Art & Text*, No. 20 (February–April 1986), pp. 62–75. 'Late Items', *Art Monthly*, No. 95 (April 1986), p. 44. John McEwen, 'Artists in Camera: The Rise and Rise of a Man of Parts', *Sunday Times Magazine* (24 August 1986), pp. 30–5.

26. 1987–89: The Case of the Foetus Earrings

Jon Underwood, 'Stop the Freak Show', *South London Press* (4 December 1987), p. 1, and 'This Man Thinks Human Foetuses Make "Art" Jewellery', p. 3. Stuart Wavell, 'Thursday People: Material Values', *Guardian* (7 January 1988). R. M., 'Human Dynamite', *Evening Standard* (30 November 1988), p. 38. Amanda Sebestyen (*Animal II* exhibition review), *Tribune* (20 January 1989). Rosalind

Coward, 'Life Outside the Womb', *New Statesman & Society* (27 January 1989), pp. 39–40. Y. Say, 'Art Less' (letter), *City Limits* (2–9 February 1989), p. 98. The Campaign for Artistic Freedom, *Human Earrings by Rick Gibson* (London: CAF, 1989), 9 pp. press release. Owen Bowcott, 'Foetus Artist Fined £500 for Sculpture', *Guardian* (10 February 1989). Caris Davis, 'Indecent Exposure', *Evening Standard* (16 February 1989), p. 29. 'Art on Trial: The Crown versus Sylveire and Gibson', *And: Journal of Art & Art Education*, No. 20 (1989), pp. 3–9, transcript of TV programme 'Art on Trial', *Signals*, Channel 4 (22 February 1989). 'Art for Artists' Sake' (Editorial), *Spectator* (4 March 1989), p. 5. 'Diary', *Art Monthly*, No. 124 (March 1989), p. 2. Sean O'Neill, 'Offal Idea', *City Limits* (13–20 April, 1989), p. 7. R. Gibson, 'Drawing the Line', *Observer* (Special Supplement on Censorship) (17 April 1994), p. 3.

27. 1988: Nude Painting Deemed Too Rude for Royal Eyes

M. Walters, *The Nude Male: A New Perspective* (Harmondsworth, Middlesex: Penguin Books, 1978). 'Get Him Orf...', *Sun* (3 November 1988), p. 1–2. 'A Fig-Leaf too Far', *Art Monthly*, No. 121 (November 1988), p. 39. Mark Currah, 'Great Scott!', *City Limits* (5–12 January 1989), p. 15. K. Love and K. Smith, 'Construction of Male Identity: The Invisible Man', *And: Journal of Art & Art Education*, Nos 18/19 (1989), pp. 38–40. Naomi Salaman, 'Paternalism and the Invisible Man', *And: Journal of Art & Art Education*, No. 20 (1989), pp. 10–11. Naomi Salaman, 'Why Have There Been No Great Women Pornographers?', *New Feminist Art Criticism: Critical Strategies*, ed. K. Deepwell (Manchester and New York: Manchester University Press, 1995), pp. 119–25. Derek Manley, If You Show me Yours, I Promise Not to Look: Some Considerations of Fetishism (London: Middlesex University, 1997), unpublished dissertation.

28. 1992: British Gulf War Painting Accused of Anti-Americanism

Nicholas de Jongh, 'Artist After a Piece of the Action', *Guardian Review* (6December 1990, p. 22). 'John Keane: The Art of Warfare Along the Basra Road', *Guardian: Environment* (5 April 1991), p. 27. 'Discussion of John Keane's Gulf War Paintings', *The Late Show* (BBC2, February 1992). Mark Lawson, *John Keane: Conflicts of Interest* (Edinburgh and London: Mainstream Publishing/Angela Flowers Gallery, 1995).

29. 1993: The House That Was No Longer a Home

Sarah Kent, 'Home Work', *Time Out* (27 October – 3 November, 1993), pp. 22–3. Sarah Dunant (chair), discussion about *House* with Whiteread and Richard Cork, *The Late Show* (BBC2, 24 November 1993). 'Housey! Housey!', *London Psychogeographical Association Newsletter*, No. 5 (1994), p. 1. James Lingwood (ed.), *House* (London: Phaidon Press/Artangel Trust, 1995); this book contains several essays and it reproduces many of the articles and letters that appeared in the press. A. Graham-Dixon, *A History of British Art* (London: BBC Books, 1996), p. 200. Lynn Barber, 'The *Observer* Interview: In a Private World of Interiors', *Observer Review* (1 September 1996), pp. 7–8. Lynn MacRitchie, 'The War Over

Rachel', *Guardian* (5 November 1996), p. 9. Simon Hattenstone, 'From House to Holocaust' (interview), *Guardian* (31 May 1997), p. 3. 'The Monument' (Vienna), *The Works* (BBC2, 18 October 1997). Kate Connolly, 'Clash Over Holocaust Memorial', *Guardian* (22 November, 1997), p. 5. Brian Masters, 'This Bust ...', *Observer Review* (29 March 1998), p. 5.

30. 1993–94: Outsiders Seek to Outrage the Art World

Alix Sharkey, 'Trash, Art and Kreation', *Guardian Weekend* (21 May 1994), pp. 24–6, and pp. 29, 52. Jim Reid, 'Money to Burn?', *Life, Observer* Magazine (25 September 1994), pp. 28–33. Matthew De Abaitua, 'K Sera', *Observer Preview* (5–12 November 1995), pp. 6–7. Kevin Hull (Director),'K Foundation', *Omnibus*, BBC1 (6 November 1995). Mike Gartside, 'Art Reviews: Watch the K Foundation Burn a Million Quid', Cornershop, Bristol', *Venue*, No. 67 (24 November – 8 December, 1995). Angie Simmonds, 'Burn a Million Quid and Call it Art: Performance, the K Foundation, Liverpool Everyman', *Daily Post* (27 November, 1995). Ben Watson, 'King Boy D', *The Wire*, No. 157 (March 1997), pp. 32–7. Miranda Sawyer, 'They set fire to £1m ...', *Observer Review* (26 October 1997), p. 1, and p. 4. Chris Brook (ed.), *K Foundation Burn a Million Quid* (London: ellipsis, 1997). Plus letters and phone conversations between Bill Drummond and the author.

31. 1993: The Artist Who Adores Little Girls

P. Overy, 'Arts in Society: On the Job', *New Society* (26 March 1970), p. 528. G. Ovenden and R. Melville, *Victorian Children* (London: Academy Editions, 1972). G. Ovenden and P. Mendes, *Victorian Erotic Photography* (London: Academy Editions/New York: St Martin's Press, 1973). P. Webb and others, *The Erotic Arts* (London: Secker & Warburg, 1975), pp. 238-9. Brian Moynahan, 'Brotherhood of Ruralists', *Sunday Times Magazine* (3 October 1976), pp. 78–84. John Hooper, 'Painter and Photographer Deny "Victorian" Fakes', *Guardian* (29 October 1980), p. 2. Francis Gibb, 'Faked Photographs Taken in the 1970s', *The Times* (30 October 1980), p. 5. Staff Reporter, 'Case of a Hoax, Principles and Laughter', *The Times* (12 November 1980), p. 4. Nicholas Usherwood, *The Brotherhood of Ruralists* (London: Lund Humphries/London Borough of Camden, 1981). Alex Bellos, 'The Arts: In the Eye of the Beholder?', *Sunday Telegraph* (2 January 1994). 'Artnotes: The Eye of the Beholder', *Art Monthly*, No. 174 (March 1994), pp. 24–5. Sally Mann, *Immediate Family* (Oxford: Phaidon, 1992). Anthony Georgieff, 'As Far as the Eye is Not Allowed to See', *European Photography*, Vol. 15, No. 2 (Fall 1994), pp. 48–52. Wendy Steiner, *The Scandal of Pleasure: Art in an Age of Fundamentalism* (Chicago and London: University of Chicago Press, 1995). H. Feldman, 'The Lolita Complex', *World Art*, No. 2 (1996), pp. 52–7. Valerie Walkerdine, 'Popular Culture and the Eroticisation of Little Girls', *Cultural Studies and Communications*, eds J. Curran and others (London: Arnold, 1996), pp. 323–33. Rosetta Brooks, 'Lisa Yuskavage: Some Girls Do', *Art & Text*, No. 54 (1996), pp. 30–2. Valerie Walkerdine, *Daddy's Girl: Young Girls and Popular Culture* (London: Macmillan, 1997).

32. 1994: Hirst's Lamb Vandalised

Nicholas Jenkins, 'A Shark on the Horizon', *Art News*, Vol. 89, No. 6 (Summer 1990), pp. 30–2. 'Freeze, But is it Art?', *Omnibus* (BBC1, 22 February 1994). Damien Hirst (guest curator), Andrea Schlieker (organiser), Richard Shone (catalogue introduction), *Some Went Mad, Some Ran Away* ... (London: Serpentine Gallery, 1994). W. Feaver, 'Murder Most Foul in all its Forms', *Observer* (8 May 1994), p. 14. Edward Pilkington, 'Life, Death and the Meaning of a Two-Tone Sheep Dip' (plus Leader comment), *Guardian* (19 August 1994), p. 1 and p. 19. C. C., 'Agitate: What the Critics Said', *tate: the art magazine*, No. 4 (Winter 1994), pp. 16–19. D. Thacker (Letter), *Observer Review* (10 December 1995), p. 6. Loura W. Brooks, 'Damien Hirst and the Sensibility of Shock', *Art & Design*, Vol. 10, Nos 1/2 (January–February 1995), pp. 54–67. Robert Chalmers, 'Dissecting Damien', *Life, The Observer Magazine* (28 May 1995), pp. 12–16. Jim Shelley, 'Pop Art', *Guardian Weekend* (12 August 1995), pp. 12–16. Carl Freedman, 'Damien Hirst' (Interview), *Minky Manky* (London: South London Gallery, 1995). Roger Bevan, 'London: Plagiarism pickled', *The Art Newspaper* (October 1995). Ian Katz, 'Damien Hirst's Cows Send New York into a Pickle', *Guardian* (3 May 1996), p. 3. Martin Wroe and Ian Katz, 'Sister Wendy Puts the Boot into Damien', *Observer* (12 May 1996), p. 13. Ian Katz, 'Designer's Art Keeps the More Famous Afloat', *Guardian* (28 May 1996), p. 3. Owen Bowcott, 'Unholy Trinity Offers Food for Thought', *Guardian* (5 August 1996), p. 2. Gordon Burn, 'Hirst World', *Guardian Weekend* (31 August 1996), pp. 10–15. 'Hirst's Cow Heads on Protest Menu at Soho Restaurant', *Guardian* (25 January 1997), p. 8. 'Art Restaurant Fracas', *Guardian* (1 February 1997), p. 10. D. Hirst, *I Want to Spend the Rest of My Life Everywhere* .... (London: Booth-Clibborn Editions, 1997), p. 161 and pp. 296–7. 'Quo Vadis Five Win Lenient Sentences!', *London Animal Rights News*, No. 30 (November 1997), p. 1.

33. 1994: Painting of Rape Too Brutal for Imperial War Museum

Robert Heller, *Peter Howson* (Edinburgh and London: Mainstream Publishing, 1993). Robert Crampton and Richard Cork, *Peter Howson: Bosnia* (London: Imperial War Museum, 1994). Richard Brooks, 'Bosnian Rape too Brutal as War Art', *Observer* (18 September 1994), p. 6. R. Strong, 'Images of War', *Sunday Times* (25 September 1994), p. 8. David Lee, 'In Profile: Peter Howson', *Art Review*, Vol. XLVI (September 1994), pp. 6–10. Noel Malcolm, 'Not by Bread Alone', *Modern Painters*, Vol. 7, No. 4 (Winter 1994), pp. 52–3.

34. 1994: Child Murder: A Suitable Subject for Art?

Mark Thomas, *Every Mother's Nightmare: The Killing of James Bulger* (London: Pan Books, 1993). 'Editorial: Counting the Cost', *Art Monthly*, No. 178 (July/August 1994), p. 25. Sarah Kember, 'Surveillance, Technology and Crime: The James Bulger Case', *The Photographic Image in Digital Culture*, ed. Martin Lister (London and New York: Routledge, 1995), pp. 115–26. Robert Hamilton and others, *15:42:32, 12/02/93* (London: History Painting Press, 1996), booklet and postcard published to accompany an exhibition of Wagg's work at The Commercial Gallery, London, March–April 1996. Blake Morrison, *As If* (London: Granta, 1997). Blake Morrison, 'Murderous Innocence', *Guardian Weekend* (1 February 1997), pp. 12–18. Barbara Ellen, 'My Shame over Denise Bulger', *Observer* (8 February 1998), p. 26. Denys Blakeway (writer/producer), *Children of Crime: The James Bulger Case* (Blakeway Productions for BBC1, 7 April 1998). Plus interviews with the artist.

35. 1996: Perversity and Pleasure – The Art of Dinos and Jake Chapman

Stella Santacatterina, 'Dinos & Jake Chapman', *Art Monthly*, No. 166 (May 1993), p. 27. Godfrey Worsdale, 'Dinos and Jake Chapman', *Art Monthly*, No. 180 (October 1994), pp. 36–7. Stuart Morgan, 'Rude Awakening', *Frieze*, No. 19 (November–December, 1994), pp. 30–3. Mark Sanders, 'The Artworld Deserves Them' (interview with D and J), *Dazed and Confused*, No. 14 (October, 1995), pp. 54–7; Talk by Jake Chapman given at Middlesex University in 1995. Charlotte O'Sullivan, 'Dedicated Followers of Fascism', *Observer Review* (24 September 1995), p. 8. Megan Tresidder, 'Brilliant Bad Boys of the Galleries', *Guardian* (7 October 1995), p. 29. Martin Maloney, 'The Chapman Bros. When Will I be famous', *Flash Art International*, Vol. 29, No. 186 (January–February 1996), pp. 64–7. Nick Land, David Falconer, and Douglas Fogle, *Chapmanworld* (London: ICA Publications, 1996). 'Interview with Dinos and Jake Chapman', *Audio Arts*, Vol. 15, No. 3 (1996). Imogen O'Rorke, 'So Who Owns Kylie?', *Guardian* (9 December 1996), pp. 8–9. Brooks Adams and others, *Sensation: Young British Artists from the Saatchi Collection* (London: Royal Academy of Arts/Thames & Hudson, 1997).

36. 1996: Punishing a Graffiti Artist

M. Kurlansky, *The Faith of Graffiti* (New York: Praeger, 1974), English edn: *Watching My Name Go By* (London: Mathews Miller Dunbar, 1974). R. Reisner, *Graffiti: Two Thousand Years of Wall Writing* (London: Muller, 1974). *United Graffiti Artists* (New York, Artists' Space, 1975). R. Castleman, *Getting Up* (Cambridge, MA: MIT Press, 1983). M. Cooper and H. Chalfont, *Subway Art* (London: Thames & Hudson, 1984). *Frontier Art: New York Graffiti* (Bologna: Museum of Modern Art, 1984). *Jean-Michel Basquiat* (London: ICA, 1984). *USA Graffiti Artists* (Rotterdam: Museum Van Boymans, 1984). H. Chalfont and J. Prigoff, *Spraycan Art* (London: Thames & Hudson, 1987). F. Coffield, *Vandalism and Graffiti: The State of the Art* (London: Calouste Gulbenkian Foundation, 1991). (News reports in) *Guardian* (13, 14, 16, 21 March, and 4, 8 October 1996).

37. 1997: A 'Sick, Disgusting, Evil, Hideous' Portrait of Myra Hindley

Vivek Chaudhary, 'Anger at Hindley Portrait', *Guardian* (26 July 1997). Myra Hindley (Letter), *Guardian* (31 July 1997). Gordon Burn, 'The Height of the

Morbid Manner', *Guardian Weekend* (6 September 1997), pp. 14–21, plus front cover. Dan Glaister, 'Academy Artists Back Showing of Hindley Portrait', *Guardian* (12 September 1997), p. 7. Barbara Ellen, 'Hindley and the Art of the Cynical', *Observer* (14 September 1997), p. 32. Brooks Adams and others, *Sensation: Young British Artists from the Saatchi Collection* (London: Royal Academy of Arts/Thames & Hudson, 1997). Dan Glaister, 'Sensation Turns Ballyhoo to Cash', *Guardian* (17 September 1997), p. 5. (Front page), *Mirror* (19 September 1997), and Tracey Harrison and others, 'I'm Just So Glad I Did It', p. 7. Julia Hartley-Brewer, 'Academy Defiant as Damaged Hindley Portrait Stays on View', *Evening Standard* (19 September 1997), p. 6. Dan Glaister, 'Attacks Force Hindley Picture Out of Show', *Guardian* (19 September 1997), p. 2. Dan Glaister, 'Hindley Art Damage "Extensive"', *Guardian* (20 September, 1997), p. 13. William Feaver, 'Myra, Myra on the Wall...', *Observer Review* (21 September 1997), p. 10. Julie Burchill, 'Art and Immorality', *The Modern Review*, No. 2 new series (November, 1997), pp. 14–19. Julie Burchill, 'Death of Innocence', *Guardian (G2)* (12 November 1997), pp. 2–3.

38. 1998: An Angel Descends on the North and Divides the Community

Mel Gooding, 'Exhibitions: Seeing the Sites', *Art Monthly*, No. 108 (July/August 1987), pp. 12–15. Brian McAvera, 'Polemics: The Emperor's New Clothes ...', *Art Monthly*, No. 116 (May 1988), pp. 31–2. Malcolm Miles and others, *Art for Public Places: Critical Essays* (Winchester: Winchester School of Art Press, 1989). Lewis Biggs and others, *Antony Gormley* (London: Tate Gallery Publications, 1993). 'Nazi ...but Nice?', *Gateshead Post* (2 February 1995), p. 1, p. 4. *Art Marathon* (BBC2, 21 November 1995). John Hutchinson and others, *Antony Gormley* (London: Phaidon Press, 1995). R. Schopen, '*Angel of the North – News Release*' (Gateshead: Gateshead Metropolitan Borough Council, 1996). P. Wason, 'Not on the Side of the Angel' (letter), *Guardian* (16 April 1996), p. 14. David Lee, 'Editor's Letter', *Art Review*, Vol. XLVIII (May 1996). Andy Beckett, 'The Angel with a Dirty Face', *Independent on Sunday* (28 July 1996), pp. 16–18. Peter Hetherington, 'On the Side of the Angel', *Guardian* (10 January 1998), p. 6. Peter Hetherington, 'Traffic Stops as Angel Spreads His Wings', *Guardian* (16 February 1998), p.1. 'The Slapper in the Angel's Wings' (Letters), *Guardian* (18 February 1998), p. 17. William Feaver, 'It Will Never Take Off ...', *Observer Review* (22 February 1998), p. 13. Belinda Williams (producer), *Angel of the North – Gateshead* (Four short films) (A19 Film and Video Production for Channel 4 Television, 1998).

39. 1998: Sculptor Found Guilty of Stealing Body Parts

Andrew Clifford, 'A Dying Art', *Guardian Weekend* (4–5 January 1992), pp. 10–12. Catherine Pepinster, 'Prince's Sculptor Casts From Corpses', *Independent on Sunday* (12 January 1997), p. 3. Kamal Ahmed, 'Judge Casts Eye Over Dead End Art', *Guardian* (16 January 1997), p. 5. Owen Bowcott, 'Artist who uses body-parts arrested in corpses inquiry', *Guardian* (9 April 1997), p. 5. Nick Pryer, 'Body snatching sculptor held', *Evening Standard* (9 April 1997), front page and p. 2. Kamal Ahmed, '"Corpses for Art" Investigation Widens', *Guardian* (10 April 1997), p. 3. Dan Glaister, 'Leonardo First in a Long Line of Artistic Body Snatchers', *Guardian* (10 April 1997), p. 3. Peter Seamark and Peter Rose, 'Bodysnatch Police Dig Up Castle', *Daily Mail* (10 April 1997), front page and article by Vicky Ward, p. 5. Jonathan Meades, 'Let Death Out of its Tomb', *Observer* (13 April 1997), p. 32. Dr Jonathan Sawday, 'Livid and the Dead', *The Times Higher* (18 April 1997), p. 14. Stuart Millar, 'Sculptor "Stole Body Parts for Moulds"', *Guardian* (24 March 1998), p. 3. Sarah Hall, 'Technician "Was Only Burying Body Parts"', *Guardian* (26 March 1998), p. 7. 'Jury Sees Body Sculptures', *Guardian* (27 March 1998), p. 7. Brian Masters, 'This Bust ...', *Observer Review* (29 March 1998), p. 5. Stuart Millar, 'Artist Jailed ...', *Guardian* (4 April 1998), p. 1 and Adrian Searle, 'Tacky Body Art ...' and Stuart Millar, 'Death Fascination ...', p. 3.

Index

Index compiled by Auriol Griffith-Jones